Advance Prai

"A poignant read about a little-known issue ... What I'm telling my friends: particularly topical in these days of bullying stories and gay teens committing suicide, this brings to light just one man's tremendous struggle."

—Julie Kane, *The Library Journal*

"Honest and triumphant! A must read for anyone battling darkness, seeking light."

—Justin Reed Early, Author of *StreetChild: An Unpaved Passage*

"In lively, poignant prose, *Shorn: Toys to Men* details the movement from fragmented conflict to balanced maturity. Bensie's unique memoir will appeal to anyone who has ever felt the heady, dangerous pull of obsession."

—Jeff Mann, author of *Edge: Travels of an Appalachian Leather Bear* and *Loving Mountains, Loving Men*

"Dennis Bensie was a 'different' kind of boy, bullied at school, humiliated, and virtually ignored by his father. His memoir tracks an initial fascination with hair to a full-blown life-defining illness, a paraphilia in extremis. At times, the story becomes so disturbing that you wonder how he can possibly emerge as a wonderful human being. But he does. This book is at once a confession and a gift. Anyone interested in the development and transformation of the human psyche should read this important and fascinating book."

—Walter de Milly, author of *In My Father's Arms: A True Story of Incest*

"In prose frank and fierce Dennis Milam Bensie bravely sets forth for us the lifelong tale of a fetish—how it was born; how it grew to become his life's taskmaster. It is moving to hear in the enormous suffering of obsession, the distinct echo of our human passion for connection. In this singular and, at moments, exuberant journey, it is ultimately the long tangled web of secrets and shame that get shorn."

—Martin Moran, Author of *The Tricky Part*

"A life in the theatre is always an adventure; and *Shorn: Toys to Men* proves that truth is more interesting than fiction. By writing this humorous and inspiring memoir, Dennis Milam Bensie gives new meaning to 'Letting one's hair down.' "

—William Ivey Long, Tony Award Winning Costume Designer for *Hairspray*

"If a father insists on giving his son a buzz-cut, remind the old man he was only in the Marines a couple of years but the kid will have to live with therapy a lot longer. Give daddy a copy of *Shorn* and little Denny will get to wear cornrows or dreads if he wants. Oddly compelling, and full of hope. Some very weird little photos, though."

—Donna Barr, *The Desert Peach*

"*Shorn* is gutsy, shocking, poignant, vibrant, painful, joyful, tear-inducing, and wickedly funny. It's a brave, ballsy, brilliantly colored memoir by a brave, ballsy, brilliantly colorful writer. Bravo, Dennis Milam Bensie."

—Jennifer Niven, author of *The Aqua-Net Diaries*

"*Shorn: Toys to Men* is a captivating narrative that is sure to grasp your attention. Dennis is a fantastic storyteller who guides his audience through a remarkably transparent story of confusion, pain, sexuality, and hair! The scenes he weaves together are as alluring as they are honest. What I appreciate most is his candid process of sharing his struggles in an effort to find belonging and peace. This is one emotion-filled story that you won't want to put down."

—Joshua Daniel Phillips, author of *1,800 Miles: Striving to End Sexual Violence, One Step at a Time*

"Dennis Milam Bensie's candid account of how he came to unknot a sexual kink twisted into his being in boyhood—of how emotional abuse fueled an uncommon fetish—is brave writing that makes for breathtaking reading."

—Richard Labonte, editor, *Bookmarks, Q Syndicate*

"For the first time in history, a ground breaking book *Shorn: Toys to Men* written by Dennis Milam Bensie, addresses the cutting of men's hair fetish. Not only does *Shorn* delve into Dennis' insatiable desire to cut men's hair, he also addresses the psychological impact the fetish had on him and others. Where some would fantasize about shearing another guy, Dennis actually does it. Reading about Dennis' adventures became almost an obsession with wanting to discover what he would do next."

—Rick Ritter, Founder and Administrator of *MensHair.org*

"Dennis is a brave, brave soul to tell this story ... to have it published for the world to read ... and made it into a play for Seattle audiences to be introduced to ... it is quite a journey for him; one that I hope now he can look back on with humor, adventure and appreciation for how it has made him who and what he is today."

—Dustin Engstrom, playwright of *The Cut* (the stage adaptation of *Shorn: Toys to Men*)

"Thank you for sharing your story and those pieces of you that help us all to be better people ..."

—TPS

"I'm always so fascinated with the growth and expansion that comes in the telling of one's truth ... and those who have the opportunity to witness are forever changed in one way or another in the presence of that truth."

—Cherise

SHORN:

TOYS TO MEN

A MEMOIR

SHORN:
TOYS TO MEN
A MEMOIR

DENNIS MILAM BENSIE

coffeetownpress

Seattle, WA

Coffeetown Press
Seattle, Washington
Published by Coffeetown Press
PO Box 70515
Seattle, WA 98127

This is a true story. Real names have been used with
permission; others have been changed.

Cover photograph by Oscar Val Verde, ovalve.net
Cover design by Sabrina Sun
Contact: info@coffeetownpress.com
Copyright © 2011 by Dennis Milam Bensie

ISBN: 978-1-60381-092-0 (Paper)
ISBN: 978-1-60381-093-7 (Cloth)
ISBN: 978-1-60381-094-4 (ePub)

Contents

Acknowledgments

I would like to offer my sincere gratitude to those who supported me in the process of writing this book: To Jeff Brady, who suggested I actually write a book about my unusual experiences; to Jim Westerland, my best friend and former roommate, who has put up with my being "Dennis-ey" for almost 25 years; to Kerry Spaulding, who helped me find my voice and encouraged me to introduce Stefeny Calvert to the world; and finally, Oscar Val Verde, the man who changed everything for me and who seems to enjoy my authenticity without judgment.

I also need to thank those who read the book in various stages and offered their thoughts: Ranny, J.R, Imelda, David, Bill, Jan, Cheryl, Eric, Stephanie, Patti, Dustin, Fried, Amy, Scot, Marta, and Bunny.

For Clyde and Barbara

Introduction—July 18, 2010

Today is my 45th birthday. I am at work and there is a big drop of blood on my hand. I am curious because I do not know if it is real or fake.

My job today is making sure all the actors are getting into costume and being taken care of for the 7:30 performance of Lynn Nottage's Pulitzer Prize winning play, *Ruined.* This wonderful play is the 117th production I have done for Intiman Theatre in Seattle since 1992.

The blood in question could be mine, or stage blood used for a story line about a desperate person who takes desperate actions in the play. Even though it is my birthday and I have done this play eight times a week for several weeks, I am still connected. I know that make-believe is serious business and lives can be changed by telling a good story.

I have worked with many teams of artists to tell other peoples' stories, but for the last several months, I have been writing my own. For many years I have questioned if I would have the voice to share what I want to share. It wasn't until I hit my forties that I knew my voice could support the story I have to tell. I am ready.

I am not as excited about my birthday as I am about finally confessing to everyone the things I have been hiding my whole life. It is amazing that the things so deeply tucked away inside me have finally surfaced. I hope that my confession will make this year the best of my life. If this story resonates with someone else, then it's even better.

I wipe away the blood on my hand; it is real. I have a tiny cut that I do not remember getting. I apply a bandage from the first aid kit backstage and move on with my evening. I am tired, but I feel good. I'll be glad when the show is over and I can clean up and go back to reality.

There is no birthday party to go to after work ... by my choice. No cake, either. I just want this birthday to be simple, quiet, and about me.

1-Doll in the Family

Novelist James Jones enlisted in the Army and left his hometown of Robinson, Illinois in 1939. His experiences during the attack on Pearl Harbor inspired his first published book, *From Here to Eternity*.

The first family photo of Dad, Mom and me

For his second book, *Some Came Running*, he used Robinson as the backdrop. This semi-autobiographical novel centers around a failed writer named Dave Hirsh, orphaned as a child, who comes home after serving in World War II to a fictionalized version of Robinson (renamed Parkman, Indiana) to find family divisions, sexual repression, and other unsavory vices. The book was described as shrill and bitter by its critics. The 1958 Oscar-nominated film was a scandal when it played at the Lincoln Theater, a few blocks away from Jones' childhood home.

My dad was a local hero similar to characters in any of James Jones' war themed novels. He returned home to Robinson from the Korean War allegedly the most decorated soldier in Crawford County, having earned four purple hearts. He married my mom in 1951, two years before the end of the war, and struggled to settle into a job and married life. He later gained an enormous amount of weight. Seldom emotional or affectionate, my dad was undoubtedly the king of our house and was never very open-minded or worldly. I knew that he loved my mom, but I saw him kiss her fewer than three times in my entire life.

The roles of men and women have always been clearly defined in Robinson. As a boy I felt I had nothing in common with my dad, so instead, my mom was my hero. Mom had a kind heart and ran our household quite well. Like my dad, she held down a factory job most of her life. It was nothing for her to make dinner, read half of a romance novel and still manage to grab an ax and chop limbs off of a tree in the front yard. My dad rarely moved from his recliner in front of the television, which he occupied every evening. When he tipped the scales at over three hundred pounds, my mom tied his shoes for him every morning before work without complaint.

My parents had been married almost fifteen years by the time I came around. We lived in the country, seven miles outside the Robinson city limits. I had no brothers or sisters, and no neighbor children lived nearby. I was a lonely and shy child. Exposure to other kids was limited to school time and family get-togethers, where I played with the five or six cousins who were around my age.

When I got my very first report card, my Kindergarten teacher, Mrs. Wallace, stated that I "seemed to prefer the company of girls. Maybe the boys are too rough?"

The comment bothered my parents. There was good reason for their concern; I ran like a girl, talked like a girl and acted like a girl. However, I don't remember ever really wishing I was a girl. I was a boy and never wanted to change that. I was simply effeminate and liked "girl" toys rather than "boy" toys.

I remember playing with dolls with my cousins at their house. I loved to play with dolls. I thought dolls were wonderful replicas of people and vastly more interesting than inanimate objects like trucks and cars. There was no one to play with at home, so I would have been content to surround myself with dolls. My dad, however, disapproved.

"I told you, Denny: boys don't play with dolls," my dad would gruffly declare.

Out of desperation, I wondered if paper dolls were somehow more acceptable than three-dimensional dolls.

The fact that all of the details were drawn on seemed to make them less likely to breach gender taboos. I negotiated with my mom and talked her into buying a set of *Archie Comic Book* paper dolls for me. I lied and said I would play with Archie and Jughead more than Betty and Veronica, but the girls always seemed to have more interesting clothes and hair than the boys. I felt sneaky when I played with them. On the rare occasions when my parents had company, I was told to hide my paper dolls in the back bedroom to avoid embarrassment.

"You don't want people to think you're a sissy, do you Denny?" my dad warned.

I wasn't sure if my parents were more worried about protecting me or themselves from embarrassment. My paper dolls were the only toy I was ever told to hide.

When the Archie paper dolls wore out, I asked my mom to buy me another set of paper dolls to replace them.

"You're too old for that," she said. I hoped my mom didn't tell my dad I wanted another set.

My grandma was always less uptight about my girlish qualities and interests. I never felt judged when spending time with her. She was my maternal grandma and the only grandmother I had left. There was a toy box in her garage that contained a few dolls I played with. They were hand-me-down baby dolls that were broken and dirty from years of play and abuse administered by my older cousins. It was very hard to muster enough imagination to enjoy playing with those dolls.

A few days later, after my mom said *no* to getting me another set of paper dolls, I asked my grandma. She enthusiastically said *yes*. Grandma helped me pick out a set of teen fashion model paper dolls that had cool outfits and a different hairstyle to go with each look. The set was special to me because there were only girl dolls. I was relieved because I didn't have to pretend to play with the boy dolls as much as the girl dolls. That afternoon, as I sat at my grandma's house cutting out the dolls, I felt liberated. She even helped me do some of the cutting. It was strange and wonderful to be sitting out in the open with a doll in my hand. I wasn't hurting anyone, and no one was going to hurt me.

Grandma and I agreed it was a good idea to leave the paper dolls at her house and made sure to hide them before my parents picked me up. Grandma and I both knew the only ones I was hiding the dolls from at her house were my parents. I hoped someday to have an interesting doll of my choice that I would not have to hide at all.

Over the years, I had a few GI Joe dolls of my own. Because of the doll's military theme, my dad never had a problem with them. I had absolutely no interest in anything military, but liked the clothes-changing possibilities of my GI Joe. I was lost for enjoyment beyond that. I loved fashion, so I designed a strapless gown for GI Joe by cutting the toe out of a tube sock. Yet, I wanted to make real clothes for GI Joe. I taught myself how to sew by hand and began making more dresses out of my mom's fabric scraps.

I really wanted GI Joe to have long hair like a girl. I quickly became skilled at making little yarn wigs for the GI Joes and taping them to their heads. I spent hours styling the action figure's yarn hair, braiding and combing the hair with a wide-tooth comb. It didn't matter to me that GI Joe had a flocked beard and mustache. In my mind, he was a beautiful young woman.

With no brothers or sisters to distract me, I spent all my free time immersed in my feminine fantasies, alone in my bedroom with the door closed. My parents seldom disturbed my playtime. It wasn't unusual to come home from school and spend the entire evening in my room with my GI Joe in drag, only emerging to eat a quick dinner or go to the bathroom.

I made sure to keep the drag GI Joe all to myself. My choices during playtime would surely be questioned by my parents, especially my dad.

Changing GI Joe's gender gave me an exciting idea when Halloween came around:

Every Sunday night I watch the Cher show.
It is my favorite show because she is funny and has
very long, pretty hair. I want my hair to look like hers
so I could have lots to play with.
If I had hair like hers I would be happy, but I know
people would think I was doing something wrong.
My Dad would be mad.
Boys are not supposed to have long hair.
I will tell Mom and Dad and everyone I am going
Trick or Treating as a hippie, but secretly I know that
my Halloween costume is Cher.

The most important part of the Cher costume to me would obviously be the wig. There were no wig shops in Robinson. It didn't matter because I decided I could make my own Cher wig. I took my mom's rubber swim cap, poked holes in it and meticulously tied long pieces of black yarn into each hole to make the wig. I spent hours and hours handcrafting the wig, trying it on many times during the construction period.

When I was finished, I was more excited about Halloween than I had ever been in the past. I was also excited because I knew I had a wig to play with after Halloween. Mom caught me wearing the wig, along with the fringed vest and bell bottom pants from my costume, and singing along with Cher to "Half Breed" on more than one occasion.

That homemade yarn wig was my favorite toy for over a month. I styled it over and over with pins and braids and anything else I could come up with. I also created many fantasy characters and situations while wearing it. I liked to pretend to be all of the things little girls pretended to be: princesses, gypsies, teachers, fashion models.

I didn't have a Styrofoam wig head so I made a block for the wig by stuffing and molding a pair of Mom's pantyhose around a large circular Crisco can. I tacked the wig to the can with thumb tacks and even drew a face it.

It eventually became less and less important to actually wear the wig on my head. It became much more interesting to manipulate the fantasy character than to actually wear the "skins" of the characters. I started altering the wig less with braiding and pinning and became drawn to more serious styling techniques that involved cutting the wig. I knew that the yarn would not grow back, and eventually, I would not be able to play with the wig in the same way. I cut the wig a little at a time, pacing myself to make the experience last as long as I could, examining all possibilities of each length. The wig went from Cher to Marlo Thomas length then ended up as a Liza Minnelli bob.

I discovered that I really enjoyed cutting the yarn hair into different styles. Cutting hair made me feel powerful. At this point, I didn't really understand what the power was or the validation it could provide. It wasn't long before my parents found out that I had a campy attachment to that homemade wig. By Christmas, the yarn hair was cut short and the cap was beyond repair. Mom wasted no time tossing it in the trash.

Once the Cher wig was gone, I became desperate for anything I could put on my head and pretend was long hair. I figured out that a bath towel could be thrown over my head to frame my face and fashion a beautiful, ultra-long head of pretend hair. The same could be done with a long silky scarf or a T-shirt. These household items let me cleverly continue experiencing my long-haired fantasies.

My dad teased me in his gruff manner, often demanding that I stop acting like a girl. His tone not only frightened me, but often made me feel like I was doing something shameful.

2-Boy Dolls

In first grade on library day, the teacher read us a storybook called *Mop Top*. It was my favorite book for many years after. The book was about a little boy with shaggy red hair who doesn't want to get a haircut. He enjoys his hair and is harassed for being a long-haired boy. It isn't until an old woman mistakes him

Lester and me, our first Christmas together

for a mop in a store, grabbing his hair and tugging on it, that he submits to going to the barber shop.

I wanted to be like the boy in *Mop Top* (except I didn't want to submit to a haircut). I was used to people affectionately patting me on the head and telling me that I had very pretty blond hair. I am sure my dad felt he was doing the right thing by having my hair cut every few weeks into a short, tapered haircut.

It was the 1970s, and there was a growing freedom in men's hairstyles. Still, my dad and I went to a traditional barbershop and got identical haircuts. On one occasion I remember crying hysterically as the barber snipped at my hair. The crying was ignored by the barber, and I looked my dad square in the face. He was laughing at my tears, which made me cry that much harder as I dug my fingernails into the barber chair upholstery.

People keep telling me my hair is pretty; so why do I have to get it cut off?
It's not fair.
There is nothing left to touch.
It's too short to grab onto after the barber cuts it.
I want to feel how soft it is.
I want to feel it blowing in the wind when I run outside.
It's so short it doesn't move.
Daddy knows I don't want to get my hair cut but he makes me anyway.
I know all boys have to get their hair cut, but he acts like he's mad at me all the time.
I'm not sure Daddy likes me.
He wants me to be more like the other boys.

Being a soft-spoken boy with a masculine-minded dad, I wasn't allowed to grow my hair into a longer contemporary style until I was in the fifth grade. It was 1976, and most boys my age were starting to grow their hair out. Repeatedly showing my dad school pictures of my male classmates with longer hairstyles finally convinced him longer hair could be considered acceptable. Even then, the length of my hair was closely monitored. After months and months of persuasion, my parents gave in. The family tradition of my dad taking me every two to three weeks to the barber shop gradually shifted to my mom taking me to a unisex salon for a "style" every four to five weeks.

Mom took me to that salon again.
Dad said that he'd better be able to see my ears when we got home from the salon, or he'd cut my hair himself.
I got scared after we left the salon, because you could see only half of my ear.
Mom told me it would be all right.

Dad only needs to see half of my ear.
He always talks about not wanting his son to look like
a girl.
I know the problem isn't just my hair.
Even with short hair, he will still growl at me all the
time for acting more like a girl than a boy.
Mom never seems to mind what I act like.
I try to stay around her.
Sometimes she protects me from Dad.

I was very excited to grow my hair out for the first time. Despite the victory in getting to grow my hair, the top was all that was ever allowed to gain much length. I had straight, baby-fine blond hair and began to develop a great deal of pride in it, hanging on to every compliment. I spent weeks watching my bangs get longer, obsessively checking the length by pulling them toward my nose.

I loved to touch my hair and couldn't wait to get my own blow dryer just like I imagined the girls at school to have. At school I studied the girls' hairstyles. I spied on my mom as she set her hair on pins and rollers. I would sneak into her room, steal pins and carefully arrange my hair, pinning it in place like I had watched her do many times. Eventually, I was alone long enough to play with my mom's tiny plastic perm rods, teaching myself the basic principles of a wash and set. I became pretty good at using her curling iron on my hair, too. I was always very sad to have to wash the curl out of my hair to avoid getting into trouble with my dad.

While I gained this little bit of freedom to choose my own clothes and hairstyle, my dad still used haircuts as a threat. I don't ever remember the threat of being grounded or spanked, but I was continuously threatened with having to get sheared back into a short haircut if I got in trouble. After years of wishing for even a little bit of length to play with, I could easily be traumatized by the thought of going back to the shorn look. Luckily, I never got in enough trouble at home to merit such severe humiliation.

Haircuts took on a whole new meaning when I first saw a doll in the *Sears Wish Book Catalog* named Lester. Willy Tyler and Lester were a popular African-American ventriloquist act in the 1970s featured on such shows as *Laugh-In* and the game show *Match Game*. Sears was selling Lester dolls, along with a few other toy ventriloquist dummies like Charlie McCarthy and Howdy Doody. I instantly became obsessed with getting a Lester of my own. Lester had little to do with girl-play. He was a much different fantasy.

Lester was over two feet tall and had a stuffed body and a plastic head and hands. He was designed to sit on a child's lap, and a string on the back of his neck could be pulled to make his jaw move. He was dressed in a gold corduroy jacket and brown pants and wore round eye glasses. I only wanted Lester because he had lots of rooted curly hair. Before I even saw a Lester doll in person, I felt an overwhelming need to cut off all of Lester's hair. I obsessively stared at the picture of Lester in the catalog.

Being sneaky wasn't enough to convince my mom to buy Lester. I had to beg my mom for the dummy, despite the fact I didn't really have an interest in ventriloquism. She was speechless when I talked about Lester. She seemed frightened by the doll, confused about whether it was appropriate for me to own.

I got Lester that Christmas. From the day I got the doll, my dad never hid the fact that he hated it. In our household the doll seemed so large and hard to ignore. Unlike other toys I got that Christmas, I was forbidden to take Lester to school. I was expected to hide Lester if we were to have company just like I had hid the Archie paper dolls years earlier. I am sure my dad's concern was that the doll would open me up to teasing. Perhaps another problem my dad had was that the doll was black. There were no black people in my hometown.

Lester was an oddity in my world, not because of his color, but because he was undeniably male. I really enjoyed touching and styling his hair, but beyond that was bored with him. Lester was big and clumsy to handle. I seldom played with him in front of anyone. Certainly not in front of my dad, who had quickly started referring to him as "that nigger doll." His face would turn bright red and he would leave the room when I carried Lester around. I became afraid of playing with Lester, for fear of angering my dad.

Knowing the hair wouldn't grow back, I waited as long as I could stand it before giving in and allowing myself to cut Lester's hair. After about a month of torturous anticipation, I ceremoniously sat the doll down before me in the privacy of my bedroom and draped a towel around his shoulders just as you would a barber cape. I remember getting very tingly and excited as I prepared to make the first cut. I wasn't like a real barber who combed and began gingerly snipping around the head. I grabbed a handful of hair and sliced it off to the scalp. I couldn't help myself. It only took about four big cuts and a few minutes before Lester was virtually bald. I loved the sight of the black curls all over the doll's shoulders and the floor around him.

Something unfamiliar and unexpected happened while I cut his hair: I got an erection. I sat there looking at the ridiculous mess I had made of Lester and marveled at my hard penis poking at my pants. I was about eleven years old and couldn't begin to process this bodily reaction.

Is this what it feels like to be a real boy?
I feel like I have been a brave hunter trying to capture
Lester since I first saw him in the catalog.
Lester is a victim just like I feel sometimes.
He has to get his hair cut like all boys are supposed to;
like I am supposed to.
I felt naughty when I cut all of his hair off.

It made me feel strong and important, like I was winning a prize.
I also feel ashamed.
I feel like I killed him, even though he is just a doll.
His hair was the one thing I liked about him and I took it away.
It won't grow back.

Despite the doll's unpopularity with my dad, there was a slight chance I would get in trouble for ruining one of my toys. The shorn Lester was hidden until I got an opportunity to bury him in the trash undetected. I can't say that I missed him. My parents quickly forgot about Lester, too.

3-Stickneyed

One of the big kids on the bus keeps teasing me.
He asks me every day, "Have you ever been Stickneyed?"
The strong boys always call all the weak boys "STICKNEY!"
"What's a Stickney?" I asked.
I pretended that I didn't know what a Stickney was.
"Stickneys take it up the butt"
No one wants to be called a Stickney.
There was a whole family named Stickney and everyone knew they were weird.
I finally told him yes: I had been Stickneyed.
I was confused.
I thought if I said I had done it, that he would finally leave me alone.
The boy told me being Stickneyed made me a girl.
He started laughing at me and telling other kids that I had taken it up the butt.
Some of the kids laughed at me and I started to cry.
Now all the kids are really calling me a Stickney.
One of the big girls was nice to me and told me that taking it up the butt wasn't supposed to happen to boys.

All sixth graders had to choose between taking Wood Shop or Home Economics. One reason I desperately wanted to take Home Ec was so I could learn how to use a sewing machine.

"Your classmates are going to call you a sissy if you take Home Ec," my dad warned.

What he didn't realize was that I would get a break from being bullied while the boys took Shop. After some negotiation, my parents let me sign up for the class I wanted. However, my father was right; things got worse when I started taking Home Ec. The bullying escalated, and being pushed and shoved by a couple of the more aggressive bullies became an everyday occurrence. My new nickname was "Sissy Sewer."

My own dad made fun of me when I brought my sewing projects home from Home Ec. I began to believe I deserved to be choked and shoved. I knew my problems were not going to get any better as high school approached. I was an empty, lonely boy who didn't identify with other boys. I didn't feel like I wanted to be a girl, either. I just wanted to be the feminine version of me.

> *Gordon told me to stop walking like a fag.*
> *I was walking how I always walk;*
> *I don't know how to walk any other way.*
> *When he grabbed me by the throat I tried to push him off of me.*
> *He got mad and squeezed my throat harder and backed me up against the lockers.*
> *He looked like he wanted to kill me.*
> *I got real scared because I couldn't breathe.*
> *All the kids that were walking to class stopped and watched.*
> *"Smear the queer, Gordon!"*
> *"Get him! He's a Stickney!"*
> *I thought I was going to pass out.*
> *I was embarrassed and angry because I am not strong enough to fight back.*

Mr. Rankin walked right past and saw me pinned
against the locker with Gordon's hands around my
neck.
He told him to stop but kept walking like he was in a
hurry.
The kids that weren't laughing and cheering did
nothing.
When Mr. Reynolds came round the corner, Gordon
let go and everyone hurried to class like nothing had
happened.
Most teachers do not try too hard to stop the bullies.
The male teachers probably secretly think I need to be
bullied.
The female teachers seem afraid to say too much.
Gordon and his friends ride the same school bus as me
so I am afraid to take the bus home.
I'll call Mom and tell her I missed it so she will pick
me up.

Mr. Robb was the P.E. teacher at Nuttle Middle School. He was in his twenties and very athletic. He had no compassion for sissy boys like me. I could not keep up with the other boys in sports or deal with their daily harassment. Mr. Robb's first period P.E. class was where I got the most abuse during the school day.

The abuse always started in the locker room. Any opportunity to slap, poke, or verbally bully any of the boys who didn't meet the masculine expectations of the more athletic guys was indulged. There was no adult supervision, and I was always being humiliated.

I refused to get naked and shower after gym class. All the boys would scream and yell at me to get in the showers: I refused. I was vulnerable fully clothed and was not willing to risk my self-esteem any further. Mr. Robb heard the commotion and called me into his office.

"Milam, what's the problem? Shower up!" he said. There was nothing anyone could do or say to get me in that shower. I ignored him and got dressed before the boys finished showering.

I continued my shower strike for several days, and the contempt for me increased from the boys as well as Mr. Robb. Pretending to be sick, I started missing school as much as I could just because of P.E. I eventually convinced my mother to write notes that would get me out of gym. Each day I would take a note to Mr. Robb claiming I was unable to participate in gym class that day. His reaction was harsh.

"What's this, Milam: another note from your MOMMY? When are you going to grow up and take my class like the rest of the students?" he snarled. I would look at him with equal contempt. Mr. Robb made it clear he had a personal vendetta against me. I would much rather have him hate me than be naked in front of my classmates. I tried to be invisible to him and the whole class.

The kids saw how much he resented me. Mr. Robb looked for any reason to single me out and make me uncomfortable.

"As you see, class, Milam is too sick and weak to participate in class. Let's all hope he feels better tomorrow. Maybe his mom will forget to write a note for him."

His jeers only fueled the harassment from my classmates, which now lasted the entire school day. School got harder and harder and that first period gym class was the crux of my anxiety.

I was withdrawing more and more into myself, barely speaking in any of my classes. I was paranoid Mr. Robb was telling my other teachers bad things about me. A few of the male teachers already looked at me negatively because of my effeminate tendencies. Because I felt there was no adult at school to turn to, I just took my harassment.

A brief, non-specific mention of P.E. class while I was at the doctor's office one summer led to a gesture of compassion. Dr. Snider had treated me my whole life, and I am sure my body language told the doctor how I felt about gym class.

"You have trouble breathing in gym class, don't you Dennis?" Dr. Snider asked. It wasn't so much a question as a statement he was feeding me. I agreed with the diagnosis as my mother sat with me. We were both confused because we were not there to talk about my lungs.

"Gosh, darn it, Dennis. You have asthma. You don't have any business taking P.E. with those other kids. Let me write you a note to get you out of gym class altogether for the whole year. How does that sound?"

It sounded like the doctor understood what was really going on in gym. He, my mother, and I all knew that I didn't have asthma. I almost cried with joy. It was the best thing I could think of to help me deal with school.

When I registered for school that fall, I handed in my doctor's note to the school nurse and was assigned study hall while the rest of my class took gym. Surprisingly, no one really noticed I had stopped taking gym class altogether. I had to stop and wonder if Dr. Snider had done the same favor for other sissy boys.

The worst humiliation I suffered didn't happen at school. There was a boy in my class named Bob. The only thing we had in common was that we were both flunking our classes. Bob was a rough kid. He looked dirty and I suspected he came from a troubled home. I used to see him smoking across the street at the motorcycle shop before and after school with all the other bad kids.

Bob was evil. If I had been an ordinary guy like most guys, I would have had no problem believing I was a better, or at least equal, person than him. After all, Bob was always getting in trouble and had even been suspended from school a number of times. Bob did everything in his power to make me feel like I was worthless. He had been torturing me for years: you're a fag, a stickney, a queer. I hated Bob. I hated him so much that I fantasized about killing him.

Bob was also known for having the longest hair of any guy in the whole school. It was greasy and looked like he almost never combed it. I couldn't explain it, but I hated Bob more than any of my other bullies, just because of his long, nasty hair.

One Saturday, Mom asked me to go to the junkyard with her to unload some stuff. I reluctantly agreed. Once we got there, my heart sank: there was Bob with some other young men whom I didn't know. I know he saw me, but I prayed that he wouldn't say anything to embarrass me in front of my mom.

Mom pulled the truck to the other side of the dumping area, which relieved me greatly. We went on about our business unloading the truck. She had no idea my nemesis was 500 feet away or that I even had such a nemesis. I never talked about things like that with her.

After about half an hour, Mom and I were done with our mission. As we started to get in the cab of our truck, Bob and his gang drove by in their truck.

"Dennis Milam is a QUEER! Dennis Milam is a QUEER!" Bob screamed from the bed of the beat-up pickup truck as it tore past us and through the junkyard gate. He was laughing so hard he couldn't contain himself.

"What did he say?" my mom asked.

"Nothing," I said, choking back the tears.

I was devastated. No one had ever made fun of me in front of my mom. She looked at me, disturbed, but said nothing. When we got home, I got into bed and pulled the covers over my face and cried for hours. It just didn't seem fair. How could someone who didn't even know me hate me so much?

Months later, the whole school heard that Bob got in serious trouble with the police for stealing and might get sent away. He came to first period one Monday morning and his long hair had been cut short, neatly combed and parted on the side. Everyone gasped when he walked down the hallway that day. He, for a change, was being laughed at. He looked much younger and completely uncomfortable with himself. I didn't dare say anything to him about his hair for fear of retaliation, but I felt fully vindicated. I could not stop staring at his head. I was even happier when Bob disappeared from school altogether before Thanksgiving of that school year.

4-The Most Important Decision She Would Ever Make

I knew my brain was different from anyone else's. Hair was the most important thing I could imagine. Every single thought in my head had some reference to hair, whether it be my own hair or someone else's.

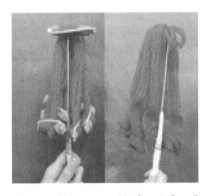

A yarn stick serves as "Stefeny Calvert"

Cutting girl's hair is a good thing: making her look prettier.
Cutting boy's hair is a bad thing: punishment and humiliation.
My dad threatens me with a haircut for being a sissy.
Bob had to get a haircut before the police sent him away.
I pretended to have power over Lester by cutting his hair.

I became fascinated by the effect a haircut could have on real people. For someone to look a certain way because of their hair and then be transformed simply by the reduction or removal of that hair seemed like magic to me. The person cutting the hair was the magician.

For a kid like myself who was immersed in fantasy, the magic of cutting hair gave me a feeling of powerfulness that I could not match anywhere else in my life. It allowed me choices, and those choices could reflect my taste or attitude. Having power in my own private fantasy world was better than having no power at all.

I developed an alternative personality on which all my fantasies hinged. I named her Stefeny. I thought Stefeny was a pretty name and didn't actually know anyone at school with that name. The name was also appealing because it sounded like the boy name, Steven. It seemed appropriate for my alter ego to have a girly-fied boy name.

When it came time to choose a last name for Stefeny, I went to the phone book and looked for a believable one that was not already taken by someone I knew in school. I liked Calvert because it wasn't too exotic or hard to say or spell, and it was near the beginning of the alphabet. I felt sorry for kids with names that began with letters at the end of the alphabet, because they were usually the last ones to get a turn—always on the bottom, placed farthest from the front in the alphabetized world. I didn't give her a name with A or B because Stefeny was humble and shy like myself and would be nervous to be first at everything life dictated.

Stefeny Calvert was everything I couldn't be because of my gender. She was a confident, feminine version of me, a side of my personality my environment had robbed me of. If my dad and the boys in school hadn't made fun of me for being girlish, then there would have been no reason to be Stefeny in private.

I think everyone can be part boy and part girl.
Maybe we're more one than the other.
I have a lot of girl in me, but I still want to be the boy I am.
Stefeny is the girl part of me and I have to keep her all to myself.
Maybe she is the stronger part of me.

Stefeny can certainly wear her hair any way she wants.
It is much easier to be Stefeny, because I can control her easier.
Nobody likes the boy part of me, so Stefeny must be my more likable side.
It's a shame no one can meet the Stefeny in me.

It was easier to be a boy in my real life, as long as I could be Stefeny when I was home in private. I had complete control over when I was and wasn't Stefeny. The private, alter ego of Stefeny was a comfortable place I could look forward to going where I could be who I really wanted to be.

Now that Stefeny Calvert was an official character in my play world, I needed a prop to support her. I had become less enchanted with wearing the hair props—scarves, towels and my makeshift yarn wig. I became more interested in actually holding a prop. This allowed me to look at the hair without using a mirror. Plus the prop in my hand was an obvious extension of my characters, almost like a puppet. The need to participate in this type of playtime seemed less shameful; I was controlling something forbidden rather than becoming something forbidden. I wanted something that could represent hair. Yarn had been a fine substitute when I made the hippie wig, so it became the key material. What I came up with was a makeshift doll.

I pulled apart a wire clothes hanger and cut a two foot piece from it, discarding the rest. I doubled the hanger and bent it into the number "7," making it stand about eight inches tall. To form a comfortable handle, I quickly wrapped a couple of feet of masking tape around the vertical part of the stick. I then cut approximately fifty pieces of yarn about eighteen inches long. I grabbed three to four pieces at a time and folded them in half, tying them evenly to the horizontal part of the stick so they dangled down beside the vertical part. I repeated this until all of the precut yarn was on the stick.

It took a lot of imagination to visualize this device as Stefeny. The horizontal part of the stick with the yarn hanging from it represented the top of her head. I would hold the stick at the bottom of the vertical part, allowing four or five inches above my hand to imagine her face. The yarn would drape over my hand and down my arm, representing her shoulders and back. Essentially, the stick and my arm together became a doll representing Stefeny Calvert.

When I wasn't immersed in Stefeny-play, I found myself informally researching the subject of hair. I loved watching Lindsay Wagner as the *Bionic Woman*, because her hair would flip and blow in the wind while she was running. *Charlie's Angels* was also one of my favorite hair shows. Most little girls were running around with toy guns pretending to be Charlie's Angels; I was prancing around waving my wire and yarn stick pretending to be Stefeny, acting like Farrah Fawcett-Majors.

I was spending about fifty percent of my secret playtime focusing on traditional female role models, just like a lot of little girls. Stefeny wanted to be a wife and mother; she wanted to be a teacher; she wanted to be a cheerleader; she wanted to be prom queen. But her biggest dream was to be a famous actress in plays and movies. Stefeny's history was erased from day to day, so one day's fantasy play didn't always correlate with the next day's agenda. I allowed myself complete freedom to be Stefeny, and her possibilities were as endless as my imagination.

Since men and boys were still pretty scary to me, their roles in my fantasies were limited to supporting ones. I virtually eliminated men from my fantasy world. Stefeny had a dad and various fantasy husbands, but they were working out of town. Her boyfriends were usually only spoken about, and when she got pregnant, it was certainly always an immaculate conception. If the offspring happened to be a boy, he didn't have much personality and usually remained an infant.

The other fifty percent of my playtime dealt with hair play. I liked giving thought to what hairstyles were pretty. I loved the versatility hair could offer to one's appearance and self-esteem. Stefeny had a fairly narrow existence. My longing to have long hair had been stifled, so her existence mostly facilitated my need to play with hair. She usually spent more time doing her hair than actually participating in teacher, cheerleader, bride, mother or actress activities. To me, a girl couldn't be popular without long, pretty hair. A teacher had to wear her hair in a bun; a woman always comes up with some special hairstyle for her wedding; and an actress had to be prepared to wear her hair all sorts of ways. In Stefeny's world, decisions about her hair were the most important decisions she would ever make.

Occasionally, my fantasies had drama. If Stefeny was suffering, it was likely her hair was, too. A bad perm or haircut always corresponded to something bad happening in the more realistic part of her life: a divorce, a death, sickness, unpopularity. Just as I was growing up feeling like a victim, occasionally Stefeny became victimized. She could scream and savagely flip her hair around in her defense. When depressed, her long hair could hang in her face, providing a hiding place from the world.

I was scavenging for materials to keep me afloat in my fantasy life. I became pretty good at coming up with substitute hair accessories and equipment. Paper and wire bread ties became useful as barrettes. Mom's perm rods came in handy when I discovered that yarn could be heat set into curls by holding the yarn in front of an electric space heater. I even tried my hand at yarn hair coloring using magic markers.

Cutting yarn with such a high degree of frequency was producing a lot of debris. My bedroom floor was often covered in fuzz and yarn slivers. Something in the back of my mind told me that this was an activity that would be frowned upon by my parents, so I had to pay close attention to cleaning up the evidence. I vacuumed my bedroom incessantly, which fed my mom's suspicion. I also knew that I couldn't simply throw away the cut yarn in my own wastepaper basket, so I had to take it directly outside to the garbage bin or try to hide it at the very bottom of the kitchen trash can.

I also had a supply and demand problem. There was only so much yarn around the house at my disposal. It was only a matter of a time before I had cut all the available yarn too short to be of use. After convincing my mom that I wanted to learn to crochet, she bought me a few skeins of yarn of my own. After a couple of tutorials, she caught on that I was cutting it up. I did the same routine on my grandma, asking for her extra yarn. When my yarn resources finally dried up, I began stealing yarn from my mom and grandma, even if it was needed for their current crocheting projects.

One of the few times I ever saw my mother lose her temper was when she discovered I had cut up an entire skein of her yarn. She was in the middle of crocheting an afghan for a wedding gift and was on a deadline. She had bought the yarn out of town and was furious that she was going to have to make an extra trip to Indiana to finish the present. The worst part was that mom warned my grandma to keep an eye on her yarn. When asked, I gave no reason as to why I needed to cut up so much yarn.

Eventually both of my parents caught on to the fact that I was pretending that the yarn stick was a doll with long hair, even though I was doing my best to hide my activities. Neither of my parents questioned me much about this strange play. My mom knew there was a large quantity of yarn going into my bedroom. After she stopped buying yarn for me, she never really questioned where I was getting it or why I needed so much. Instead of initiating a discussion about my behavior, my mom simply took my props away and threw the yarn stick in the trash. This was only a minor setback. I would just make another one. My dad continued to mock me under his breath for playing with yarn and pretending it was hair. He always had a disappointed look on his face that made me sick to my stomach.

I wondered if the son of a barber would be treated the same way.

5-The Stefeny Calvert Show

(A big sparkly sign comes down from the sky. It says; THE STEFENY CALVERT SHOW in big letters with lights. Stefeny enters. She looks beautiful. She has on a pretty blue dress and her hair is long and amazing.)

STEFENY
Hello everyone and welcome to the Stefeny Calvert Show. I am Stefeny and I am so happy to be here!

(Applause)

Today on my show we are going to talk about me: Stefeny. I know you all want to know more about me, so today I am going to take questions from the studio audience.

(Applause)

Thank you. Thank you. All right everyone, who has a question for me?

AUDIENCE MEMBER
Are you single? Do you have a boyfriend?

STEFENY
Awwww. Sweet question. You may have seen me around with lots of different guys. Right now I'm dating

Grant Goodeve from the TV show *Eight is Enough*. He's the dark-haired guy on the show. He's really cute and we're in love. We plan on getting married soon. I already have my wedding dress and everything. We're so happy right now.

(Applause)

Thank you. Who has another question for me?

AUDIENCE MEMBER
Do you want to have a baby?

STEFENY
Oh my God. Yes. I do. I want to be a mom real bad. I want to have a baby to love me and who I can take everywhere I go. I think it will be so special to be pregnant with a baby inside me. I can't wait. I'll have to get all new clothes.

AUDIENCE MEMBER
What were you like in school?

STEFENY
That's a great question. Thank you.
I love school. I love to learn. I get all As. Also, I'm a cheerleader, and I was the prom queen. My teachers loved me and I always had a lot of friends. I never did any sports or liked the sports too much, just the cheerleading.
Next question? You ... over there.

AUDIENCE MEMBER
Are you still a teacher?

STEFENY
Yes. Yes, sometimes I am a teacher and sometimes I am a professional actress. I love acting, especially the serious

plays—the more serious the better. I do comedies every once in a while, but my favorite are the dramas. I have won a lot of awards for acting.

AUDIENCE MEMBER
What are some of the plays and movies you have done?

(Applause)

STEFENY
Awwwww, thank you, again. Thank you so much.
I was Lucy in *Dracula*. I got to scream a lot in that play. I love to scream in plays. I played Mary in *Vanities*—lots of cussing. I got to say "fuck" a lot.

(The audience giggles)

My hair was long for those two shows.
I played Martha in *The Children's Hour*. I was a lesbian and killed myself in that one. I had short hair then.
Abigail in *The Crucible*—more screaming.
I loved stabbing the guy with the scissors in *Dial M for Murder*. My hair was all curly for that one.

(The audience gasps)

Let's see …
I was very, very sad in *Glass Menagerie*.
And nobody loved me in *The Heiress*. I wore a big dress, and my hair was all pulled back in a very tight bun in that play.
I had a heart attack and died in the first act of *Deathtrap*.
I was plain in *The Rainmaker*. People liked to see me be ugly because they know I'm really pretty in real life.

I am also developing my own play version of *The Bell Jar*. It is about a woman who wants to kill herself.

AUDIENCE MEMBER
Do you ever do musicals?

STEFENY
Oh, yes. I played *Evita*.

(Applause)

Thank you.

It's my favorite role of all time. It has it all. I am sexy and powerful, and then I get dramatic and die. I had a million hairstyles for this musical. I love to sing.

I played Effie in *Dreamgirls*. I had a big dramatic number in that one. Everyone loved it. But I had to wear a fat suit to do it.

I have a wonderful costume designer named Dennis. He designs all my costumes.

AUDIENCE MEMBER
Wow. That's great, Miss Calvert. Which ones did you win awards for?

STEFENY
Well, I won the Best Actress award for *Evita*. I also won the award for *Dreamgirls*. I got to sing my song on TV for that one.

I hope I win for *The Bell Jar*, too. We'll see about that one.

I have won more awards for stuff than anyone in my town, but people still like me and respect me. I am not stuck up at all.

AUDIENCE MEMBER
Can you sing a number for us now, Miss Calvert?

(Applause)

STEFENY
Of course I can. I would love to.
(Applause. A piano is rolled out on the stage)

I am going to do one of my best numbers. It is from
Evita. I am sure you have heard it. It is "Don't Cry for Me,
Argentina."

(The full orchestra plays and a balcony rises out of the
floor. Stefeny is bathed in beautiful light. She has magically
changed outfits and her hair is pulled tight into a low bun.
Stefeny finishes the song perfectly. Wild applause. The lights
fade out. Patti LuPone would be proud.)

6-We Girls Can Do Anything

I was in awe of Mattel's Barbie-marketing slogan "We
Girls Can Do Anything." Barbie had become a modern
woman. The company was widening the appeal of the
fashion doll by being less specific. The doll was originally
conceived in the late 1950s as a more traditional young
woman focused on poise and glamour. By the 1980s, Barbie
became more of a career-minded toy, encouraging girls to be
more goal-oriented. Barbie, and those who played with her,
could be anything—a teacher, a doctor, an astronaut, a
cowgirl, or an ambassador for world peace. She could even
work at McDonald's.
    Grandma's toy box didn't have any Barbie dolls, so the
only place I could play with a Barbie was at my cousin
Angel's house. She was a few years younger than me and had

several Barbies of her own. There seemed to be a sanctioned way to play with Barbie with other girls. The doll-playing had to be interactive. It was hard to indulge in Stefeny-play with someone else in the room. I had to really fight to stay interested in group play and not become disengaged.

> *I have to pretend to be a regular boy playing with a girl doll.*
> *I act like I am playing with the dolls only to entertain Angel.*
> *This is not at all how I want to play with a Barbie doll.*
> *I cannot be Stefeny and play this way.*

Eventually, I didn't care if I looked too much like a sissy in front of Angel. I had limited time with a real doll and I didn't want to waste it. As we got older I became less and less interested in maintaining the act around other kids, and they were becoming less and less interested in playing with me.

One weekend, I got sucked into my own world of Stefeny-play with Angel's Barbie dolls. I ignored her and she quickly grew bored with the dolls and wanted to play basketball outside with her brother and some of the other neighborhood kids. I wasn't interested, so she went outside, leaving me alone in her bedroom. This was a cherished time for me, because it was the first time I was alone with my favorite toy. I had the opportunity to engage in Stefeny-play however I wanted.

> *I feel happy and more myself playing with a doll than any time in my life!*
> *I feel creative and smart and the world is on my side!*
> *Barbie has long blond hair just like I want to have; just like Stefeny has. Angel doesn't play with her dolls the way I do.*
> *She is silly and doesn't care like I do.*
> *If I had this doll I would never get bored.*
> *I need this doll to be Stefeny.*

Angel has many dolls and will never miss this one.
She is a girl and her mom will buy her however many
she wants.
She doesn't even take care of them. I must have this
doll!

That afternoon was pivotal because it was then I decided that I had to have an actual doll of my own, even if I had to steal it. I was a desperate, hollow child who ached for a toy that most girls took for granted. A real doll was going to put a vivid face on Stefeny Calvert. Barbie was the ideal feminine toy. I already had a few years of continuous role-playing under my belt, years in which I felt like I was missing a real doll. This doll was the key to fleshing out my hair fantasies.

I quickly tucked the doll into my tube sock, pulling the leg of my pants down over it. I was terrified of getting caught, knowing my dad would be embarrassed for both of us and would want to punish and shame me. I couldn't wait to get home and close the door to my bedroom and play with my doll.

I got the doll home without anyone knowing. I was delighted and felt like something wonderful and important had happened to me. I spent hours braiding, combing and styling the doll's long blond hair. It didn't matter that she only had the one evening gown that had been on her back when I stole her. I put her in GI Joe's clothes, including all the homemade dresses I'd made for him, and cinched in the waist. I felt like I had graduated or passed some tough initiation. I no longer had to rely on my crude yarn stick to support my fantasies.

Possessing a real doll heightened and enhanced the world of Stefeny Calvert. There was only a minimal amount of guilt from the theft of the doll. I quickly became too engrossed in actually playing her to care about my cousin Angel's loss. I could now blend a real doll and Stefeny and pretend I was one of the girls at my school.

A few of the most popular girls in middle school started to get their hair cut into short, Dorothy Hamill-style haircuts. The famous figure skater's look was popular all over television. The haircut was all the rage and everyone was talking about it in class. One by one, other girls got their hair cut, too. It became an epidemic. I was fascinated to sit in the cafeteria before school and watch a newly shorn girl come into the room. All the other shorn girls would gather around and admire the girl's new haircut. It was like she had joined a cult. By the end of the school year, there seemed to be no girls left with long hair. If I had been a girl with long hair, I would have cut my hair like the others in a heartbeat, just to be popular.

Being a boy, I wasn't allowed to have long hair to cut like the girls, but Stefeny Calvert was. I held out as long as I could. After about two weeks of intense play with Angel's stolen Barbie doll, I decided to allow myself to give Stefeny one haircut: to her shoulder blades.

Just as when I'd played with the yarn stick, the doll was a tool to pretend to be Stefeny. I felt like I was Stefeny, so cutting the doll's hair was like getting a haircut as her. Not at all like the real haircuts forced on me by my dad. Cutting the doll's hair allowed me to fit in and be prettier. I was emulating my female peers at school.

I set the scene up in my head much like I imagined a schoolgirl makeover to be. Just as I had witnessed girls at school go through different looks and hair changes, so would Stefeny. Cutting the Barbie doll's hair was going to be carried out with much more fanfare than any of the haircuts I'd performed on the yarn stick. This haircut would be the closest I had ever come to the kind you got in a real beauty salon.

I became a dramatist as I developed a fantasy story line for Stefeny to justify the makeover.

*I have been growing my hair out for years. I am ready
to get my hair cut before the school concert.
My mom scheduled the appointment after school the
day of the concert. She is as excited about the change
as I am and helped me pick out a new hairstyle from a
magazine.
I haven't told anyone that I am going to do it. I'm a
little bit nervous.
I'm just going to show up at the concert with a new
look!
Everyone will be shocked.*

There was some last minute indecision, but finally the
haircut began. I definitely had mixed feeling about cutting
this doll's hair. I knew I wanted to perform the haircut, but I
also knew that that if I kept cutting her hair, the doll would
eventually become less interesting to play with. This doll
wasn't like the yarn stick; I couldn't put more of the same
hair on her head. Despite the doll's impending depreciation,
it was clear to me that the whole point of my playtime was to
eventually give a haircut. It was the climax of my fantasies.

I carefully draped a piece of cloth around the doll's
shoulders and wet and combed her saran hair, sectioning it
off. I was mentally performing double duty at this point,
pretending to be the hairstylist as well as Stefeny receiving
the haircut. I let out an audible gulp after the first cut. It was
too late to turn back.

"Oh my God! I can't believe I am doing this!" I said out
loud, as Stefeny and as myself.

I gently sliced off each section. A couple of strokes of
the comb, a little evening up and the makeover was
complete. Stefeny had a new look.

A Barbie doll haircut was vastly more fulfilling than a
yarn stick haircut. An hour or two later, I felt I needed to do
another makeover. By the time I went to bed that evening,
the doll was bald and I no longer had the valuable tool for

my playtime. I was depressed, like I had bottomed out from a great high.

> *I am so mad at myself.*
> *Having the real doll in my hand helped me really get lost inside Stefeny.*
> *I feel like I had something wonderful and exciting for a few minutes and now I am back where I started.*
> *I have nothing.*

The next day, it was back to the same yarn stick I had relied on for years. I tried making Barbie a yarn wig, but it wasn't the same. I was already trying to think of a plan to get a new doll.

Because we lived in the country, my bike stayed at my grandma's house where I had city streets to ride it on. My parents both worked, so I traditionally rode my bicycle to my grandma's house after school and waited the hour or two for my mom to pick me up. I hated taking the school bus because it was the place I got harassed the most by other kids. This was an arrangement that had been going on for a few years to help me feel safe from bullies. This was golden time to me because it allowed me a dose of freedom from school and my parents.

Many stores lined the town square of Robinson, which surrounded the big brick county court house. It wasn't unusual for me to take a spin through the square and do some shopping after school with my allowance. My favorite store was a small department store named The Index Variety Store. I always found myself drawn to the doll aisle. Despite the aisle being tucked away in a quiet corner of the store, I was terrified to actually spend time looking at the dolls, for fear of a classmate catching me. My time in the aisle was limited to just a few minutes of me trying to look indifferent, yet aching to touch or own a doll.

My parents kept close tabs on how I spent my allowance, so I started faithfully saving my lunch money. I wasn't happy to be skipping lunch, but I knew it would be worth it when I finally got the doll in my hands. After about two weeks, I had the money. I was a wreck at the thought of actually having to pick up a doll, carry it to the counter and pay for it in front of a sales clerk and anyone else who was standing in the checkout line. Serious consideration had to be given to this purchase, but I had starved without lunch—and without a doll—for too long not to go through with it.

After school one afternoon, I rode my bike to The Index with determination. I decided that the direct, no nonsense approach was the best. I rapidly marched into the store, grabbed the doll off the shelf and walked to the counter. I was very nervous, but I paid for the doll and got on my bike and rode away. A few blocks from the store, in a residential neighborhood, I stopped and carefully pulled the doll out of the box. I unhooked her from all of the cardboard packaging and put just the doll in my book bag. It was a lot easier to smuggle just the doll into my house, so I dumped all of the packaging in a nearby trash can.

I got the new doll home without incident. It was even better than the first, which had been played with long before I had her to myself. The doll even smelled new. An added bonus was that I still had the outfit from Angel's doll. Now I had two real Barbie outfits, plus all the homemade dresses from GI Joe.

Playtime commenced with fervor. However, I was repeating my patterns. Within three days of getting the store-bought doll, it had no hair. Now I had two bald Barbies and a definite addiction.

By the eighth grade, most girls were beginning to give up their Barbie dolls, but I was just getting started. I felt left behind. Other boys my age were consumed with cars and sports and were beginning to discover the opposite sex. I was still dependent on the pretend world in my head—a world of femininity and obsession with hair.

7-Doll Withdrawal

*The west side of Robinson Square
in the 70s. I spent a lot of time at The Index.*

*I can't sleep or care about school anymore.
My cravings to cut hair keep getting stronger, much
stronger than cutting yarn.
As soon as I get my hands on a doll, I just have to cut
its hair.
My thoughts go so fast when there is hair to cut, I
cannot keep up.
Next thing I know I have done it.
I am not sure if Stefeny is a good thing or if she makes
me want to cut more.
I can't eliminate Stefeny any more than I can
eliminate the need to cut.*

I went back to The Index. I lurked around all of the toy
aisles and finally got up the courage to walk down the Barbie
aisle again. The store was particularly quiet that day, so I felt
a bit more at ease as I glared at the shelves of Barbies and
Barbie accessories. I stood there amazed and depressed. I
couldn't imagine what I had done to deserve such anxiety. I
was being tortured at school and now I was torturing myself
over a toy I was convinced I needed but wasn't supposed to
have.

*I wish I could hide in the dressing room until the store
closes at night.*
*I would come out after everyone has left and play with
all of the dolls.*
I would love to cut and style their hair.
Stefeny could be beautiful over and over.
*There would be no reason to fantasize about this if my
dad and the kids who make fun of me understood.*
*THEY have made me what I am, and I don't know how
to change.*

I decided I wasn't leaving that store without a doll. I
opened up a Barbie box, released the doll from her
packaging, and quickly tucked her into my coat. I walked to
the front of the store and left without paying for the doll. I
was twice as scared stealing this doll as I had been buying
the one the week before. I was trembling as I rode my bike to
my grandma's house.

When I got home to my bedroom, the fear died down
and I was relaxed enough to play with my doll. I was
delighted that this doll came with a different outfit. Now I
had three.

Despite having the brand new stolen doll, I went back
to the store the following day after school. It seemed so easy
to steal the day before. I was so miserable it didn't even seem
relevant that stealing was wrong. I certainly didn't feel as
guilty as I did after I stole from my cousin. I wanted to steal
again. I knew that I would be cutting the new doll's hair, so it
made sense to prepare for the future. When I got to the
store, the open package from yesterday was gone. The store
was the same as it always had been.

I opened up another Barbie package and stopped. I
realized I didn't really need another whole doll ... just the
head. I had two doll bodies that were perfectly good. I swiftly
popped the head off of the doll and put it in my pocket.
Stealing felt even easier this time. I wasn't nearly as nervous
as on the day before. I was careful; no one had seen me. I

was also glad to not have to hide an entire doll under my coat. I felt almost relieved. I opened up another package and tore another doll head off. I then swiftly proceeded to the store exit and biked to my grandma's house.

> *I really did it.*
> *Today something went right for me.*
> *I was strong and brave and TOOK what I wanted.*
> *The world wasn't against me and I was rewarded*
> *with the stuff I need.*

I replaced the bald doll heads with the new long-haired stolen ones. I now had a reserve. I knew that my new skill at theft was going to make things go a lot smoother in my private fantasy world. The possibilities seemed endless.

I was content for a few days, but suffered an expected loss as I cut one doll's hair. It felt like I had waited enough time for things to settle down in the store, so I planned a trip back. This time, however, I took along a seam ripper, which had a sharp point on the end. This would allow me a little bit of speed when opening up the packages. I could simply stab the clear plastic window of the box and reach in and yank the doll's head off. I was cocky as I strolled into the store, and I made my selections like I had all the money in the world. I decided to not waste the trip, so I got a few Barbie outfits to go along with the four doll heads I was stealing that day.

I became paranoid that the store clerks knew that I was the Barbie thief and were preparing a sting operation to catch me. I branched out and started stealing dolls from other stores. I even became brave enough to steal stuff while my mom was shopping in other parts of a store. Yet no one, including my mom, seemed to catch on to what I was doing. I felt like I was winning a prize every time I came home and emptied my pockets. I had to find a box and a special hiding place for my stash. I found that there was some dead space between the bottom drawer of my dresser and the floor. One would have to take the drawer out or actually move the dresser to find my hiding place. That seemed very safe. It wasn't long before I had quite the collection of dolls, clothes ... and bald doll heads.

My determination got the best of me one summer while on a Barbie stealing binge. Having taken a break from The Index, I found a fantastic supply of Barbie dolls and Barbie clothes to steal from another neighborhood store called Town and Country. I rode my bike there with my trusty seam ripper in my pocket. Their toy aisle was in the back corner of the store, which I thought would afford me some privacy. I was wildly cutting packages open and pulling out the contents out when I noticed a store clerk watching me from around the corner. I quickly dropped all the merchandise and exited the store empty handed.

Angry with myself, I decided I needed to go back to the store and get the pile of stuff I left behind. I knew I could not go back as myself, so I decided I would try and disguise myself to elude the store clerk who had spotted me.

I rode my bike to the Goodwill store downtown and bought a cheap women's wig for one dollar. My next stop was my grandma's house, where I secretly borrowed a blouse from my cousin Donna who was staying there. I bicycled back to Town and Country, where I put on my disguise in the parking lot before re-entering the store.

The disguise was not successful, because the minute I made my way into the store the same clerk spotted me and made no attempt to hide the fact the she was following me from aisle to aisle.

"Can I help you?" she asked, holding back her giggles at my disguise.

"No ... I'm just doing a little early Christmas shopping." I answered in a falsetto voice I hoped approximated that of a mature lady.

I sheepishly realized that my plan was an embarrassing failure. The clerk wasn't going to let me get near the Barbie aisle, so I turned around and exited the store, empty handed and feeling like a fool.

My afternoon at Town and Country had not discouraged me one bit. I rotated back to other stores with Barbies. I had become as engaged and obsessed with stealing as I had been with my fantasy world. The power of stealing began to rival the power of cutting hair. I was quick to steal every time something else in my life went wrong or I had a bad day. I was in a downward spiral and had no idea where I was going or what was going to happen to me.

Returning to The Index one afternoon, I was faced with a chilling image: surprisingly, no one had removed the debris from my shoplifting spree the day before. On the shelf before me were six headless Barbie dolls still in their boxes. I was operating faster than the store could keep up. For just a moment I was breathless and couldn't believe what I saw. I was responsible for the damage, yet still unaccountable, not only to the store, but to myself.

8-Karma

By the time I was a freshman in high school, I had built up quite a head of steam as a Barbie doll thief. I had reached a point where I had about six or seven dolls at a time and tons of doll clothes and accessories. I started making doll clothes for Stefeny when Mom wasn't watching the sewing machine. I was totally engrossed in the world of Stefeny Calvert that I had elaborately set up.

One evening, while sitting up late and reading her romance novel, my mom called me into the living room.

"Denny, I found your dolls this morning." she announced.

Her tone was serious, yet she didn't seem to be judging or mocking me. I instantly felt sick to my stomach. My contraband had outgrown the hiding space under my chest of drawers. I had become careless and had been hiding the sizable stash in a box under my bed. She hadn't been nosy, but had found them while changing my sheets. I was embarrassed and started to cry. I was a thirteen-year-old boy who had been caught with several hundred dollars worth of dolls. I couldn't imagine what my mom was thinking.

She calmly asked, "Don't you think we should get rid of them before your dad finds out?" This wasn't really a question; it was a statement with which I knew I would have to agree. I didn't want my dad to find out for fear of even more humiliation. I was certain he would make me get my hair cut short as punishment.

The only question my mom asked was, where had I gotten them? I told her I bought the whole box at Goodwill for ten dollars—a highly unlikely explanation since I had at least five hundred dollars worth of new dolls and clothes in the box. I knew I could not tell my mom that I had stolen the dolls. The truth would have surely got my dad involved. I was already mourning the loss of the dolls, and I didn't want to suffer any more. I wasn't a kid who got in trouble a lot, so my mom clearly believed my story.

I asked her what she planned on doing with them. She said she would take them to my aunt and uncle's house and give them to my cousin, Penny.

Penny's family didn't have a lot of money, and my mom was certain she would be delighted with the gift. She said she would take the dolls to Penny the next day.

How dare she do this to me?
How on earth will Mom explain having a box of new Barbies to give away?
Those dolls are the only thing holding me together.
They are MY dolls.
I ask for so little from this world and everyone is against me.
I am not hurting ANYONE by playing with dolls.

No one even has to watch me doing it.
She found doll heads with no hair or bodies.
This is the perfect time for her to really look at me and
ask questions.
I am scared of her asking questions, but I still want
her to.
I want her to listen and understand me.
She is the only person in the world on my side.
I want her to help me.
She didn't even look up from her book to talk to me.
I must deserve everything I get.
Maybe it is karma: years ago I stole the doll from
cousin, Angel, now my mom is taking my dolls and
giving them to cousin, Penny.

The next day she surprised me by telling me that she
would buy me another toy to replace the box of dolls and
asked me what I wanted. I had become a fan of *The
Muppets.* I had already collected hand puppets of Kermit the
Frog and Animal. I had desperately been asking for a Miss
Piggy puppet, as well as Fozzie Bear. Miss Piggy was the
most expensive of the set, so Mom had clearly been avoiding
buying her. I seized the opportunity and told my mom I
wanted the Miss Piggy puppet. She agreed. Miss Piggy had a
huge mass of hair that could be combed and styled.
Essentially, my mom was replacing one doll with another
that was more socially acceptable—an animal rather than a
human woman.

Losing my dolls was only a minor setback. It had been
too easy to shoplift the collection of dolls and clothes. Within
a few weeks, I was well on my way to building my doll
collection back up. However, this time I appreciated what I
had and was much more careful about hiding the stuff. I
emptied the beans out of my bean bag chair and hid all my
Barbie stuff inside. I got the Miss Piggy puppet as promised.
It was no surprise when she, too, was given a short haircut
while taking on the role of Stefeny.

When I entered high school, my need to play with dolls and cut their hair intensified. Stefeny was growing up right along with me and I continued to fantasize about being a typical teenage girl. However, the real me was being bullied more than ever. I was branded a homosexual before I was even thinking in those terms. There was noticeably more malice in the ridicule I was facing. Other boys were getting physically stronger. I remained completely defenseless.

Shoplifting was becoming more than just a means to get dolls for playtime. I loved the physical and psychological rush it provided. I shoplifted every time I went into a store. I started stealing more conventional items—magazines, school supplies, clothes, candy. I even boldly walked out of a store with an Atari computer game system while a clerk was distracted.

My parents continued to be oblivious as I came home with all kinds of stuff I hadn't purchased. I always had a clever excuse as to how I got stuff: it had been purchased from Goodwill, friends had given it to me, I had won a contest. Or I simply lied about how much things cost. I once stole a pair of Calvin Klein jeans from Roots—Robinson's most upscale clothing store. I took the label off the pocket, re-stitched it on upside down, and told my mom that I got the designer jeans for $10 because they were a factory mistake. She believed me and I turned the label back right side up.

Mom and Dad never questioned anything I told them. I made a conscious decision not to care about the lies or the stealing. There were so many painful things going on in my head, the deception didn't seem to matter. I got to a point where I didn't even pay attention to what I was taking. It was common to come home after an afternoon of shoplifting, empty my pockets; and find stuff that I had no memory of stealing.

9-Branded

There was a black and white movie from the 1960s that played on TV every couple of years called *Five Branded Women*. The premise was that five Yugoslav women are shorn as punishment for consorting with the Nazis. The commercials themselves would send me running and crying to the other room. I could never even think of watching the movie. The film, and the commercial, actually showed these women getting their long hair buzzed off with clippers by angry looking men. Seeing or thinking of a woman getting her head shaved for any reason would upset me greatly. That kind of humiliation was Stefeny's and my worst nightmare.

As this was happening, I developed a phobia about allowing anyone to touch my hair. I, more than ever, wanted to keep my hair long. I was gradually becoming more and more uncomfortable with the idea of barbers and stylists. At the peak of puberty, my mom and I almost came to blows over a hair appointment.

Mom picked me up from high school when I was a sophomore to take me to a salon to get my hair trimmed. I had a full-blown panic attack in the car and couldn't breathe. I refused to go and started gasping and crying hysterically. I thought seriously about jumping out of the car right there on the highway. My mom had never seen me so unhinged.

I can't do it.
I don't want people to see me getting my hair cut.
I won't be able to control what is happening.
I'm afraid of getting it cut too short.
I do not trust anyone.
If the stylist doesn't like me she can cut my hair too
short on purpose and pretend it's a mistake.
Even the haircutting cape upsets me; it takes away my
arms and legs.
A cape makes people look weak; like they are all
bound up.

45

*Sitting while the stylist is standing doesn't seem fair,
either.
Standing gives her power over me.*

Mom had to pull the car off the road. She just sat there,
alarmed, and tried to reason with me. Getting a haircut that
day would have been so terrifying that I would have hurt
myself trying to avoid it, and my mom could sense this.
Seldom had she seen me so upset. The truth was, I was now
equating cutting a man's hair with humiliation. It was a
humiliation I wanted to inflict, not receive.

"What do you plan on doing the rest of your life? Your
hair obviously isn't going to stop growing," she said.

She had been cutting my dad's hair at home for years
and asked me if I would be comfortable letting her cut my
hair.

"No!" I snapped, ""I will cut my own hair!"

"Do you think you can do a good job?" she asked.

"I know I can do it," I assured her. She was hesitant but
agreed.

The truth was my mom wasn't too keen on salons
either. That was how she learned to cut hair. She had gotten
a bad perm when she was a little girl from one of the
overhead chandelier perm machines with the metal coils
that make you look like Medusa. The machine burnt all her
hair off. She never went to a salon again. She cut her own
hair by taking a piece of cardboard the length she wanted
her hair to be and carefully cutting each section by lining it
up to the piece of cardboard.

No cardboard was needed when Mom cut my dad's
hair. Watching her cut his hair always made me very
uncomfortable. The relationship between haircutter and the
one getting a haircut didn't seem appropriate between
people who are suppose to love each other. I could not make
sense out of it.

My years of secret haircutting on dolls had afforded me
the ability to cut my own hair, which I did while locked in

the bathroom. Mom was surprised and complimented me on a job well done. She later confessed that she hadn't expected me to do a good job, and that she would have taken me to the salon to get my hair fixed if necessary.

When I started cutting my own hair, Mom decided to invest in a nice pair of haircutting shears. She let me help her pick them out. She made a big deal about keeping the barber scissors in her haircutting kit so they would only be used for their intended purpose. Her kit also contained a pair of black Oster clippers with five snap-on length guides, a comb, and a white cape. Whenever it was time for me to cut my own hair, I always had to dig the good scissors out of Mom's kit.

I had no use for the electric clippers on my own hair, but was fascinated by them. They seemed so elegant. I enjoyed the vibration and the humming sound. It was interesting that the casing got very warm after they had been left on for a few minutes. I found myself looking for an excuse to use them.

I pretended to shave GI Joe's head and beard with them once. This was a very clumsy task because the clippers were much bigger than the doll's head. When I started growing pubic hair, I hated it so much that it was a pleasure to use the clippers to keep it buzzed off. I felt such power just holding them in my hand that I always got aroused. It seemed only natural to rub the warm clippers on my erect penis. I buzzed my crotch every week, and each session I found myself spending more and more time rubbing the clippers on my cock. The intense warmth of the clippers gave me a warm feeling all over my body. I learned to get a fantastic rhythm going with those clippers.

One evening I found myself enjoying the rubbing and vibration with more intensity than I had ever felt in my life. With the clippers grinding on my erection, I had my first orgasm, shooting semen five feet across the room.

I was horrified watching my body turn into a man's body. It was like I was turning into a monster. I sank into a serious depression. Since I had met very few men I trusted, I certainly didn't want to become more like them. As I matured, I found myself believing all men were malicious.

When I sprouted my first whiskers, I remember my dad teasing me that I was going to have to start shaving. The thought of shaving my face made me sick. Dad made a big deal about it, acting like he was proud of me, but I do not remember him ever teaching me to shave. Mom quietly left me a razor and shaving cream in the bathroom, and I figured it out by myself.

10-Get a Haircut

I was a sophomore in high school when I first realized that I was attracted to men. But even my sexual attraction to men seemed screwed up. I had some idea of traditional homosexuals in my head. Having never had a male friend aside from my cousins, I had never really touched a guy's body. I admired a man's ass and how his jeans fit. I also had curiosity about penis size. However, I was extremely turned on by any man who had a beautiful head of hair. Men with little or no hair were of no sexual interest to me at all. Every day I masturbated while thinking about cutting a man's hair.

Brent McMann

It was the early 1980s and men's hair had become more sleek and groomed over the last decade. Hair approaching shoulder length, parted in the middle and feathered had become common. I was completely obsessed by men who carried that look well. While sizing up the guys sexually, I seemed to be way more interested in dark hair than blond. Curly or straight didn't matter as long as it was well cared for and long and thick. It wasn't hard to figure out whether or not a guy was vain about his hair. Guys who touched their hair fondly were especially exciting to me. If I saw a guy comb his hair, I was in heaven. If a guy didn't have hair I found attractive, then I rarely found anything else attractive about him.

Brent McMann was the first guy I ever found sexually attractive. He was a grade ahead of me in school and on the football and track teams. We were in the same Consumer Math class my sophomore year. He never made fun of me like a lot of other boys in school did. I don't think he even noticed me. He had a beautiful head of shiny, light brown hair that hung in his eyes; he flipped it out of his face constantly. Just as I had experienced with the Lester doll years earlier, I had an overwhelming urge to cut it all off. There were other guys in school I found attractive for the same reasons, but Brent was my favorite.

> *He LOVES his hair.*
> *His hair makes him a happy person.*
> *I can tell within a week when Brent will get his hair cut.*
> *He gets it trimmed every four or five weeks.*
> *I can just imagine him giving his stylist instructions on how to cut it:*
> *"Don't cut too much off"*
> *I wonder what he would look like with short hair.*
> *What if he was bald?*
> *No one would notice him anymore.*
> *I can't stop looking at him and his hair.*

My childhood fantasy world was overlapping with my newly discovered sexuality. I was still involved in doll playing and shoplifting to support my time pretending to be Stefeny. I fantasized about Brent as a supporting character

49

in the playtime. Since I had a crush on Brent, so did Stefeny. In the privacy of my bedroom, I spent hours combing, styling and cutting my Barbie doll's hair ... and pretending to be Brent's girlfriend. In my fantasies, Stefeny would cheer for him at his football games. Yet Stefeny did not want to cut Brent's—or any other guy's—hair. She was proud of Brent and loved him just the way he was.

By the age of fifteen, I was certain I was gay, but only admitted it to myself in the most negative of terms. I began to slowly break away from fantasies of Stefeny Calvert and indulge in a certain amount of traditional gay sex fantasies. Yet, hair remained the most important element of any fantasy. I invented a very strange sexual scenario of admiring a guy who had the kind of hair I found appealing, then wanting to rob him of the one thing I found most attractive.

I want him alone and all to myself.
Tricking him is the only way to get his attention.
He is under my complete control.
I want to worship his hair,
Letting him know I like it.
He can watch me touching it just like he touches it;
just like girls have touched it.
Then I want to slowly take all of his hair off.
Clippers are brutal; they quickly peel hair off the head.
Scissors are a tease.
The more he squirms the more I like cutting his hair.
I'm aroused, but I know he's not.

I got quite a surprise when I found out that my Aunt Rima was friends with Brent's mom. I spent the night with my cousin, Louis. We went through a box of old pictures for fun, and I found a small school picture of Brent from Kindergarten. I was shocked to see that he had a buzz cut. His hair couldn't have been more than half an inch long all over his head. Obviously a clipper cut. I quickly snatched the picture when no one was looking.

Once I got the picture home, I couldn't help but stare at it. He looked enough like himself in the photo, but younger. Same face, same smirk. His hair was a little blonder, but other than that, it was clearly Brent. I got an erection looking at his hair that short. I started touching myself. I pretended that the picture wasn't him in Kindergarten, but him after I had sheared him down. I didn't see an age at all. All I saw was the buzzed hair. In my mind, what the picture didn't show was the long pieces of hair that I had cut off of him. Despite his age in the picture, it was golden to me. This picture was probably the only way I would ever get to see him with very short hair.

My fixation on hair was more shameful to me than being gay; it was something so far removed from normal that I had never heard of anyone else dealing with anything like it. I would have been paralyzed if my obsession had ever been discovered, especially by the guys who were the objects of my desire.

Brent and I never had any personal interaction in reality. I was too intimidated to ever make eye contact on the rare occasion he was within a few feet of me. I would have been terrified if he'd known what was going on in my head. That didn't stop me from memorizing his class schedule and routines so I could get a good look at him from a safe distance. I knew he drove a red Mustang with two white stripes across the top that went from trunk to hood. I also knew he had a girlfriend named Janice he often walked to class. She was very pretty and popular, and I did my best to ignore her. I couldn't wait for the yearbooks to come out so I would have another picture of him. Occasionally, his picture would be in the newspaper during the football and track seasons. I clipped any sports mentions from the newspaper and saved them in my yearbook.

After spending most of my sophomore year fantasizing about Brent, I started to feel desperate. I was faced with the same kind of compulsions I'd had when I cut a doll's hair or shoplifted. I felt cheated and entitled to some crumb of satisfaction. Shoplifting offered an adrenaline rush, along with the payoff of getting to keep what I stole. I found that danger very exciting. Cutting hair was a way of leaving my mark on something. My infatuation with Brent had grown to a point where I needed to act out and achieve the same kind of high.

I felt very silly about having such a huge crush on someone who I had never spoken a word to or looked square in the face. There was no comfortable possibility of ever doing so. I would have been satisfied with many innocent gestures—shaking his hand, looking him in the eye and smiling, or just saying, "hello." In the politics of high school, all of those things were simply impossible to do without creating a potentially embarrassing situation. I decided I wanted to hear his voice. It seemed safe enough for me to call him on the telephone anonymously.

I will settle for his attention for a few safe seconds; something I can store away in my memory.
I don't need to do it more than once, but I want the call to be something he and I will both remember ... even if it is weird and confusing.

I found Brent's parents' telephone number in the Robinson phone book and weighed the pros and cons of making a crank call. I knew I would have to disguise my voice a bit. It seemed a safe bet that he would never know who was calling him.

I really didn't know what to say. Certainly I couldn't say anything that would give away my identity. I knew I wouldn't be able to keep his attention on the phone for very long. I didn't want to threaten or anger him, so I thought long and hard about what I could say that would make an impression.

One morning before school I got up the nerve and dialed the phone. I was having the same rush I got from shoplifting. A woman I assumed was his mom answered the phone, and I asked for Brent in the deepest, most realistic voice I could muster. She excused herself and called out for him loudly enough for me to hear on my end of the line. I heard footsteps approaching the receiver and then he picked up the phone.

I quipped in a deep voice, "Is this Brent McMann?"

When he said yes, I said with as much confidence as I could fake, "Get a haircut."

He repeated without much comprehension, "Get a haircut?"

I hung up the phone.

I could barely breathe. I ran to my bed and crawled under the covers to catch my breath. I didn't feel like I had accomplished anything with this phone call. I was neither disappointed nor relieved. I had certainly gotten his attention, but he couldn't have understood what was going on. I was dying to know what he thought of the call, but had absolutely no way to find out. The call was a futile effort. It was the only time I ever spoke to Brent.

About two months later, I was experiencing the same pangs I'd had before, feeling like I needed his attention. Another small, distorted piece of attention was better than nothing. I gathered the courage to act out again. I thought about what to do next. I wanted him to know that my newest prank was tied to the phone call, but I would still remain anonymous.

Padlocks on the lockers at my high school were optional, and students had to provide their own if they wanted one. Most kids, including Brent, didn't bother with locks at all. I knew which locker was his and decided that leaving him a gift would be my next stunt. I made a simple sign that said:

"GET A HAIRCUT—HERE, IT'S ON ME!"

Below the words on the sign, I attached an envelope with ten dollars inside. I went to school very early one morning and taped the sign in his unlocked locker.

The sign was better than the call.
It was a gift and a harassment.
Since cash is universal, I was sure he couldn't refuse
my gift. I'm sure he spent it on something other than a
haircut.
How could he not realize the sign and the call were
from the same person?
I wonder if he had a clue that it was me who did this?
I hope he thought about my pranks every time he got
his hair cut.
Maybe he shared the story with his stylist.

That was my last contact with Brent McMann. Since I wasn't close to anyone in his circle of friends, I never heard anything about the sign. I fantasized that he joined the military right after high school and had to get an induction haircut during basic training. It wasn't until five years later that I saw in my hometown newspaper that Brent had become a policeman. There was a picture of him with a short article. He was obviously a bodybuilder. He had very nice biceps bulging out of his uniform. His hair was shorter, but still appealing. I clipped the picture and kept it in my yearbook, along with all of the sports clippings about him from high school.

11-A Poem: Eight Ball

My head is turning
I am so confused
My life is worthless
I don't understand.
My life is a cue ball
Without a rack.

The stick is chalked
The remark is made,
The aim is perfect
The laugh is called
And my head is rolling.

I hit the ten ball
Ten is anxiety.
Then I bounce to the side.
I meet the four and eleven balls.
Four is anger.
Eleven is Hostility.

I roll down the center of the table
With the path all clear,
Except for the eight ball at the end.
Unlucky eight: suicide.

As I nick suicide,
I roll off the table into the corner pocket
Off the table of life I go.
Scratch.

The cue is replaced,
But this is not me.
Another white ball is alive.

I was fourteen years old when I wrote "Eight Ball" for
extra credit in my freshman English class. My teacher, Mrs.
Hazel Henderson, kept me after class one morning to praise
me for the poem. She probably wasn't surprised by the frank
and dark tone, because I think she knew that I was a very
unhappy teenager.

Suicide was something I had contemplated on many
occasions, and I wore my unhappiness on my sleeve. She
asked if I would allow the school newspaper, the *News N'*

Everything, to publish the poem. I was petrified at the idea, because I didn't want to draw any attention to myself. I was already an outcast and didn't want to add fuel to the fire. I was also uncomfortable getting involved with the school newspaper because Brent's girlfriend, Janice, was the editor.

I finally agreed, but insisted the poem not have my name listed with it.

The paper published the poem as being written by an anonymous author and it was a big mystery for some to try and figure out who that author was. The poem was a cry for help, and I showed the newspaper to my parents to grab their attention. They seemed genuinely proud of my accomplishment, but never questioned me about the sincerity of the suicidal theme. Later that school year, Mrs. Henderson encouraged me to enter the poem in a national high school poetry publishing contest. I didn't win anything, but the poem was published in an anthology along with poems from other students across the United States.

Mrs. Henderson, also the drama and speech teacher at my high school, became my friend and mentor. She was the first adult who ever took me seriously. She was about forty years old and had begun her career in theater, fully planning to become an actress. Fate intervened and she fell in love, got married and went back to college to become an English teacher. She was a throwback from the sixties and something of a radical, free thinker compared to most people in Robinson. I loved her style and absorbed everything she said to me. She always claimed to see a spark in me. She took me under her wing and began molding my creative side, challenging me and making me think in ways no one ever had.

Mrs. Henderson encouraged me to do more creative writing and join the school newspaper staff. I had a handful of creative writing featured in the paper, all under fake names to protect my identity. I got over my paranoia of dealing with Janice and found her to be a good editor who could easily inspire me. I am certain she never figured out that I was fascinated with Brent and was harassing him about his beautiful hair.

I quickly realized I was less driven to write than to perform. Mrs. Henderson invited me to participate on the school speech team, taking part in such events as verse reading, prose reading and acting. This was the one thing I felt good at and was on the team for the last three years of high school. I even performed "Eight Ball" along with a handful of other poems. I eventually won my district and sectional meets and qualified for state competition senior year. I was the only student in my high school's history to do so. My parents never watched or read anything I performed in speech contests.

Every time I stood in front of an assembly and performed "Eight Ball," I would get a little choked up. The passion and honesty with which I performed it was intense, which probably contributed to my success in speech. It was strange to be performing a poem I wrote out of desperation and pain—a poem no one knew I had written. We competed out of town most of the time, where I didn't know anyone. As I recited the lines of my poem, I could tell which of the students and teachers in the room felt my pain. I wondered if some students suspected that I wrote the poem after all.

Students participating in extracurricular activities had to maintain a C average in their classes. It was a good thing that nobody checked my grades the week of the state speech finals, because I was close to flunking out. It was hard to attend school and live with the continuous harassment. I seldom attended an entire week without an absence. On more than one occasion, I had considered quitting school and pursuing my GED instead. My parents never asked why I wanted to quit school, but agreed to let me do so, reasoning that neither of them had finished high school. It was Mrs. Henderson and my success in speech and drama that kept me from dropping out. In fact, she was the only person who asked me what my plans were after high school. I hadn't really given the future any thought. She encouraged me to think about college. My parents never did.

My high school didn't actually do school plays, but my hometown had a very active community theater affiliated with the drama department of Lincoln Trail College, located in Robinson. They did two productions a year. I got very excited when I read an audition notice in the town newspaper for an upcoming production of the musical, *Oliver!*, based on the Charles Dickens novel, *Oliver Twist*. I wanted to play the lead role of Oliver but was too old. However, I won the role of The Artful Dodger and was very enthusiastic about the production. I immediately felt comfortable performing on stage and with theater people. I had spent years in my bedroom pretending to be someone else; it seemed only natural for me to want to become an actor. I was more terrified to go to school and be myself than I was to perform on stage. I quickly knew I wanted to work in professional theater.

The following year I was cast again in the musical, *Mame*, based on the book, *Auntie Mame,* by Patrick Dennis. Since there were no Asians in my hometown and I was the right age and size, I was cast as the Japanese houseboy, Ito. I gave a completely stereotypical performance, jumping and giggling with drawn-on Asian eyes, my hair spray-painted black. *Mame* is large-scale musical, and I was in awe of all the fancy costumes and wigs. Since I knew how to sew, I was eager to help out the costumers.

I became rather fascinated with one wig in particular. It was to be worn by the actress paying Agnes Gooch. In the play, Agnes goes through a transformation from a plain-Jane secretary to a vamp who eventually gets pregnant out of wedlock. The wig picked for Agnes was a waist-length, chestnut-brown wig with lots of waves and curls. The wig was to be worn up in a bun and then be taken down to go with a low-cut red dress she wore for her sexual awakening scene. When she returned, pregnant, the wig was to be back in a bun.

I had never seen a wig this long. It was shiny and beautiful, and I fantasized about playing Stefeny with this wig. With no trouble at all, I stole the wig and a Styrofoam wig block during dress rehearsals. I played hooky from school the day after I got the wig home. With the whole day to myself, I styled the wig into every imaginable style. Just as with Barbie dolls, the wig was cut shorter and shorter until there was nothing left.

The wig was certainly missed and searched for at the theater. I did feel guilty for stealing it. But the guilt didn't match the need I had to use it for Stefeny-play. In our production of *Mame*, Agnes went from a chestnut brunette to a mousey blonde, and no one was ever the wiser as to what had happened to the original wig.

Both my mom and my dad supported my interest in theater and drama, although they didn't identify with my artistic interests at all. Aside from my mom's crocheting, neither parent had a creative bone in their body. But they said I should be free to do whatever I wanted as long as I was happy. This was the first activity I had found outside of my bedroom that came close to making me happy.

My mom and dad came to see me perform in my productions. Neither was accustomed to seeing live stage plays, and would have never chosen to see it had I not been in them. My dad openly said he didn't want to go, but Mom always convinced him to go at the last minute. He had trouble sitting through an entire play, due to his obesity, and always left the auditorium in the middle of the performance. I still remember singing and dancing my heart out and noticing his large figure getting up out of his seat and walking up the aisle to the lobby. This would be his routine throughout my community theater acting career. Dad never once stayed for an entire performance and eventually found excuses to not come at all.

12-It Starts With the Letter "A"

While snooping in my grandma's attic, I found a picture of my mom. She is alone in the black and white photo and obviously on a fishing trip. She smiles while standing up in a small boat on the banks of a river proudly holding up an impressive catch of fish. On the back of the picture a date was handwritten: June, 1965. I was born on July 18, 1965. My mom has a tiny waist in the photo. I returned the photo and never told anyone I had found it. The mystery of the photo made me feel lost, even angry. I didn't know where I belonged or where I'd come from.

My mom on a fishing trip a month before I was born.

There were a handful of rebellious girls that I hung out with on occasion throughout middle school and high school. They were misfits who also seemed lost. The girls were nice to me, but I felt like a "pity friend." They didn't know what to do with me. All of them were sexually active, and I was the only boy they let in their circle they didn't have sex with. I felt ridiculous getting too close to most of them, because I wasn't really one of them, nor remotely like them. I felt like their pet.

A girl named Shawni was part of that crowd. I felt differently about her than the rest of the misfits. We were in the same grade and had known each other since grade school. She was very pretty but rebellious. She went to parties and drank, smoked and occasionally did drugs. She had sex with a lot of guys who were in their twenties. She freely told me about all of her adventures. Her parents were the opposite of mine: they stuck their nose in her business constantly.

I got close to Shawni through my cousin, Donna, who was also in our class.

The two girls were very similar and the only other teenagers with whom I felt comfortable. Donna quit school and got married at sixteen, leaving Shawni and me to get closer during our sophomore year with Donna no longer around.

Shawni would let me style and re-style her hair over and over. I helped her dye her dark hair red once. She never touched up her roots. I drew roots on my Barbie dolls so Stefeny would have hair just like hers.

Shawni started asking me, "If you knew a deep, dark secret about a friend, would you tell them?" I mostly ignored her question until she continued asking me almost every day with a sincere look on her face. At lunch one day we sat outside on the school lawn and she rehashed her same question. This time I pressured her to tell me what was going on.

"Is the secret about me?" I asked.

"Yes," she said.

"Is it bad?"

"I don't know. I am not supposed to tell you," she confessed with a worried look on her face.

"Who told you the secret about me?"

"I can't say. I don't want to get into trouble."

"What if I guessed it? Then would you tell me?" I offered.

"All right," she said. Shawni looked like she was getting nervous.

"What letter does it start with?" I asked. It felt like I was on a game show.

"A," she said.

I knew immediately what the secret was. "I am adopted, aren't I?"

"Yes!" she screamed. Shawni looked terrified. "Yes, Dennis! You're adopted! You are adopted! Oh my God, I am so sorry. I can't believe you knew what it was. Please don't tell your parents who told you."

Who are my Parents?!?!

The school bell rang and we walked toward the school building together. I asked her how she found this information out and she explained that Donna had told her.

"A lot of people at school know. It really bugs me that your parents never told you the truth. I would want to know if it were me."

I didn't ask her who my biological parents were. I was too scared.

I wasn't sure if what she told me was going to ultimately make me happy or sad. I numbly went to my next class and sat quietly and calmly. I didn't comprehend a word anyone said to me the rest of the day. There were the usual gay taunts, but for the first time in my life, the cruel words coming from my classmates didn't sting.

The picture of my mom in the boat; it all makes sense now, although I think I knew before I ever saw the picture.
Mom and Dad are so much older than the parents of kids my age.
I don't really look like either of my parents.
I have no brothers and sisters.
It also explains why there are only two baby pictures of me before I was a year old.

After school, I went to my grandma for answers. I sat down across the table from her that afternoon and burst into tears. It was the same table where we had cut out paper dolls years before. She gave me a warm smile and took my hands in hers. She explained that she thought that my mom and dad needed to be the ones to explain the truth to me. She hugged me and sent me home. She immediately called my mom to warn her that I had found out the truth and was on my way.

Minutes later, I walked into the house and found my mom trembling in the kitchen. My dad came into the room and the three of us burst into tears.

We cried for several minutes in one another's arms. It was the very first time in my life I felt like we were a family, yet I was about to learn the story of how we were not.

My cousin Janet is my birth mother?
Pregnant at fifteen and she kept me for almost a year.
I never liked her very much.
She doesn't take very good care of the two boys she has now.
Thank God my parents really wanted to adopt me or I am sure I would be dead.
Of course, now I understand why Janet acts weird around me.
No wonder she's the black sheep of the family.
Even she doesn't know who my dad is?
I just wish they would have told me sooner.
I don't believe my parents when they say they were going to tell me when I graduated high school.
How can I believe a word they say now?
This is why we never talk;
If we talked, then there is risk of revealing the truth.
We have pretended to be a full fledged family, when there have been secrets and lies.
They have lied to me for sixteen years.
Perhaps they have been lying to themselves, too.

My dad sheepishly explained that he had a bad case of the mumps when he was a teenager, which left him sterile.

"Denny, will you please forgive your mom and me?" my dad asked with tears in his eyes.

"Yes," I said with a lump in my throat.

Hiding my adoption is the perfect example of my mom and dad's main parenting technique: denial. If they pretended something was the truth, then it became the truth to them. Deception was so common in my house while I was growing up that I didn't even know it was wrong. No wonder I didn't have a grip on my reality. My parents didn't have a grip on theirs.

I took the information they finally gave me and tried to put it into perspective. There were still a lot of unanswered questions. Things only my birth mom could address. She lived in Robinson. I knew she probably wouldn't be going far and would be there when I was ready to talk to her, something I knew I wouldn't be ready to do for a few years.

What is a mom?
My birth mom certainly hasn't been a mom to me.
She is my cousin.
But my mom—my adoptive mom—what has she been to me?
Maybe there is something to be said for blood relations, yet I don't feel like I relate to anyone.
I don't know who I am. I don't know anything.
I look at complete strangers and wonder if I am related to them.
I don't especially want to know who my birth father is, but I'd like to know what he looks like.
Have I seen him and not known?
Maybe everyone knows who he is and is still lying to me.
Maybe I am a reminder of something my parents couldn't produce.
Am I a substitute child?
Have I been raised with substitute love?
Would they talk to a blood child more than me?
Could they have stood to raise me if I had known the truth all along? Would that have been too much for them?

After the truth finally came out, I still thought of my adoptive parents as my parents. They raised me, and I still loved them. However, I was hurt and confused and nothing could change that.

My parents let me stay home from school for a couple of days to gather my thoughts. I wasn't sure what to do. My whole world had changed on the inside, but everything was exactly the same on the outside.

I hid in my room and played with my dolls the way I always had. However, being Stefeny and cutting doll hair didn't seem like enough. I wanted more. I needed to cut something alive. Perhaps cutting could release some of the pain if I could cut something real, something outside of my fantasy world.

I decided to try my handiwork on the cat that always hung around our yard. There was a friendly yellow tomcat that we saw quite often but had only a simple collar with no tags. Perhaps he belonged to one of the neighbors; we didn't know which one. My mom had a soft spot for this particular cat, so she gave him a treat and a scratch on the head from time to time. I was always indifferent to cats in general, but this one seemed sweet.

I secretly got the family haircutting scissors and went outside to find the cat curled up on the back porch as usual. I sat on the porch steps and put the cat between my legs. He was on his back looking up at me. I rubbed his belly. He purred as I reached for the scissors in my pocket. All the feelings of the last few weeks were bubbling up inside me, but were disconnected. Without further thought, I took the scissors and sliced a chunk of the fur off the cat's belly. I felt slightly tingly. Not aroused, but that cut made me feel in control for a second. I took another slice. The cat showed no response. I felt alive for the first time since the day I had been told I was adopted. I cut several more chunks of fur from the cat all over his yellow body.

The cat suddenly stood up and ran away, trailing his cut fur behind him. I hadn't hurt the cat at all, but I felt both sinister and satisfied. Being covered in his fur felt meaningful—victorious in some sport without ever having to break a sweat. By the time I had finished cleaning up the mess, I felt ashamed. An hour later, the emotions all went away and I was back to feeling empty.

The next day, my mom came in from mowing the yard, upset.

"Did you see what someone did to that tomcat?" she asked my dad.

"What?" he said. I was in my bedroom eavesdropping.

"Some awful person hacked all his fur off! What kind of sick person would do such a terrible thing?"

I could tell Mom had no idea that I was the awful person in question.

13-Outstanding Drama Student

The Christmas after I found out that I was adopted was different from any of our past Christmases. It was my junior year of high school and the first year we didn't put up a Christmas tree or any decorations. I was given money by my parents to go buy my own gifts. My mom claimed she wouldn't know what to buy me. My parents insisted I not get them anything, either.

Christmas during my senior year was no better. There was no gift exchange in our home at all. To compensate, I shoplifted even more around the holidays.

My senior picture

It's very hard to watch the whole world be happy this time of year.
People seem to appreciate their families more; things are terribly distant in mine.
I am afraid I have ruined my parents' illusion of "family."

*It seems like they really believed the lie and got some
sort of enjoyment from pretending we were
biologically linked.
Once they had to face the truth I became a reminder of
their shame.
I feel like they are punishing me for making them be
honest with themselves.
I watch people Christmas shopping.
They are worried, tired, enthusiastic and busy with
shopping for all of the important people in their life.
I find myself "acting" along with them.
I'm stealing for me, but pretending to be shopping for
important people in my life that do not really exist.
There is no one important in my life.
I turn my mind off and I just keep stealing things.
By Christmas day, I will want to choke.*

A new director named Kirk Wahamaki took over the
LTC Community Theater and he immediately began to shake
things up. He was much younger than the previous director
and had a more innovative spin on the arts. His pick for the
spring musical was *Godspell*, and all the drama folks were
quite excited. *Godspell* is a hippie rock musical from the
1970s based on the Gospel according to St. Matthew. The
show was popular on Broadway and around the country
after other rock musicals like *Jesus Christ Superst*ar and
Hair paved the way. Was Robinson ready for this?

I didn't give a good audition and was quite
disappointed when I didn't get asked to be in the show.
However, a week into rehearsals, I was asked to be the
assistant director and assistant stage manager for the
production.

It seemed only fitting that Stefeny would get cast in
Godspell at home. I took some of her doll clothes, drew
peace signs, hearts and daisies on them and distressed them
like the costumes from the real show to add realistic touches.
Time after time she gave stunning renditions of the song,

"By My Side." At this point in my life, Stefeny Calvert already had a resume Ethel Merman would envy.

One of the Saturday performances of *Godspell* was the same night as my senior prom. I was torn. I cared deeply about the show, but whenever I discussed the prom, I pretended I didn't care. Kirk asked me if I wanted the night off to attend my prom. The truth was that I had never been on a date of any kind. I couldn't imagine who I would go with. The old slogan, "The show must go on" didn't help take away the sting of missing yet another ritual of growing up. To cope with the loss, I made a beautiful prom gown for Stefeny. She had long since broken up with Brent McMann. She was the belle of the ball and showed up at imaginary prom with John Stamos, who played Blackie Parrish on *General Hospital*. They both had beautiful hair and were crowned King and Queen. It was a night I will never forget.

I was barely going to graduate high school. My class rank was 140th out of 165 students. As graduation approached, I became miserable. I was due to receive a speech award from Mrs. Henderson for my accomplishments, but didn't want to get up in front of the whole school to accept it. I was afraid someone would yell, "Faggot!" or do something worse to embarrass me. Since it happened every day in school, there was no reason to believe it wouldn't during the ceremony.

Mrs. Henderson begged me to go through the ceremony. She was proud of me, and I was the first of her students to qualify for state finals in speech. I realized my success was an important accomplishment for her as my teacher. I felt like Mrs. Henderson had put my life back on track. I sometimes wondered if she, in fact, had saved my life. The least I could do was go to the ceremony on her behalf. I realized that I had to face my fear and get it over with. It seemed silly for me to be able to perform live on stage in a play, yet not be able to walk across the gymnasium and receive my diploma and drama award.

I finally agreed to attend and, without incident, accepted my diploma and a very nice silver cup with "Outstanding Drama Student—1982-83" engraved on it. My dad stood alone in the back of the school gymnasium so he could come and go as he pleased, while my mom sat up front where I could see her smile the whole time. Immediately after the graduation ceremony, my fellow students were hugging, saying their goodbyes and taking pictures. I didn't speak to anyone. I quickly turned in my cap and gown, went to my car and drove away. I got home from the ceremony before my parents did.

When my senior yearbook arrived, I was shocked to see that I had no listings of clubs or honors by my senior picture and name. My classmates all had their achievements listed, but mine were not. I had done speech and worked on the school newspaper throughout my four years at Robinson High School. However, there was nothing but blank space where my achievements should have been listed. I had been somehow omitted. The error seemed somehow fitting. I was glad to be done with high school.

14-Bursting Out of Me

I am free.
I am happy ... happy without a doll in my hand.
I feel like nothing can stop me.
The more successful I can become, the more I can show all of the people who beat me down that I'm strong.

I am the first one murdered in the LTC production of
Ten Little Indians.
Photograph by Rembrandt Studio, Robinson, Illinois

Making it through high school seemed like the
beginning of a new life, and I was ready to be a college
student. Having done a few shows at LTC Community
Theater, I took Mrs. Henderson's advice and enrolled as a
full student at Lincoln Trail College to pursue my general
studies. It was comfortable there, but I had to work very
hard to teach myself scholastic discipline. At the end of the
first semester, I made the honor roll for the first time in my
life. No one in college seemed to bother with gay taunting.
Not once was I ever called a name.

During my first quarter as a full-time college student,
Kirk cast me in the Agatha Christie murder mystery, *Ten
Little Indians*. I was playing a very British character named
Anthony Marston, who was a bit of a scamp. In rehearsals, I
rebelliously turned the character into an effeminate sissy. I
got an ironic high from the reactions of others to my being
over the top. It was my job to act gay and nobody wanted me
to subdue my interpretation.

My character was only on stage in the first thirty
minutes of the play. My mugging ended when poison was
put in my character's unattended drink and I got to choke to
death on stage to thunderous applause. Two hours later,
when I came out for curtain call at the end of the night, I got

a standing ovation. Finally, there was a payoff to acting like a fairy. Whether they were cheering my performance or the death of a flaming homosexual, I do not know.

My real life had a relatively normal tone, yet I remained sexually ambivalent. I stayed in the closet and the haircutting fetish seemed to be overshadowed by my college studies and busy lifestyle. The better my life seemed to be going, the less dependent I was on my old vices. I didn't have time to hide in my bedroom anymore and I didn't feel compelled to shoplift. I didn't need the rush anymore.

I felt strong enough to get rid of all of the Barbies I had kept for the last few years as a Stefeny security blanket. One morning before my classes at LTC, I meticulously dressed them, brushed and braided their hair one last time, and ceremoniously donated them to Goodwill. Deep in my heart, I hoped a little boy would buy them and find comfort playing with them just as I had for almost a decade.

I was an eighteen-year-old college freshman and my depression was lifting. Yet I started having vivid memories of the summer before the second grade. Slowly I began to confidently piece together an event that had lingered in the back of my mind for almost twelve years: when I was seven years old, I had been molested.

It seemed like the minute I was psychologically strong enough as an adult to process what happened, it started bursting out of me. I knew it wasn't just a dream. I remembered telling a kid on the school bus about it and everyone laughing at me for weeks. The rape itself and my classmates teasing hurt so much that I turned the truth off like a faucet. Kids brought it up for a couple of more years, and I told them it wasn't true after all. I desperately tried to believe it wasn't true, too.

After the feelings re-surfaced, I relapsed for just one day and mindlessly stole a package of batteries from Pamida, a local department store. The batteries were for a micro-tape recorder I used in my Biology class. I don't really remember putting them in my pocket, but I knew I was being followed out of the store by a store manager with a big blond mustache. I barely heard a word the man said to me as he questioned me about the contents of my pockets. He took me to his office in the back of the store. He showed concern for me. He was more upset about my arrest than I was. My first thought was how glad I was I hadn't been caught stealing a Barbie doll head.

I was eighteen and handled by the Robinson police as an adult. I felt numb while I was being booked. The man who fingerprinted and photographed me had a nice mustache just like the store manager from Pamida. It was a strange feeling for the man to be touching my hands while he took my fingerprints. I couldn't remember a man with a mustache ever touching my hands. Almost all of the men at the police station had mustaches. I was intrigued that so many mustached men were focused on me at the same time.

My parents were shocked by my arrest, to say the least. I had gotten away with many things, but had never really gotten in serious trouble. I didn't really care that I got caught. In fact, I was relieved. I finally had my parent's full attention. They were confused and angry, just like I had been my whole life. They bailed me out of jail and were poised and ready to listen to me. I knew that they expected an explanation for the shoplifting; instead I told them the whole story about being molested. I was sobbing hysterically like a floodgate had opened.

We were even. They had kept an important secret from me for years. Without realizing it, I had done the same thing to them.

My dad looked me square in the face and said, "If you had told us about this sooner, we could have done something about it."

Neither of my parents wanted the gory details of the molestation. They just sat there looking down at the living room floor. My mom cried, while my dad was clearly angry—

I wasn't sure at whom. I was so relieved to tell them what had happened. It felt good to not have to hide the secret from them anymore.

I decided I had nothing to lose by unloading another secret off of my chest. I took the opportunity to tell them that I was gay.

"No, you're not," my dad interjected. He seemed less angry by my latest confession.

"You couldn't possibly know if you're gay because you haven't been on a date with a woman yet," he said, vigorously shaking his head back and forth.

My mom remained silent.

How dare you say I'm not gay?
You've been telling me I am a sissy for years.
I finally embrace who I am and you think it's a mistake.
I've been trying to be a different person just to please you my whole life.
I can't do it anymore.
I don't blame you for my being molested.
It happened and I have to deal with it.
What I can't stand is that you said, "If you had told us about it sooner, we could have done something about it."
That's like saying I'm guilty of something, too.
What would you have done had I told you when it happened?
I've been crying for help for years and you've done nothing.
Would you have had the man arrested?
After the kids on the bus found out that I had "taken it up the butt," they continued to tease me.
I cannot imagine what my life would have been like if there had been publicity and parents, teachers and students who knew there had been a child molestation in Robinson.
I'm an adult now and can't change the past anymore than you can.

What I need is support and love and understanding NOW.
I have enough to figure out about my past without YOU laying anything heavy on me.

That was the end of the discussion about my sexuality. It was the only time my dad had ever spoken to me about sex. I told my parents that I wanted to see a counselor, and they agreed. I wanted to begin to heal from being molested. I wanted to figure out what impact that summer had on me as an adult, then put it behind me.

I was more hopeful that a therapist could cure me of my unusual fixation on hair. I reasoned that the molestation was over and done with, yet I had to find a way to live my day-to-day life with my nagging obsession.

I was shocked to find that my name was published in the *Robinson Daily News* the day after my arrest. It was a funny feeling to have my name publicly attached to a crime I had committed, after making a big deal about not wanting my name printed with the poem I wrote in high school. I was embarrassed, but discussed the details with a few of my new friends. Everyone I talked to seemed shocked, yet supportive. I went to court and was fined, which my parents paid on my behalf. The judge told me that if I didn't get into trouble for the next twelve months, he would erase the incident from my record. He also suggested I get some professional help. For the first time in my life, I had plenty of constructive attention. Help was on the way and I never felt the need to shoplift again.

15-I Want To Go Home

With the long overdue prospect of getting the therapy I craved, I began to emotionally sort out all the things that I wanted to fix. Every day since telling my parents about being molested, I had picked through my brain, trying to remember anything and everything I could about that fearful and confusing time of my life.

There were four Stickney brothers. All four of them had thick, dark, greasy hair. I noticed that immediately at my cousin Betsy's wedding. She was a happy, peaches-and-cream bride and her husband to be, Donnie Stickney, had extremely dark

Peter and me trick-or-treating, Halloween, '72

hair. Betsy's fair-haired little brother, Peter, stood out like a sore thumb as ring bearer next to the other three Stickney boys serving as groomsmen. Shawn, Michael, and Glenn Stickney were all in high school and looked like triplets dipped in ink.

Peter and I were quite the energetic pair of boys. He was a year younger than me and we were very close. I was mad that he got to be the ring bearer at Betsy's wedding. I wanted to wear a tuxedo and get all the attention. Peter was always better at sports and I was always better at arts and crafts. He had three brothers and a sister to keep him company, while I had nothing but my fantasy world. We often joked that we wanted to trade places.

Newlyweds Betsy and Donnie had settled into a small house on the west end of Robinson by the beginning of that summer. The week after school was out, my mom began routinely dropping me off on Betsy's couch every weekday morning around 6:30 am, before heading to work across town at the Robinson Transformers plant. My Aunt Jan would do the same thing with Peter. A couple of hours later, Betsy, Peter and I would wake and begin our day. Donnie had usually gone to his job by the time we all had breakfast.

Betsy had actually married Donnie Stickney in the middle of her senior year of high school. There was definitely a feeling of Betsy "practicing" being a housewife and mom for all of us. The truth was she was barely eighteen years old and not beyond participating in Peter's and my fun and games. Our days were filled with watching cartoons, games, swimming and running all over town in a car with no air conditioning. Betsy had a beautiful voice, and I was in awe every time she sang along with the radio. "(It's So) Nice to Be With You" by Gallery was the number-one song in the country most of that summer, and I could count on Betsy singing along to it every day. I loved the song and it rang true every time.

Occasionally Betsy had errands to do that required her to leave us alone for a few hours. Sometimes she would just drop us off at the city pool to swim, but other times she would leave us at her in-laws house across town. Almost immediately, I noticed the atmosphere at the Stickney house was in sharp contrast to the time spent at Betsy's. I was an awkward boy who didn't blend comfortably with the three rough-and-tumble, dark-haired boys who were also home from school for the summer. I felt like prey the minute Betsy's car pulled out of the Stickney driveway, leaving Peter and me there for the afternoon.

Glenn was the youngest. He was more approachable and always engaged Peter and me in playtime more than his older brothers did. One afternoon, our time with Glenn resulted in fantasy-play in an old, beat-up station wagon abandoned in the backyard under a large tree. Glenn turned very sinister that day, forcing me to take off my pants while lying in the back of the station wagon. He gave me no choice. Our "play" became very serious. Glenn Stickney touched me while Peter watched. I could tell immediately that Peter already knew this game. He was pushed aside. He was to be a spectator this time. Glenn gave me stern instructions on how to please him. I was expected to be quiet and submit to his desires.

> *He's trying to push his thing in my butt.*
> *It won't go in.*
> *It hurts real bad.*
> *Peter is watching.*
> *Quietly.*
> *This car is very dirty and I don't like Glenn holding my face down in the dirt.*
> *Crying, I can't breathe.*
> *I am real mad.*
> *I want to go home.*
> *I want to go inside; anywhere but here with Glenn.*
> *I know this isn't supposed to be happening.*
> *It still won't fit in.*
> *He is trying to jab it in so hard; too hard*
> *I can't be quiet.*
> *I am mad.*
> *It hurts too much.*
> *Peter knows.*
> *Glenn holds me down.*

I am out of my head.

He told me, "This is what grown-ups do."
I believed him.
"This is supposed to feel good," he said to me more
than once.
I cried even harder because it didn't feel good at all. I
thought something was wrong with me because I wasn't
enjoying it. I tried to get out of the car, but he stopped me.
Peter continued to watch, almost frozen in fear. There wasn't
much fight in me, just guilt and rage. Glenn penetrated me
hard and I bled. I almost passed out from all the crying and
the pain.
"Don't you tell anyone what we just did or you'll get in
trouble," he warned.
I was too scared to even think of crossing him. My
mouth and my spirit were sealed. I don't remember anything
else about that day.
A part of me died in the back of that car.
My memories of the rest of that summer were flooded
with fear. There was a second rape. I have a vivid memory of
being mad at myself for letting it happen again.
After that, it was a cat-and-mouse game. My intuition
told me that this was a family activity and they were all out
to get me. I didn't trust any of the dark-haired brothers. For
the remainder of the summer, I developed survival rules to
stay safe: I would not let myself be alone with any of the
Stickneys for any reason. I would not go to the bathroom at
their house, and was even inspired to stand outside in their
yard by the street, visible to cars driving by, while Peter
played alone with Glenn in the station wagon.
I often sat in the Stickney living room in a chair by the
window ready to jump out if necessary. It seemed the safest
place for me in the whole house. All three Stickney brothers
asked me why I was so distant. Taunting me one minute and
trying to comfort me the next. All three of the boys tried to

lure me to other parts of the house. I would not budge. It felt like they were offering me a truce: no more grown up games. I didn't believe them.

Country and Western music played all the time in that house. My last memory of that summer is sitting in that chair for what seemed like hours while the Stickney boys played a 45 rpm record of the Johnny Cash's song "I Want to Go Home," over and over. It felt like they were playing it just for me. I was humiliated. They knew I really wanted to go home, and I knew I would never let any of them touch me again.

16-It Was Like He Hadn't Heard a Word I Said

Although my family knew no one who had ever participated in professional counseling, I knew I was taking a step in the right direction by asking for therapy. My mom took me to our family doctor for referrals. Getting started with a therapist was tricky. The first problem was that there were no therapists in Robinson. All of the referrals were at least thirty minutes away. It was also expensive, but my parents continued to support my request. It seemed as though therapy was for rich people and television characters. I didn't take the privilege for granted.

The first counselor I went to was Dr. Israel in Terre Haute, Indiana, about an hour's drive from Robinson. He seemed interested in treating me only while my mom was in the room. I couldn't begin to talk about my list of problems in front of my mom. After two visits, I finally asked if I could talk to him alone. Once we had some privacy, I talked to him with relative ease. I told him about my adoption, being molested, the doll playing, being gay, and the shoplifting. I decided to leave the obsession with hair for later. I was shocked to hear him say that I was simply experiencing the same sort of issues that most people my age experienced.

Before I got therapy in 1985, I drove past the house where Peter and I were
molested in 1972. The tree in the backyard was still there
(Inset—One of the Stickney brothers, yearbook picture.)

Did most teenage boys play with dolls? I wondered. It was
like he hadn't heard a word I said. He didn't offer me any
information or feedback beyond that. I really didn't bond
with him at all, and after four sessions, I was ready to try
another therapist.

I asked my parents to send me to another one of the
referrals forty minutes away in Vincennes, Indiana. His
name was Dr. Burns. I was quite intimidated by his office,
which was located in an upscale part of a town. He had a lot
of very expensive-looking furnishings all done in dark colors.
The room was darkly lit as well. He was obviously a safari
enthusiast. Large pictures of him on various expeditions
lined his walls, as well as many safari animal heads and
skins. I wondered if he had killed, stuffed and mounted his
office decor himself. He was a large-framed man who
dressed in expensive suits and sat behind a huge desk. It was
creepy to imagine a therapist who murdered animals. He
seemed a million miles away from me in distance and in
spirit: very uninterested and unapproachable. My parents
were no more impressed with Dr. Burns than I was.

Over a month later, I went to the last referral—also the hardest one with whom to schedule an appointment. His name was Dr. Simms, and his office was located in Olney, Illinois, less than an hour's drive from home. When I entered his office and sat down for the first time, he stared at me like he was very interested and was waiting for me to start the conversation. I couldn't help noticing his thick red mustache, and began fantasizing about shaving it off. I tried unsuccessfully to put the sexual thoughts out of my mind.

I'm here for this man to help me.
I'm obsessed with his mustache after only five minutes in the room with him.
I'm getting a hard-on just thinking about touching and shaving his mustache off.
What am I going to do?
What kind of person am I?
Can he really help me if I am obsessed with his mustache?
I have to focus ...

He didn't say a word. He waited for me to talk. I started spilling my guts about my fantasy world and the years of doll playing. He started taking notes. I would stop talking and he would silently return my looks. He would give me a nonverbal signal to continue, and I would explain more of my dilemma, pausing for his response every few minutes. We sat there for an hour. I was talking almost nonstop and he didn't say a word. At the end of the session, he finally spoke.

"You are a very unusual young man," he said. "I think I may be able to help you."

I enthusiastically set up the next appointment.

Wow!
He called me a "man."
No one has ever called me that.
This guy is good.

He's ready to help me.
After talking with him, I stopped thinking about the
mustache because he seems to respect me.
He isn't disgusted by me or my weird life.
I keep waiting for him to flinch, but he really believes
me.
He didn't say much of anything but I truly believe he
can help me change.
I can see it and feel it.

The next visit, Dr. Simms had more to say. He asked
me about my obsession with men's hair and my haircut
phobia, which I had only hinted at the week before. I
elaborated and began confessing that I was sexually aroused
by the thought of giving a guy with nice-looking hair a severe
haircut against his will. Yet, I wouldn't let anyone cut my
hair. I cut my own hair because I was terrified of letting
anyone cut it for me. He closed his file folder and got up out
of his chair and gently took my arm. He announced that he
needed a haircut and he wanted to take me with him on a
field trip to the barber shop at that moment. He suggested
that I should get my hair cut, too. I panicked, believing he
was serious. All of my fears came back to me in a flash.

I will NOT go to a barbershop with him or anyone!
There might be guys my age there that will make fun
of me.
I might get aroused watching a haircut in person.
I can barely handle the guilt of getting aroused
watching it on TV, but I will just die if a guy is in the
same room getting a haircut.
I'm terrified that a barber will cut my hair too short.
I can't bear the thought of sitting in a barber chair
with a cape around me.
I can't let myself ever be that vulnerable ... no arms
and no legs and everyone looking at me with no
power.
There has to be a way to get better without
humiliating me like this!

I must have looked like a terrified animal (one that Dr. Burns would have killed), because he quickly let go of my arm and sat back down and continued writing in my file. It was a test to see what my reactions would be. He apologized and shared with me that he wanted to see how serious I was about the phobia. I was impressed with his scary approach. I think I was as fascinated by him as he was by me. However, I wasn't sure if that was good or bad.

Things become clearer and clearer after talking to Dr. Simms.

This is the best thing to ever happen to me.
It's so good to say things out loud that I was barely able to think before.
I'm beginning to feel like nothing was really my fault: the molestation, the urges to steal and play with dolls.
I feel like, for the first time, I can look forward to the future.

But after about six weeks, Dr. Simms became distant and seemed depressed himself. He announced that I needed to exercise. I was dumbfounded. All of a sudden, he was as caught up in my femininity as my dad was. He crudely explained that if I exercised and conditioned my body into a more masculine one, people would treat me differently and I would feel better. I had hung on everything this man had said to me for the last few weeks. I had cherished and believed in him like he was my personal savior. As he spouted his new therapeutic strategy, I didn't believe him for a minute.

Dr. Simms set up an exercise routine of sit-ups, push-ups, and jumping jacks for me. I was to exercise at home every day. He started expecting me to perform my exercise plan in his office during my sessions. I thought he was insane. We stopped talking altogether and I spent an hour exercising while he did other paperwork in front of me. I wanted to rival his mean barbershop trick by insisting he exercise with me or I wouldn't pay his fee. But I didn't. This went on for a few weeks. I kept thinking we would start talking again.

> *I get the impression that Dr. Simms has overbooked himself because he seems tired and works on a lot of other files while he makes me exercise.*
> *Either that or he doesn't know what to say to me anymore.*
> *I'm very upset.*
> *I hate exercise and I don't think exercising is going to change my obsession with hair.*
> *I can tell he doesn't either but still makes me do the exercises.*
> *Even if I build up my body, I am still a gay man with a low self-esteem and weird problems.*
> *I'm even more depressed than I was when I started talking to Dr. Simms.*
> *I'm angry.*
> *This was supposed to be my time to put everything in place.*
> *I know I cannot do it alone.*
> *Dr. Simms has given up for some reason.*
> *He was the first man I ever trusted, and now he is just like every other man who has been in my life.*
> *He wants to turn me into something I'm not, nor can ever really be.*

I never told my parents anything about what Dr. Simms and I discussed. Telling about his exercise theory would only prove to my dad he was right: I had to fight my femininity and become masculine. I became disappointed with Dr. Simms and gave up on therapy altogether. I announced to my parents that I didn't want to see him again.

My parents never questioned that decision. My mom even said I didn't seem to be acting any different and she was relieved to not be spending so much money on all of the doctors.

17-Friends Forever

In the spring of 1984, less than a year after finishing high school, I got cast as a tap-dancing sailor in a production of *Anything Goes* at LTC Theater. This was the first show I designed costumes for. It was also the first show I did after being arrested for shoplifting. I was afraid my fellow thespian friends may treat me differently, but no one ever mentioned my brush with the law. In fact, I was awarded the Phil Evans Theater Scholarship at Lincoln Trail College. This $200 cash prize was awarded yearly to a theater major at LTC. I was honored, since Phil Evans was my first director from *Oliver!* and *Mame* years earlier.

The wild and enthusiastic ensemble of local talent that gathered for this play was more than ready to live up to the play's name. It seemed to be a personal turning point for several individuals in the company, most of who had been together for years. Some old relationships ended between the cast and crew during the run of the play. Some new relationships began as well.

I met a woman named Jessica who played a character named Virtue. She was eight years older than I was and had bright auburn hair. She was also about sixty pounds overweight. Family and friends always complimented her beautiful hair and assured her, "If you would just lose some weight, you'd be gorgeous." Despite being the thinnest I had ever been, I still thought of myself as being fat and unattractive. Jessica and I had a lot of the same issues with depression and relationships. It wasn't a surprise that we emotionally bonded so quickly.

She was a small town girl, the youngest of three kids. She had been sheltered by her parents much the way I had been. They didn't listen to or understand her any better than mine did. She was only a small step ahead of me sexually, having had only one partner—a brief affair with an out-of-town, married Schwan delivery man who made rounds delivering frozen food in a big, yellow truck.

Jessica was as smart and artistic as I was, but life seemed to continuously pass her by. We became close friends during the spring months. I had no idea she had something more serious in mind. It wasn't until she seductively invited me over to dinner one night that I figured out she was sexually attracted to me. To my knowledge, no one had ever been attracted to me before. When she leaned over and planted a kiss on me, it was a very awkward moment. It took me completely by surprise. It was my first romantic kiss. I felt like I had no choice but to go through the motions and sample a relationship with a woman. It was what society expected of me. I knew it would also please my dad.

My attraction to men didn't change a bit. I still had crushes on men I saw around the college campus, although it was emotionally impossible to let myself get too close to them. Due to all of the teasing I experienced in high school, I still had a general mistrust of men. It was easy to keep that side of my personality under wraps, because there were no outlets for homosexuality in my small hometown anyway. Dating Jessica hadn't diminished my obsession with hair. I was still fantasizing about cutting a man's hair as well as more traditional homosexual sex. I couldn't change or ignore that subject.

Jessica became more and more sexually aggressive, and I eventually I lost my virginity on Good Friday, 1984. The experience was clumsy. I had a lot of trouble keeping an erection and felt hollow and fake the whole time. I didn't even ejaculate. Jessica, on the other hand, seemed to have a great time, but I think her enjoyment had little to do with me as a person. She could have found pleasure with any man who paid attention to her sexually.

I was putting on an act. I began doing the things Jessica wanted a guy to do and saying the things she wanted to hear. For the first time I had someone who really, really wanted to be with me. I couldn't bear the thought of disappointing her. I really wanted something to work out between Jessica and me because I liked the built-in companionship. I was a "boyfriend." I felt unlovable and I truly believed that she was my only chance at a relationship. It seemed like a great idea to put our two weak lives together to make each other a little stronger.

I enjoyed Jessica's company. We were best friends. I desperately wanted to feel needed. It was a wonderful, new feeling for me to think of myself as being "taken." I also desperately wanted to move out of my parents' house and saw Jessica as my ticket. Four weeks after we consummated our relationship, I moved into her apartment. Within days, I proposed marriage to Jessica. I was afraid she would stop needing me, and I was anxious to show the whole world that I was a man after all. She was shocked by my suggestion. After a few weeks of contemplation on her part, we immediately started planning a wedding for the following winter: December 1, 1984.

Jessica's parents reacted to the announcement with skepticism. Her dad made me uncomfortable from the moment I met him. I always felt like he saw right through me. My parents seemed to completely forget that I had announced that I was gay less than a year before. I certainly didn't remind them.

Jessica and I wanted to be the "All American" couple, but we didn't even look like a typical couple. As we planned our wedding, people looked at us strangely, finding it hard to believe we were engaged. I looked closer to sixteen than I did to nineteen. Jessica was a heavyset twenty-seven-year-old who had a bookish quality. We looked more like a high school teacher and student than a romantic couple.

Jessica is saving me.
I feel strongly that it is destiny that we met.

I know that I must be with her right now, although I
am not certain of what our future is going to be like.
She is a wonderful person and I love her.
I have never loved anyone before.
I know she loves me, too.
Please God, if I am making a big mistake, let Jessica
not get hurt.
She doesn't deserve to be hurt.

Despite the marriage being my idea, I was in a state of panic. I wasn't remotely ready to process or reveal too much about my sexuality, but I knew I was gay. I was also pretty certain Jessica suspected as well. With no other homosexuals around for me to pursue, it didn't seem to matter. As our wedding date approached, we were determined to be happy and not look back. The problem was that we were both too naive to look forward.

There was a heartwarming television show in the early 1980s called *Love, Sidney*, starring Tony Randall and Swoozie Kurtz. The premise of the show was an older gay man who lived platonically with a single mother and her daughter and developed a nontraditional family situation. It depicts two people coming together and making a happy life. By the time Jessica and I had met, the show had been off the air for a few years, but I remembered watching it. We both remembered the lyrics to the show's cute theme song, "Friends Forever."

Admiring the song and oblivious to the show's premise, Jessica and I naively decided to use "Friends Forever" as the theme for our wedding. We found the sheet music and gave it to our soloist to learn. We wanted it sung right after we were pronounced "man and wife" by the pastor. The slogan was printed on whatever wedding paraphernalia we could find. It was a perfect choice for unfortunate reasons. We were sincerely good friends, but no more of a romantic couple than the characters from the television show.

I must marry Jessica.
This wedding is the most important thing I have ever done.
I want people to look at our wedding and feel we are successful.
I never in a million years thought I would ever get to have a wedding.
Neither did Jessica.
I have felt so different from everyone else my entire life.
This is the one time I get to do something just like everyone else.
I am done.
I don't have to worry about relationships anymore.
People will stop assuming I am gay or different.
I can't wait for the wedding announcement to come out in the newspaper.
Then I can throw myself into being Jessica's husband.
She needs me and I want to make her happy.
That makes me happy.

Neither Jessica nor I had been to church in years or had any religious affiliation. We were pretty dumbfounded when it came to choosing a church for our ceremony. We decided on the Baptist church my parents were married in thirty three years earlier, because we liked the big brick building. We also agreed that the church's green carpet would look nice with our December wedding colors of burgundy and pink.

Despite her full figure and age, Jessica chose a ruffled dress with large hoop skirt. Strands of marabou trim adorned the bridesmaids' dresses and flowers. We even found bride and groom stuffed Teddy Bears for our gift table. We both agreed to have the ceremony and reception videotaped, even though we didn't own a VCR.

Jessica had no trouble at all choosing her attendants; she picked her sister, sister in law, and a friend from work. However, I had a great deal of trouble finding three men to accompany her three women down the aisle. I had no male friends near my age. Only a year and a half out of high school, I had never let myself get comfortable around guys. I was still scared of men. I automatically assumed they would torment me like in high school, or even worse, figure out my secrets. I choose two older friends from my community theater and Jessica's brother to be my groomsmen. None of them were under thirty five years old.

As our wedding day approached, I became more and more nervous. I struggled with the idea of being a husband, because I knew in the back of my head there was a great deal of my life yet to figure out. The marriage was only a slight distraction from the issues I had in my life prior to meeting Jessica; I still had a haircut obsession.

The day Jessica and I went to the jewelry store to buy our wedding bands, I spied in the corner a beautiful porcelain Victorian bride doll. A music box inside her tummy played the Wedding March. The doll was over two feet tall. Only its hands and head were porcelain; the body was stuffed and covered by a beautiful period wedding gown made from very nice fabric. The doll had long curly-blond hair topped with a veil and silk flowers. It was the most beautiful doll I had ever seen in my life.

Jessica wasn't a fan of dolls, but I was. Despite the impracticality of the doll, I felt like the "grown up me" needed that doll. I knew it wasn't a doll to be played with. The hair could never be combed and you could never undress the doll. I thought about the doll for a few days and decided I needed that doll as a symbol of my own "growing up." For the same reasons a grown woman would want to own such a precious doll, I wanted the doll. I bought the doll as a gift for Jessica using the $200 scholarship money I had been awarded. I knew she would be confused by the private gift on our wedding day, but I was delighted to have that doll be a part of my life.

When we met the pastor of the church, he showed us five sample vows to use in our ceremony. We picked the least preachy of them. I had a great deal of trouble with "love, honor and obey."

It seems ridiculous that Jessica should have to obey me.
She's eight years older than I.
She's the breadwinner.
I've barely graduated high school.
I don't even have a job.
No one has ever obeyed me.
People don't even listen to me or think of me as a real man.

Distraught, I resorted to some of my old methods of coping. I bought a Barbie doll to play with; only now I was hiding a doll from my future wife rather than my parents. There was even a day before the wedding that I was so distraught that I dug Jessica's wedding dress—hoop skirt and all—out of the closet and wore it around the house as Stefeny Calvert while Jessica was at work. By 5:00 that day, I had worn the dress longer than she ever would.

I, Stefeny Calvert
Take you, Richard Gere,
To be my wedded husband.
To have and to hold,
From this day forward,
For better, for worse,
For richer, for poorer,
In sickness or in health,
To love and to cherish
till death do us part.

Jessica and I agreed to eliminate the word "obey" from our vows and the pastor agreed to marry us without question.

18-I Just Want Someone to Listen To Me

A few months before our wedding, I began noticing a guy walking around the downtown area most afternoons. He appeared to be over six feet tall with broad shoulders. The man was very masculine and always chain smoking. He wore a white dress shirt and tie and seemed to be a salesman of some sort. He had beautiful dark hair and a very thick, dark mustache. I was immediately taken with him and began fantasizing about meeting him and cutting his hair.

I started planting myself in my car downtown every afternoon in hopes of getting another glimpse of him. I followed him daily at a safe distance as he ducked in and out of offices with a briefcase. I wanted to get a closer look at him, so one day I parked the car, got out and placed myself on foot in his path so he would have to walk past me. When he did, he looked right at me and smiled. Seeing him up close made me even more interested.

It seemed like the closer the wedding got, the more obsessed I became with this man. I couldn't decide whether I would rather kiss his beautiful dark mustache or shave it off. It was very dense and completely covered his upper lip. His head hair was also thick and layered around his face, touching his shoulders and covering his ears completely. There was a slight bit of wave to his hair, which gave it a healthy appearance.

I think about his hair more than the wedding.
Sometimes I think about him as a person.
I wonder what he's like.
Is he nice?
Does he have a deep voice?
He looks like he would have a deep voice.
Would he be cruel to me like most guys have been?
I want to touch his mustache.
I have never touched a mustache.
I want to shave it off, too.

I want to cut off all of his hair, just like I wanted to do to Brent.
Yet I know that I can't do that, even though my urges seem uncontrollable.

My urge to be with this guy, to touch him, to cut his hair and shave his mustache was getting stronger and stronger. I began to wonder if I could control it or not. It was the same feeling I had as a child, standing in the Barbie doll aisle of a store. There appeared to be no one or no way to ask for what I wanted.

I would finally reach a point where my brain just flipped and I had to do something. A deep sorrow would come over me, giving me the permission to take what I felt I needed. The potential consequences were of no concern.

A lot of time and money had been spent on an upcoming wedding to a woman I cared very much about, but it didn't matter. Perhaps getting married was a mistake and this was the easy way out.

I had been fantasizing about the man constantly for over a month. I needed to get him in a room alone and have his undivided attention. My brain had trouble processing what I was going to do to convince him to let me cut his hair. I decided that our paths had to cross in some way, but I hadn't figured out how yet. My fantasies usually started with him already in my custody and continued without him fighting back or being able to resist. The fantasies began to feel more like a calculated plan of action.

Jessica worked during the day and I got out of classes in the early afternoon. Following the same routine I had established over the last few weeks, I went downtown to find the man. I was terrified and had no real idea of what I was going to do or say once I had his attention. I parked the car and approached him on foot. I walked right up to him and introduced myself as Thomas. He smiled pleasantly, shook my hand and said his name was Kory.

I steeled myself, looked straight into his big, brown eyes and asked him what he did for a living. He said he sold office supplies to businesses.

"Would you mind if I interviewed you for a class project?" I asked.

I had just read Studs Terkel's book, *Working*, and explained the book's premise. Terkel had interviewed several dozen people about their jobs. I told him my project was to conduct my own interviews on the local level.

My lies must have been convincing, because he seemed interested. I asked him if he had time to come to my home to conduct a tape-recorded interview. He agreed and we started walking to my car.

I'm on autopilot.
It feels like I'm going to go through with this.
I'm so scared my mouth is dry and I can barely form
complete sentences.
I just have to get him home alone without anyone
seeing us.
An hour from now I could be touching that mustache
and cutting that hair off, but I don't know how it's
going to happen.
He's bigger and stronger than I.
I'll have no way to defend myself if we get into a fight.
I don't want to fight anyone.
An hour from now, I could be dead or in jail.
I could fake an interview and let him go,
But that's not the action my body has chosen.
This is unbelievable.
A side of myself I have never seen.
It's like I am watching myself on TV or something.

It was a short drive to my home, and I could feel myself moving farther and farther away from reality. Somehow I was able to carry on an intelligent conversation with the guy. He continued to ask me questions about my study and I answered them believably. The conversation continued all the way home, where I offered him a seat in the living room. By this time I was finally able to think ahead.

The plan in my head ended with the arousing haircut. I couldn't come up with a conclusion as to what would happen after I cut his hair. Certainly murdering the man wasn't my goal. It had never crossed my mind. I guess I naively thought he would go away quietly and I would masturbate. I simply want to perform the shave and haircut, just like I had with Lester. Only this time I could not bury the guy in the bottom of the trash and hope no one would find out. I had become a desperate, angry little boy caught in a wave of insanity.

I continued talking to Kory and walking around the apartment from room to room like I was preparing to do the interview. He sat calmly while I went into the kitchen. It was a pivotal moment; I realized I either had to go back into the living room and conduct a phony interview with him about his job, or somehow subdue him. With little thought, I grabbed a small, heavy cast-iron skillet from the kitchen, hid it behind my back and walked to the bedroom, continuing to talk to him the whole time. He was sitting in the chair with his back to me. He seemed completely relaxed and at ease. I continued talking to him as I walked up behind the chair and hit him over the head with the skillet.

This is surreal.
Time has stopped, and, for once, I feel entitled.
Entitled to his attention.
Entitled to his respect.
His mercy.
I have never had control over any man.
My life is at a climax.
For this moment, I am no longer a lonely boy.
This man is my victim.

Something inside of me stopped me from putting all of my strength into the blow. I didn't hit him nearly as hard as I could have. I'm sure I hurt him, but he was far from down.

Kory leaped out of the chair and started waving his fists in the air after the skillet cracked him on the head. He was ready to fight. I backed as far away from him as I could and started yelling that I was sorry. I was crying and desperately trying to make peace.

I screamed at him, "I JUST WANT SOMEONE TO LISTEN TO ME!"

He stopped and looked at me. It was the first honest thing I had said to the man since I had met him less than an hour earlier.

A switch in my head flipped me back into reality. He and I stood across the room from each other, breathing hard and not daring to take our eyes off of each other. We both calmed down. He didn't seem seriously hurt. I saw no evidence of blood. I became very scared of what was going to happen to me. All of a sudden, the consequences that didn't matter to me before now meant the world to me. This man had every right to press criminal charges. It was just over a year since my shoplifting charge. I could go to jail. My mind was racing feverishly as I imagined having to explain to Jessica and my parents what I had done. It was obvious I wasn't going to get the chance to act out my fantasy after all, and I would have a lot of explaining to do.

I don't remember much of what I said to the man while trying to keep him calm. I babbled and babbled, saying anything to make him feel pity for me. I also stressed how sorry I was for hitting him. Now he had control and superiority over me. I never gave a reason why I wanted to hit him over the head and knock him out. He never asked. The scene played itself out like I was just a crazy, confused kid who needed some attention, which wasn't far from the truth.

Kory lit a cigarette and shared with me that he was a pretty confused and unhappy person, himself. For a moment we seemed to have something in common.

It became clear after listening to me babble that he really did feel sorry for me and had no intention of calling the police. I think he was embarrassed that he fell for my class project story so easily. He and I were both ready to put the incident behind us.

"You should get some professional help," he said.

He left me the number of his own counselor. I didn't mention to him that I already knew I needed help and had tried getting help from three different therapists a year earlier. He smiled and shook my hand before he left the apartment. For a brief instant, I thought he might even give me a hug.

I felt like a very lucky person. I could have lost everything I had that day.

The stunt hadn't changed my fate or entitled me to anything at all. Instead, at the end of the afternoon, Jessica came home from work, and we talked about our upcoming wedding. It was like nothing had happened.

Less than a month later, I was married.

19-Wedding Proofs

My Aunt Rosie commented that I looked so nervous when I came out to the altar to meet Jessica that she thought I was angry.

Our ceremony went off without a hitch. My new brother in law made a comment that it was more of a play than a wedding. I wasn't sure if that was a compliment or not.

Almost all of my family that lived in Robinson or nearby came to the wedding. Very few members of Jessica's family showed up. One of Jessica's guests took me by surprise; the mustached store manager from Pamida who caught me shoplifting walked up to me in the receiving line. He was the husband of a friend of Jessica's. He shook my hand, patted me on the shoulder and congratulated me, while I tried to hide the fact that I was staring at his mustache. His mustache distracted me from the wedding. I have no idea if he remembered me stealing the batteries from his store.

The big day and the big doll

After the service, Jessica and I met our sixty or so guests in the church basement for the reception. We cut the cake and politely fed each other to some cheers from the small crowd. After only a few minutes at the cake table, we were rushed back upstairs to the altar by the photographer for more pictures. The pictures took forever, and when we returned to the basement an hour later, almost all out guests were gone. There were only a few of the teenagers and my mom left to catch the bouquet and see us off in Jessica's car, which had been decorated with shaving cream. We couldn't afford a honeymoon, so we just drove home when we left the church.

The morning after our wedding, I gave Jessica the beautifully gift-wrapped box containing the bride doll. I was more excited about this moment than I was the wedding. She opened the box and looked very surprised, perhaps at a loss for words.

"Oh my God. I have never seen such a beautiful doll."

She was hesitant to take the doll out of the box. I helped her stand the doll up on the table and wound up the music box. Jessica was stunned.

"I love that you got me such an extravagant gift. People always give me such practical stuff."

Jessica would not touch the doll. I could not keep my fingers out of the doll's pretty, blond hair. The doll found its home on our bedroom dresser. It was a challenge for me not to cut and restyle the doll's hair.

When we got our wedding picture proofs from the photographer a few weeks later, we had a little bit of a dilemma. We were not satisfied with the shots taken at the cake table. Either they had heavy shadows that looked weird or the soft focus made the flames of the candles look too exaggerated. We picked a shadowy 5x7 sized print of us cutting the cake from a side angle for the newspaper announcement. For our big wall portrait, we picked a large 20x24 inch print of a soft focus shot. It was a good shot, except that one of the candle's flames was shooting up right over Jessica's face. The exaggerated flames upset me terribly, but I kept my thoughts to myself.

Despite being newlyweds, it didn't take long for our sex life to dry up. On the rare occasions when we were intimate, I was privately fantasizing about men's haircuts in order to get an erection. When we were at our best sexually, it was still a far cry from enjoyable or satisfying for me. Likewise, it was becoming more challenging for Jessica, due to my obvious lack of enthusiasm. We were living in a bubble. As hard as we tried to be a normal married couple, we just weren't. We immediately started talking about having a baby, yet we had all but stopped having sex.

I had a scholastic meltdown the quarter after the wedding. I was racked with shame and worry. I couldn't concentrate and I was in danger of flunking all my classes, so I dropped out of Lincoln Trail College. Jessica was alarmed but said nothing about it. I agreed to get a job, but we both knew jobs were few and far between. I was seriously depressed and slept a lot. I played with the one Barbie doll I had from before the wedding, and when her hair was gone, I made a yard stick to facilitate Stefeny.

Jessica and I lived in a tiny house on Plum Street, not too far from the high school. The one thing I had to look forward to everyday was the string of attractive, long-haired high school boys who walked through our backyard on their way home from school. I was only a year or two older than them. I was alarmed to hear them talk their tough boy-talk. I am sure they would have made my life Hell if I had still been in school.

I borrowed a set of binoculars from my Grandma and began closing the blinds, leaving just enough room for me to peek at them and masturbate. I would have given anything to give them all clipper haircuts. I felt stuck. There was absolutely nothing I could do to get rid of my haircutting impulse. And I couldn't think of a safe way to explore it, either. My strange impulses weren't even recognized by the world, as far I knew.

My father had a connection with a private security business in Robinson. He suggested I apply for a job as a Security Guard. I had a hard time imagining myself as a guard, let alone someone taking me seriously in that type of uniform. I did apply, but was never even called to interview. I applied for a handful of other jobs, but was not considered for anything. I had no job history and few skills that were useful in my hometown.

Money was tight, so my dad offered to pay for Jessica and my lawn care. We did not have a lawn mower so we had to pay the landlord to do it for us. I was shocked to hear that he wanted to hire my half brother, Jacob, to mow our yard for us. I had no real relationship with my birth mother or either of my half brothers, despite them being legally my cousins and living in Robinson.

The offer was kind but left me terribly conflicted. Janet and her two sons had long since distanced themselves from all the family functions. I had not seen any of them since I was a young kid.

What the Hell is that all about?
Why is my dad forcing Janet on me?
I don't think I am ready to have a relationship with her or the boys.
But does this mean she wants to have a relationship with me?
Is she glad I found out the truth?
I know I am glad.

I was uncomfortable that my dad wanted Jacob to mow my yard, but I accepted his offer. I made it clear to my dad that Jacob could come over to mow, but not to visit.

One Saturday afternoon, while Jessica was shopping, an unknown truck pulled into my driveway. Jacob got out and started to mow my lawn. I was stunned; I knew he was only sixteen, but he looked very grown up. I had not seen him since he was six or seven years old. The first thing I noticed was the long blond hair hanging down Jacob's back; the second was his muscles and tight body frame.

I hadn't known he was coming that day. It was like I was hit in the face with a shovel. He might as well have been a stranger. I immediately found him attractive and wanted to cut his hair. I lowered the blinds and masturbated while I watched him mow the lawn, just as I did with his fellow high school students.

It made me sick.

20-The Real Odd Couple

There was an episode of *Tony Orlando and Dawn*, the 1970s music and sketch comedy show, where long-haired

Tony goes backstage to get his hair "trimmed." Dom DeLuise plays the barber and hacks off all of Tony's hair (a realistic wig) while he is asleep in the barber chair. Tony awakes, is furious, and runs all over the backstage area. Nobody recognizes Tony anymore with short hair. Even as a small child, that scene titillated me. I never forgot the scene and wished I could watch it over and over again.

Jessica and I bought our first VCR at The Family Variety Store. We had to apply for a small loan at the bank to make the frivolous purchase. Both sets of our parents were outraged that we got the VCR. We had told them money was tight and they were helping us pay our bills.

As far as Jessica was concerned, the biggest incentive for purchasing the VCR was to watch the video of our wedding. Since I had quit college and wasn't working, I was most excited by the opportunities to rent movies that offered stimulating men's hair scenes. I started watching what I considered "haircutting pornography" while Jessica was at work. I kept a constant eye out for anything on television that might contain a haircut scene and taped it.

The home video rental was just becoming mainstream. The day after we bought the VCR, I couldn't wait to rent a film called *Angel*. The movie was about a serial killer who murdered prostitutes. I had been extremely curious about this film when it was running in the theaters. In the trailer shown on television there was a very brief hint that a man shaved his head. The commercial was no real indication of how much haircutting was shown in the movie.

Jessica was upset by violence and wouldn't watch a movie like this in a million years, so there was no question that I would be allowed to watch this movie alone after she went to bed. I fast forwarded through the film, looking for the scene. My heart was beating a mile a minute. This was the first time I could watch a haircutting scene with enough privacy to masturbate.

Toward the end of *Angel*, the man indeed shaves his head to disguise himself from the police. The whole scene is underscored with creepy music. The killer stands in front of a sink and mirror in some sleazy room. He grabs a lock of his brown hair and twists it around two fingers, then methodically cuts it off with scissors. He repeats the action a couple of more times, then starts maniacally hacking off all of his hair. There is a glimpse of the hair piling up in the sink. The scene cuts away, and then returns to him lathering and shaving his head with a scary knife. When I rented the video, I was afraid the scene would be faked with a wig and bald cap. However, it was obvious that the actor really was cutting his hair.

To me, that ninety-second segment from *Angel* was the most sexually explicit scene I had witnessed since the scene from *Tony Orlando and Dawn*. I couldn't have cared less about the plot of the film, but I liked the scene's tone. The motivation for the man shaving his head was powerful and sinister. It was a shocking image and made the character in the movie appear to be even more of an outcast. I loved watching how the haircut transformed him. It was a sacrifice that changed his entire demeanor. I experienced a powerful orgasm as I watched the scene over and over in slow motion. I secretly rented the video many times. Eventually, I kept the film, and Family Variety charged Jessica and me for the replacement.

The VCR offered much better hair prospects than watching teenage boys in the yard. I rented and watched many movies to investigate possibly arousing scenes. Haircut scenes were pretty rare on TV and film, so the payoff from this hobby was sporadic, making the demand more intense. I felt so guilty masturbating to scenes from television and video, I might as well have been watching illegal, black-market kiddy porn.

Films dealing with military basic training or prison were likely to contain a haircut scene. *Midnight Express* and

Tribes were a couple of my favorites; both contain scenes where men get their heads buzzed. It was a dead giveaway to see a commercial or movie preview where an actor has long hair in one scene then short in another. *Death Be Not Proud* was a made-for-TV movie that came out on video. I knew the movie dealt with brain surgery, and the video box showed pictures of Robby Benson with a full head of hair. It was easy to figure out that somewhere in the movie he has to get his head shaved.

Sometimes I could get aroused just fantasizing about the possibility of a haircut without actually seeing it. I found no shortage of media that featured men with hair I found sexually attractive. The 1980s were an era of long hair for men. Music videos were just getting their start on MTV at this time. Jessica didn't like them nearly as much as I did, so they were a perfect excuse to not go to bed with her and stay up all night. I thought John Oates (from the rock duo Hall and Oates) was very good looking. His dark, thick mustache and dark, curly hair were beautiful.

Not having a job or a purpose in life and having all this new visual stimuli was too much for me to handle. Without giving any details, I asked my parents if I could go back into therapy. They agreed, and I was referred to a counselor in nearby Olney, Illinois named Dr. Jan Berty. Both my mom and Jessica took me to my first appointment.

I was scared I was getting hooked up with another ineffective professional, but I immediately found Dr. Berty to be sweet and compassionate. It didn't take long for me to realize that I still wasn't ready to talk about my impulses to cut men's hair. My focus was trying to be straight and make a life with Jessica. The doctor told me during the first session that she thought that she could help me embrace heterosexuality (if that is what I truly was), but she could not guarantee that Jessica was the woman for me. It seemed fair enough.

It was much easier for me to talk to a female counselor than a male one. I liked Dr. Berty a lot, and she got me back on track enough to again enroll at LTC full time. Jessica and I continued acting in the LTC plays, both of us getting cast in a production of Neil Simon's *The Odd Couple*. We became the theater's power couple as we hosted many parties, and our circle of friends widened. I felt vital and authentic in the theater, but was lost and living a lie at home. Jessica and I really were an odd couple, and we were fast drifting apart.

Many of the people involved in the theater lived up to 40 miles away so we became accustomed to letting people sleep over at our tiny house. We did not have a spare room, so we set up the dining room, which shared a wall with our bedroom, as a guest room. Dr. Berty was quick to point out that we were sabotaging any chance of having any alone or romantic time with each other by welcoming a constant string of overnight guests.

The theater held auditions for a production of *Fiddler on the Roof*. Jessica was cast in the chorus, and I was cast as Fyedka, the Russian soldier that takes the Jewish daughter, Chava, away from her family. I was delighted to have the part. Not long into rehearsals, our director Kirk pulled me aside and told me he wanted to work with me privately. I was alarmed but welcomed the special attention.

"Okay, Dennis, I want you to be aware of your posture. Stand up straight for me," he said as he patted his own chest with one fist. Kirk gently molded me into a more confident posture.

"Now we're going to get you some big soldier boots, and they'll help you walk with more pride. I need you to walk more like a man."

I quickly realized that he was giving me lessons on how to be more masculine. Kirk was the same director that let me be as gay as I wanted in *Ten Little Indians*. I was a little shocked, but I listened to what he had to say. He coached me alone for about twenty minutes, and I took everything he said to heart. I wanted to be an actor and do a good job, but I had mixed feelings. I had never been successful at being masculine, but I had never tried hard, either.

> *Is there something wrong with me?*
> *Am I so ridiculous that I have to be coached on how to be a man?*
> *If you only knew about Stefeny.*
> *She should be playing Hodel or Tzeitel.*
> *You wouldn't have to coach her to be a girl.*

I did as I was directed and had a great time with the role. I loved taking a curtain call as one of the three men who marry the three oldest sisters. I had never been categorized like that before. Maybe the counseling with Dr. Berty was working. Already being a married man perhaps sold the director that I could pull it off. I got really worried, however, because I was developing a big crush on the actor playing Motel Kamzoil. Jessica quickly figured it out and confronted me about it. For the sake of our marriage, I did the best I could to stay away from him.

Things got much worse for Jessica and me with our next production, the Rogers and Hammerstein musical, *Oklahoma!* I was asked to design the costumes and had a small walk-on role as a farmer, while Jessica was cast in the chorus again. From the first day of rehearsals I couldn't deny the intense chemistry with a young college student named Stephen. He had a dark mustache and would be playing a cowboy. I had never been with a guy, but all signs indicated that Stephen could well provide my first sexual encounter with a man. I became obsessed with Stephen and wanted to explore both his body and his mustache.

At a cast party, Stephen and I disappeared into my car for some privacy. Jessica stormed outside moments later and screamed through the windshield,

"ALL RIGHT YOU TWO FAGGOTS, IF YOU WANT TO BUTTFUCK EACH OTHER, GO RIGHT AHEAD!"

I had not actually cheated on Jessica with Stephen, but the intention must have been clear to her. *Oklahoma!* would be the last show I would do at the community theater, and this period marked the emotional end of our marriage.

I finished my Associate degree at Lincoln Trail College. Upon the recommendation of Mrs. Henderson, I accepted a place in Southern Illinois University's theater department. SIU-Carbondale was her Alma Mater, and she always spoke fondly of her time there in the 60s.

Jessica and I had already been preparing for months to move 175 miles away to Carbondale so I could get my bachelor's degree. We were stuck with each other. Our plans had been finalized before the whole mess with Stephen. She had given notice on her job. We had given notice on our house. Jessica had nowhere to go, so I let her come with me. We discussed a truce and the possibility of working on our marriage once we got settled into our new environment, but I think we both knew it was over.

21-Mrs. Eddie Bensie

There was one piece of personal business I felt I needed to deal with before I left Robinson: I wanted to talk to my birth mother. My parents had said very little about my adoption since I had found out the truth four years earlier. I went to my dad and asked how best to talk to Janet. He suggested inviting her to my house for an afternoon. She was a heavy coffee drinker, so he advised me to make a pot of coffee for her visit.

My dad was clearly acting like a business agent, but I wasn't sure if he was representing Janet or me. He insisted on making the calls and arrangements between the two of us. I insisted on speaking to her privately. He agreed and made a big deal of telling me how he had instructed Janet not to lie to me, which was ironic because Mom and Dad had

been lying to me for years about my
adoption. I sent Jessica away for a
Sunday afternoon, made a pot of
coffee and waited for Janet's arrival.

I couldn't remember the last time
I had seen Janet, certainly not since I
had found out about the adoption. She
didn't come around the rest of the
family much. Her car pulled into the
driveway and my stomach sank. I was
scared.

*I just want the truth.
This woman gave birth to me and
I owe my existence to her.
I want her to know how I feel.
I want to hear her side of the story.
I think my parents tell me only what they want to
believe.
She can help me understand what happened and
maybe how it affects me now.*

My birth mother,
pregnant with me

I answered the door and she gave me a hug. I poured
her a cup of coffee. Her hands were trembling as she lifted
her cup. We went into the living room and sat down. Once
we were comfortable, I asked her to tell me her side of the
story of my adoption. It was immediately clear that the
woman had never gotten over giving me up. She pulled a
dog-eared baby picture of me from her billfold. She still
thought of me as her baby.

Her side of the story mostly matched my parents, but
was revealed with more detail. I asked about my birth dad.
She didn't know for sure who he was: one of four men she
had slept with. The name given to me at birth was "Dennis
Wayne Bensie." She married one of her good friends she
knew wasn't my birth father in order to give me a name. Her
new husband, Eddie Bensie, disappeared not long after I was

born. Janet told me she was surprised when he became abusive to both her and me. I could tell she still had a soft spot for him. The marriage was very short and she never saw him again.

Ultimately, she had really loved me and wanted to keep me, but being a teenager, she'd had minimal resources. While telling her tale, she became emotional, racked with guilt. I was afraid to touch her, for fear she would not want to let me go.

> *I feel terrible for this woman.*
> *She is a stranger to me but she thinks she knows me.*
> *This is a torn and fragile woman.*
> *I respect Janet and understand her pain, but I am freaked out that she still thinks of me as her son.*
> *Maybe she thinks giving me up was a mistake.*
> *I don't think it was at all.*
> *For all of my parents' misdeeds, I have been provided for in a manner this woman could have never achieved.*
> *I feel like I want to, or need to, do something for this woman.*
> *Do I owe her something?*
> *What does she need from me?*
> *Could she ever get enough back from me? I doubt it.*
> *She is profoundly affected by me: just being in the same room.*
> *I think it's best to get the information I want and put the rest of this behind me.*

Janet elaborated on how she was forced by her mother to hide her pregnancy. My parents were ready to adopt me the minute they found out she was expecting. I got the sense from her that they were pushy with their offer. Rather than supporting her, the whole extended family was against her raising me. She resisted for as long as she could after my birth. She kept me for a while, but when she found she had no money to feed me, she realized she needed to accept the offer and gave me up eight months after I was born.

My parents served as my foster parents before they could adopt me. An exhaustive search for Eddie Bensie took place. Despite the fact that everyone knew he wasn't my biological father, he was still named as my father on my birth certificate. He was in the military and located overseas. My parents had to bribe him under the table and pay his way back to Illinois to sign my adoption papers. It was then that I finally became "Dennis Wayne Milam."

I was curious about Eddie Bensie. I asked Janet what he looked like. She surprised me when she opened her purse and briefly showed me an old, beat-up copy of his senior picture. I studied the picture long enough to see that he had thick, dark hair and glasses before she quickly tucked it back in her purse. I wanted Janet to indulge me with more talk of her first husband, but I could tell it was difficult for her. I dropped the subject.

There came a point in the afternoon when there was nothing left to say, but she didn't seem like she was going to leave my house. I had to politely explain that Jessica was due home and that she should go.

I felt bad. Her whole life had seemed like a continuous dismissal. I knew she had been married a few times. One of her husbands used to beat her. She even had a rocky relationship with the two teenage sons she had given birth to after me. All three of her boys had different dads and none of us ever had those men in our lives.

She gave me a final hug and sobbed on my shoulder. Then she turned and ran to the car. Before she left, she sat in her car and sobbed for several minutes.

I'm numb.
This was important, but I don't feel enlightened.
I expected to be fulfilled in some way from this
meeting.

Instead, I'm left cold and empty.
I don't really fit in anywhere and don't know who I
am.
I'm too twisted up inside to even belong to myself.
All the dolls and hair in the world can't balance me.
Jessica can't fix things for me, either.
How I wish I could just erase my past and reset for the
future.

The timing was good for Jessica and me to move. I wanted to get away from Robinson. Two weeks after the meeting with Janet, Jessica and I left town and started a new chapter of our lives.

22-Married Student Housing

Jessica and I left a small town of 7,000 people in favor of a thriving college town of 27,000. Southern Illinois University at Carbondale was known as a "party school." It wasn't exactly hard to get accepted into the university, and students chose the school for its liberal feel and reasonable tuition. For years, the city hosted an infamous Halloween street fair that brought drunken revelers in from miles around. The yearly festival often went dangerously out of control and was eventually abolished in the 1990s.

My life changed drastically as I got busy with classes. After having to be coached on how to be a man, I gave up the idea of becoming an actor. I knew how to sew and got a work study position in the costume shop. I was awarded a full tuition talent scholarship to major in Costume Design, which I was more than happy to accept. I was slated to design my first show in the spring.

Within weeks of our move, I was the happiest I had ever been in my life and Jessica was miserable. Our relationship was tense. We rarely saw each other. She had difficulty adapting to the new environment and trouble finding a new job. Depressed and discouraged, she stayed in bed most of the time and filled her few waking hours overeating. Jessica gained over fifty pounds the first six months after we left Robinson.

The loneliness that drew me into this marriage is wearing off.
I have outgrown Jessica.
I'm embarrassed to be married, so I try to hide it.
Everyone knows I am gay.
The word is out and people are snickering about me.
I just want to scream to them that I KNOW I am gay.
I just got married because I didn't know any better three years ago.
It is clear to me now; being gay is not a curse.
There are plenty of guys around just like me ... and they are happy, fun people.
I am finally figuring out who I am and how I can be happy.
My life will never work with a wife.
It is not fair to Jessica or me to remain married.
It is going to be so very hard to end this, but I know it is the best thing to do.

The drama department had a drama prom for its majors. I was excited to finally attend a prom. I had not included Jessica in any of my school activities. It seemed odd to bring her to the event, so I chose a lesbian friend as my date. We wore matching tuxedos. Jessica was hurt not to be included and stayed in bed the whole weekend.

In the summer of 1987 after my first year at SIU-C, I got my first out-of-town theater job stitching on a production of Shakespeare's *The Tempest* for Colorado Shakespeare Festival. I told Jessica that I would be moving out of married student housing when I returned and that she (not being a student) would have to find a new place to live as well. During my six week stay, I told no one in Colorado that I had a wife back in Illinois.

When I got back from Colorado, Jessica and I followed through on our plans to separate. I was in the process of moving out of our apartment and, while walking to campus, was picked up by a handsome man with a mustache. I was on my way to work in the costume shop. He drove past me a couple of times and finally stopped and asked if I would give him a blow job. I had my first sexual contact with a man in his car in broad daylight in a secluded corner of the Mae Smith Tower parking lot on the SIU-C campus.

I had finally lost my "gay virginity." I wasn't too excited about the oral sex, but I was like a wild animal playing with his mustache. I had never touched one before. It was almost like his penis didn't count. For me, the adventure was all about the mustache. My trick looked at me like I was crazy. An anonymous encounter in a car wasn't exactly how I wanted my first time with a man to be, but I was glad to be initiated into homosexuality. I had also delved deeper into my obsession with real hair.

I dashed to work in the costume shop that afternoon feeling like a new person. I had so much energy from my encounter that I made a fake fur coat—start to finish—in one afternoon. Still, I was a little bit upset by what I had done. Jessica and I weren't actually divorced yet. We were days away from separating, but I felt that by telling her I would hurt her more than I already had. I decided to keep it to myself.

After three years together, Jessica and I separated and eventually divorced. The divorce papers filed by her claimed she had suffered "extreme and repeated mental cruelty." It was strange to see it worded that way, but I had to own what had happened between us. I was relieved to see that Jessica wanted to take her maiden name back. I signed the papers without contest. I was a twenty-two-year-old divorcé. My parents paid her the settlement she was due on my behalf, while I was awarded the opportunity to live my life as an openly gay man.

23-The First Cut

I was having great success in my theatrical studies as a costume designer at SIU-C. My senior year I was given assignments to design *Little Shop of Horrors* on the main stage and *Snoopy!* for the department's Black Box Theater. It was no accident that this was a career choice that would indulge my haircutting interests. Often the drama department would do period plays requiring men to get their hair cut short. Budgets were tight at the theater, and actors were expected to take care of their own hair needs. Sometimes students didn't have money to go to a salon. I was slowly getting up the nerve to offer my services as a barber.

After years of cutting doll's hair and making and cutting yarn wigs, I had some crude sense of hairstyling. I had absolutely no formal training but did possess instinct and skill. I had started cutting my own hair in middle school because of my phobia. I had even cut my mom's and Jessica's hair a couple of times. Cutting women's hair had never been erotic for me, unlike cutting a man's hair. However, I had never cut a man's hair other than my own.

I was nervous at the idea. I had associated men's haircutting with humiliation since childhood, and it was hard for me to disassociate myself from that notion. After my fixation on Brent in high school, I had become accustomed to fantasizing about cutting guys hair while I masturbated. It seemed likely that I would become sexually aroused while cutting a guy's hair. As opportunities became available to cut hair at the theater, I knew that I wasn't going to get the opportunity to experience giving a haircut from a sexually obsessive perspective. I was going to have to hide my sexual feelings and show some restraint. I still wanted to do it. Badly.

An opportunity to cut a man's hair occurred when I was designing costumes for a production of *Of Mice and Men* at SIU-C. The play was based on John Steinbeck's classic novel and was set in the 1930s. There was no apparent need for any haircuts at the beginning of rehearsals. The men in the cast had agreed to maintain their own hair. However, right before dress rehearsal, an actor named Brian came to me out of desperation. He had promised the director he would get his dirty blond hair cut much shorter and had forgotten to make arrangements. Since I was the costume designer, he assumed I would help him. He asked me to cut his hair.

At first, I had to say no. We were between classes and he wanted me to drop everything and cut his hair immediately. But Brian kept harping on me to do it. Finally, I said that I would do the haircut because I was afraid I would lose the chance and he would find someone else to help him out. I told him to meet me in twenty minutes and went to the bathroom where I took a moment to pull myself together. This actor was around twenty years old and somewhat handsome. His hair wasn't particularly interesting to me, but I was certainly turned on by the idea of cutting it short. I arranged my erect penis in my pants in the least noticeable way possible and psyched myself up to perform the task.

> *I wish my hands would stop shaking.*
> *If he notices my hands, then he'll see I am nervous.*
> *If he thinks I am nervous, that will make me more nervous.*
> *I have to come across like I'm confident.*
> *But I'm not confident.*
> *I'm scared to death I'll mess his hair up and make him mad.*

A few friends gathered in the dressing room where I was cutting his hair. It quickly became somewhat of a social atmosphere. With more people in the room, it was easier to hide the fact that I was nervous and aroused. He instructed me to cut about two to three inches of hair from the top on his head and to taper and clean up the sides, giving him a much more masculine look. I had to use a great deal of concentration to pull my focus away from my throbbing cock and pay attention to cutting his hair. Brian didn't seem to sense any unrest, and I remained somewhat composed as I finished his haircut. He seemed pleased with the look.

After the haircut, I ran back to the restroom and masturbated, reflecting on what I had just done. I felt somewhat guilty for having been aroused during the haircut. I couldn't help wondering what Brian would think if he knew what was going on in my mind and in my pants. I tried to give myself permission to remember the event without torturing myself with guilt. After all, there was no real harm in what had just happened. My first male haircut went off without a hitch, and word quickly spread around the theater department that I cut hair. It wasn't long before other guys were approaching me to cut their hair for shows.

A month later, a new script written by a student was being produced in the smaller experimental theater. The play had a military theme. All of the boys in the play would be expected to have short hair. All of them already did—with one exception. There was a guy named Cody who had a long, blond mullet hairstyle. He came to me and asked me to cut his hair short for the show. He had been referred to me by Brian.

The stakes got a lot higher with Cody because he had beautiful hair that I found very arousing. He was a handsome guy and I was more than happy to do the cut. He obviously liked his hair long and wanted to wait until the last minute to cut it off. We set an appointment for the haircut over a week in advance. Each day prior to the haircut when I saw him, I became aroused, anticipating what I was going to do to him. I thought about the upcoming haircut constantly and experienced jitters not unlike what one feels before a first date.

I'm a wreck.
I don't want to embarrass myself.
I wonder if he is a wreck, too.
I want things to go perfectly so I can remember this day for a long time.
I just wish I could really fulfill my obsession and touch myself while I cut his hair off.
I don't get to cut his hair as short as I'd like, so I have to control myself.
But it's cool that I'm going to have his undivided attention.

Cody showed up for our appointment right on time. I was much more prepared for this haircut, having arrived early to prepare the room and arrange my equipment. I also took no chances and arranged my penis in my pants like I did for Brian's haircut. He sat down and I caped him and arranged the long hair on his shoulders. What made this haircut interesting to me was the fact that Cody obviously didn't want to get it cut. But it had been stipulated that in order for him to get cast in the play, he would have to do it. I understood it had been a tough decision. He was nervous and vulnerable—two emotions he probably didn't display to many people.

The conversation before I started cutting was as erotic as the actual cutting. I asked him as many questions as I could about his hair, making sure they were innocent enough so I would not give away my sexual interest.

"Is this the longest your hair has been?"

"How often do you get your hair cut?"

"Were you trying to grow it out longer?"

As I continued talking, I took my first slice out of the back of his long hair.

As I had fantasized over the last week, I wanted to make the first cut without warning from the longest part of his hair. Cody flinched as he watched the hair fall to the ground. I felt my cock throb in my pants at the same time. I also noticed in the mirror that my face had turned bright red. Luckily, Cody was looking at the floor more than me. I continued cutting and asking him questions about his hair. He eventually stopped flinching, but my cock kept throbbing and causing me great discomfort.

I finished the haircut and was shocked at how different he looked. Cody seemed pleased with the results but made a point of telling me he would immediately grow his hair back out after the show closed.

> *That was cool.*
> *Not only was it a turn-on, but he seems like a nice guy.*
> *He's a straight guy, but seems like he is unaffected by my femininity.*
> *He was vulnerable about the haircut.*
> *I realized today that there's something very tender, and even honorable about haircuts.*
> *Despite my sexual turn-on, I bet he doesn't show that vulnerability to many other guys.*
> *Come to think of it, one man cutting another man's hair is one of the few times two adult men can touch and it is socially acceptable.*
> *I'm still uncomfortable when men touch me.*
> *It's odd to me that he trusted me to cut his hair.*
> *No guy has ever seemed to need and trust me like that. It's a good feeling.*
> *I want to feel this again: the sexual turn-on and the power from a man's vulnerability.*

Cody stopped me in the hallway a few days after the haircut and thanked me again. He had been getting nothing but compliments about his new look. People were even complimenting me directly about his haircut. Not only did I gain praise from the experience, I also inherited eight inches of his hair. I was going to remember this dramatic haircut for a long time, and I decided to keep a few locks of his hair to stimulate my memory. I never did anything perverse with the locks of hair. I simply liked to look at them and touch them. I kept his hair for a few weeks and then threw it away. I felt sinister having it.

Brian and Cody were very charismatic and grateful for my attention and skill. I was grateful for their respect and trust. It was a positive exchange that helped me understand how I had grown since I had assaulted the man years before with the frying pan. I was enthusiastic and anxious to learn more about this part of my life.

24-Gay Niche and Cut

After my anonymous encounter in the Mae Smith Tower parking lot, I had a sexual dry spell. I longed to touch and be touched. Having been starved of positive attention from men, I became obsessed with finding affection and love but had trouble finding either. My parents had been married for 35 years, and I felt pressured to go out and find the gay version of a marriage: a lover with a house and a yard with a picket fence. I even toyed with the idea of being a gay dad someday.

For the first time in my life I didn't have to answer to my parents, Jessica or anyone but myself. But opening the closet door hadn't guaranteed me anything as far as romance was concerned. Being a single gay man only created new problems, but I was more than happy to face those challenges. I felt like I was learning to walk on my own two feet. I was ready to experience all the things that other gay men were experiencing. It seemed the only logical thing to do was become comfortable as a gay man. I tried not to think about my obsession with men's hair.

I became buddies with a colorful guy named Jim Westerland. He was an acting major at SIU-C and the gayest person I had ever seen. We met during the last months I was married to Jessica, and he quickly deduced that I was gay, despite the wedding ring. He became a great friend and helped pave the road out of the closet with his bold energy and sarcastic sense of humor. Despite his brashness, I looked up to Jim and felt safe with him. Under the bright clothes and his dyed red hair was a sincere and caring person.

I wasn't having any luck dating. None of the gay men around me wanted to be more than friends. I was a horny young man and didn't feel like I could wait for a relationship to have more sex. It wasn't long before I had my next sexual encounter with a man. Jim pointed out that there was a restroom in the basement of Morris Library where men cruised for sex. I went there to investigate.

It seemed like the restroom was designed for anonymous sexual encounters. It was located in a deserted part of the building. The first time I went in, I had no sooner found a stall and sat down than a hand signaled me from under the stall partition. The man in the next stall wanted me to kneel down and slide my cock under the partition so he could suck it. I did what he wanted and got my first blow job from a man. I left the restroom wildly unimpressed. There was no affection, which is what I was craving more than a quick ejaculation. I dependent more on a face and hair rather than a hard cock for visual excitement. However, it didn't stop me from going back on a regular basis in hope of something more stimulating.

I spent the next several years engaging in sexual activities with numerous partners. Public restrooms, lakeside bushes, public parks, and parking lots all became fair game for a sexual encounter. I was hoping to find love, acceptance and validation. I was constantly disappointed when all I ever got was empty sex. However, empty gay sex was better than heterosexual sex for me. Despite not having any emotional connection with my partners, I felt more at ease having with sex with a man than I ever had felt with my ex-wife.

Without realizing it, I was setting up a pattern of selecting my sex partners based on how attracted I was to their hair. When faced with a man I found attractive, it was common for me to fantasize about shaving the guy's head and create a separate fantasy about being his boyfriend. However, it was doubtful that I'd still find the guy attractive if he was bald, and I would be too embarrassed to date a guy whose head I had shaved.

I graduated from Southern Illinois University at Carbondale with my BA in Theater Design in the spring of 1988 and went on to graduate school at Illinois State University in Normal, Illinois the following fall. Normal was six hours north of Carbondale. Robinson was exactly three hours between the two college towns. In contrast to the happiness I'd found going south to finish my undergraduate degree, the trip north to Normal was almost immediately and equally disappointing, both scholastically and personally.

ISU was much more conservative that SIU-C and I had trouble finding a gay niche, let alone an outlet for my hair obsession. I missed Jim and my friends from Carbondale and felt anything but normal in Normal. I was twenty-three years old when I finally mustered up the courage to ask a guy to indulge in my fantasy.

I clandestinely met a man in a porn shop parking lot—Normal's cruising spot—and invited him back to my apartment for what was meant to be typical sex. He was in his early thirties and rather ordinary looking. He gave me a lot of eye contact and seemed open and intelligent. This man didn't have interesting hair, but I couldn't take my eyes off his beautiful blond mustache.

I had previously had sexual encounters with men who had mustaches, but seldom felt comfortable focusing on their lips. I threw caution to the wind here, however, and began to indulge in my desire more than ever before. I loved kissing him, rubbing his face and chewing on his mustache. He also got aroused when I pulled and yanked on it. I started rubbing my cock all over his mustache, which was an amazing feeling. The sex we had that evening took me to a new level of excitement. I found myself wanting to take it even further. I felt a special rapport with this man. I decided I had nothing to lose by asking him if I could shave his mustache off while we were having sex. I could tell that he probably wouldn't be offended by my request. Either he would say yes or he would say no.

I introduced the topic by saying, "There is something I would like to do to you that would really turn me on."

Without hesitation he asked what it was.

"I would really love to shave your mustache off and cum on your naked lip."

Much to my surprise he said, "Go right ahead. Until this afternoon I had a full beard. I wish we would have met yesterday. I would have let you shave the whole thing."

I almost fainted.

We took a short break and I ran and got a pair of scissors, razor, shaving cream and a bowl of water. I sat them on the table beside the bed and got back on top of him and started kissing him fiercely all over his face. After getting ourselves worked up again, I got him positioned on his back and I sat on his chest with my erect penis near his chin. A devilish smile came across his face as I took the small scissors and cut his mustache hair down to stubble with only three or four clips. The hairs flew all around his face and I knocked them out of the way on to the sheets. I lathered up his lip and gently scraped it clean. Having only experienced shaving my own tender face, I was surprised by how rough his skin was as I dragged the razor over it.

I kissed his naked lip and he seductively asked, "Is that better?"

The truth was he was much better looking with the mustache, but I lied and said he looked great. He looked younger, but more ordinary. I had robbed him of the one quality that I found interesting. We continued to have sex, but I was disappointed because I expected a sexual boost from indulging in my obsession. I didn't even ejaculate. He eventually left. I felt confused. I certainly found the experience interesting, yet it hadn't measured up to my expectations.

After the guy left my apartment, I sat alone and reviewed the event, as well as my whole budding obsession.

I have to figure this out.
Why do I want to cut hair?
It's obviously not a negotiable part of who I am; and not just a hobby.
Sometimes a haircut is interesting and sometimes it isn't.
This guy's mustache gave me some sexual freedom, but left me unsatisfied.
I feel like a failure.
What did I do wrong with this guy?
What should I have done to turn me on?

Perhaps it isn't what I should do, but more about the guy getting his hair cut.
The more drastic a haircut, the better.
A long-haired guy getting his hair cut short is the most sexual for me.
If a long-haired guy gets a trim, it isn't all that interesting.
It also seems the more nervous or unenthusiastic the guy, the more turned on I am about the haircut.
I don't get excited by a guy getting beat up or anything, but if a guy is mentally tortured by the thought of a haircut, it is very sexual to me.
Is my turn-on a male vanity issue?

If I had really knocked the guy out back in Robinson in order to shave his mustache and cut his hair, I doubt I would have been too turned on, because I would have been too scared.
I think I need to feel somewhat safe to be aroused.

Cody back at SIU was very arousing.
He had long blond hair that had to be cut short.
He didn't want to get it cut.
I loved the experience because of his resistance.
I was safe the whole time.
I was the lucky haircutter, but I was safe and HE was vulnerable.

The guy whose mustache I just shaved: he was WAY too into me shaving him to get me aroused.
The stakes were not high enough for a big turn-on.

It makes sense to me now.
In order to fulfill the perfect sexual situation, I have to meet a long haired guy, get up the nerve to ask him to let me cut his hair and hope that he doesn't want a haircut.
He needs to be tolerant of my sexual arousal during the haircut.
It would be most arousing if he squirmed and flinched while I cut his hair but presented no danger to me.

It is also important he keep his mouth shut about what happened between the two of us;
I am not comfortable with people knowing I am turned on doing this.
This is terrible.

What a twisted life I have.
It's so unfair that I have these stipulations to my sex life.
Will it ever be possible for me to be sexually satisfied?
Can I ever get over the shame?

These feelings are too strong to ignore, but I don't know if I have the courage to explore them much further.

My problems had escalated from needing to play with dolls. By the time I was twenty-four, I had already found the courage to come out of the closet, divorce a wife, and be sexually active with men. I would have to find even more courage to deal with my present situation. I was becoming more and more distracted by my obsession. I felt my brain was already wired, but wired completely differently than anyone else's.

25-The Professionals

My debut project for the costume design graduate program at Illinois State University was to design a production of the long-running musical, *The Fantasticks*. My overall experience at ISU had been anything but fantastic. After only a year of the three-year program, I was asked to leave by my advisers. I was more than ready to get out ... not just out of ISU and Normal, but the entire Midwest. I wanted to start earning a steady paycheck, so I began sending my résumé to professional theaters across the country.

I got a gig designing a summer stock production of *The Odd Couple* (only this time it was with a female cast) and working in the costume shop on two other shows at University of Connecticut in Storrs. Storrs might as well have been named *Snores*. The most exciting thing that happened that summer was catching crabs from my dorm room mattress and hiding my erection while I gave a handful of shaggy-haired boys short haircuts for the production of *Bye, Bye Birdie*.

In the fall of 1989, I packed my bags and moved to Chapel Hill, North Carolina to work for PlayMakers Repertory Company on the campus of the University of North Carolina. PlayMakers is a professional theater affiliated with the drama department of UNC. Students, faculty and professionals from around the country make up the labor force for the organization both on and off stage.

I was hired to work in the costume shop, as well as be the dresser for all the performances. I would occasionally be assigned to work with wigs and hair. It was a milestone because it was the farthest I had ever lived from my family.

Before I made the cross-country move, I lined up a roommate named Pilar, who was an actress and graduate student in the drama department. Despite having a roommate, I liked the feeling of independence the distance gave me.

Chapel Hill's population was around 38,000, and it was located in the tri-city area next to

The Professionals were not so professional.

Raleigh and Durham. The college town had a small gay
scene and a couple of gay-friendly bars. There were larger
gay populations in the nearby cities, a short drive away. I
found all the stereotypical charm of the south to be engaging
at first—architectural and natural beauty was abundant—but
it didn't take long to feel the pace was too slow and drippy
for my taste. Despite Chapel Hill's reputation for being one
of the state's cultural and liberal meccas, I still felt stifled
and out of place because of my sexuality and my obscure
interest in cutting hair.

It was still difficult to meet guys to date, and I was
becoming paranoid that the problem wasn't the guys as
much as it was me. I knew I wasn't unattractive, but I was
needy. This kind of frustration only heightened my
obsession. If I couldn't have attention from men one way, I
would try and get it another.

I began reading the national gay magazine, *The
Advocate*, when I stumbled across it at a small alternative
bookstore that was run out of someone's house on the sly.
Neither the campus nor the mall bookstores seemed to carry
any gay magazines. There was a classified ad for men who
were sexually interested in other men's hair:

> MEN'S HAIR -If you find yourself looking at
> another man's head of hair before the rest
> of his body, you are not alone. There is a club
> for your fantasy ...

I responded to the ad with a self-addressed stamped
envelope and a short note proclaiming my interest. I got a
nice letter back from a man named Rick Ritter in California
who was starting a fetish club called "Men's Hair Club." I
was one of his first club members, and we became pen pals
for a number of years. He produced a monthly newsletter
that included stories, alerts to media containing interesting
hair content, pictures, and a growing list of other members

who were interested in sharing their fetish. It was wonderful to know that I was not alone. I contributed everything I could to the newsletter. By the late 1990s, the club had to change its name to simply "Men's Hair" due to trademark issues with "Hair Club for Men," a hair restoration company. The club blossomed over the years and made a healthy transition to the Internet.

In the back of *The Advocate*, there were a few advertisements for gay phone sex companies. I was intrigued. I thought about the possibilities for a few weeks; then I was compelled to investigate. I called a phone sex company called "The Professionals" with a couple of questions. The picture that accompanied the ad featured two muscular attractive guys talking on the phone and tied together with the phone cords. The dispatcher who answered the phone took a few minutes to explain how a phone sex date worked. The setup was as follows: you described the physical characteristics of the guy you wanted to talk to and the scene you were looking for. For forty dollars, someone who had been informed of your interests by the dispatcher would call you back. Your phone date would talk to you until you climaxed.

Knowing I was looking for something specific and unusual, I asked what limits there were to the scenes, and the receptionist explained that a caller had to be at least eighteen years old. Everything was fair game except for sex with animals or dead people. He mentioned a few favorite kinky fetishes: food, uniforms, pissing, bondage, underwear, prison scenes, and military scenes. The guys calling back were all over eighteen, so you could even pretend a guy was a minor. I knew how turned on I could get while a guy talked to me about his hair and how he didn't want it cut. The advantage to the phone sex situation was I could ask for exactly what I wanted. It was also safe sex. I decided to go for it.

I told the dispatcher I wanted to talk to a guy in his twenties with long dark hair and a mustache. I wanted the guy to be calling me to set up a haircut and a shave for a job interview, despite the fact that he really didn't want his hair cut. I explained that the guy should be very, very nervous— the more nervous, the better. The dispatcher seemed to understand what I was looking for and then asked for my credit card information and my phone number. I hung up the phone and prepared for my date to call me back. I found some pictures of guys with long dark hair in my collection of hair pictures and began to masturbate right next to the phone. Sure enough, ten minutes later the phone rang.

My phone date told me his name was Will, and we exchanged some small talk. I finally broke the ice and said, "What's on your mind today, Will?"

"Well, I've got a job interview this afternoon and I need to get cleaned up," he replied in a deep voice.

I pretended this was news to me, "How cleaned up do you have to get?"

"Well, it is a pretty conservative firm. I need to get a short haircut. I guess I should lose the mustache, too," he said.

We continued talking. I had him describe his hair and mustache in great detail, and I continued to jack off. I didn't ask anything about his body or penis. I could tell Will was puzzled by my kink. He would start to steer the conversation in a more mainstream sexual direction by suggesting we sixty-nine each other, and I would quickly get him back on the subject of the haircut. We were playing a verbal game of cat and mouse. Then he started acting like he wanted to get his hair cut after all.

"Yeah, man. Cut all of my hair off. That'll be hot," he said.

I tried to turn the situation around by dropping a few hints to my phone date. "I bet you really don't like getting your hair cut, huh?"

129

Finally, it became apparent that he understood my need for him to be unenthusiastic about a haircut and he began protesting. I got excited by his resistance. I played along and began convincing, even shaming him into letting me cut his hair. We began arguing about it.

"NO, motherfucker, I ain't letting you cut my fuckin' hair. Get away from me!" he yelled. He had taken my fantasy too far and wasn't going to verbally agree to the fantasy haircut after all.

I tried to get the conversation back on my track. "You're very hot and I would love to cut off all of your hair ... and maybe I'll cum on your head when I am done," I announced. Will seemed to calm down, but I could tell he was still struggling to find out how best to get me off.

Fifteen minutes into our telephone call, it was time to get down to business. I talked us through the haircut scene in great detail and continued to masturbate. As I began "cutting his hair," he started making sounds like he was aroused, too. I found myself doing all of the talking while he moaned. After a couple of minutes, I suspected that he wasn't even listening to me. The more aroused he got, the less aroused I got. I felt like Will should be paying me for my time rather than vice versa.

The illusion was shattered. I was only minimally excited at this point. I finished my description of the haircut and moved on to the mustache. After my wordy description of shaving it off, I was out of hair I wanted to cut. I was also out of patience. I faked an orgasm, which my phone date matched. Will reminded me of his name and said he would love to talk again. I wasn't sure if he was serious. I hung up the phone and felt like I had wasted my time and my money.

A couple of days later, out of desperation, I decided to try phone sex again and called the company back. I specifically asked for a different partner. I tried explaining myself to the dispatcher very clearly. My phone date had to eventually submit to the haircut, but shouldn't enjoy or be aroused by the haircut. I didn't want to hear moans or any enthusiasm from my date. The second telephone call was no better than the first. It took longer to explain what I wanted to the dispatcher than the actual date lasted.

I then switched to a different company called "Dial-a-Daddy." This company was slick, offering you an account code and a strict thirty-minute time limit. My first date arranged by this company was with a bubbly, effeminate-sounding guy. When I asked him to describe his hair, he explained that his hair was six feet long and trailed the ground when he walked. From the very beginning of our conversation, he sounded like he was going to have an orgasm—without even listening to me. I couldn't get him to bring up or acknowledge that he was calling about a haircut. When I finally suggested that he might need to get a haircut, he gasped and started making a fake crying sound. He was way over the top and I quickly hung up on him. There was nothing daddy-like about him. I called the dispatcher back immediately and got another call issued to me that was only mildly interesting.

The prospects for this being an outlet for my obsession seemed bleak, but I had trouble giving up on it. Talking on the phone about my fetish was better than nothing. I became determined and called back "Dial-a-Daddy" a third time. The dispatcher told me my fantasy was impossible to fill and implied that I shouldn't bother to call back ever again. This really made me feel like a freak. I was being rejected by a phone sex company.

A month later when I got my credit card bill, there were charges on my statement to "Tahiti Vacations" along with my phone sex charges. I knew all these charges weren't legitimate and I called my credit card company to investigate. It was no surprise when the Visa agent found a discrepancy. The charges to "Tahiti Vacations" and "The Professionals" had the same vendor number. I called "The Professionals" and asked to speak to the manager. The dispatcher connected me to another man and I began to explain the wrong charges. He hung up on me mid-sentence. "The Professionals" appeared to be professional scam artists. Visa quickly removed the false charges from my records, and I noticed "The Professionals" were not listed in *The Advocate* much longer.

26-Shave Him or Date Him?

I never really felt comfortable living in the South. There were plenty of gay men and women around Chapel Hill and UNC, but they seemed repressed. If you didn't know someone personally from work or school, or were not one of the few who frequented the nearby gay-friendly bar, the only place to find other gay men was in one of a few public restrooms on the college campus. I was no stranger to anonymous sex in restrooms, having relied on them heavily since I was a college student myself. It became too easy for me to spend hours of my free time looking for attention in a restroom.

I crossed paths with a variety of guys who had unusual kinks and agendas equal to mine. I was still learning about my fetish, and I was ready to dig deeper into my own psyche and bond with more open-minded people. I fucked a few men in the bathroom stalls. I met and brought home a man who liked to be urinated on. There was also a man who liked to be punched in the face during sex (which I didn't want to do, so he left my house completely unsatisfied). There were even a couple of older gentlemen who offered me money to have sex with them. It seemed that in this quiet, southern city, I wasn't the only one with unusual desires. I was game to try just about anything once. I always hoped to find a key to my own peculiarities in someone else's. I kept making myself available while hoping any gay man I ran into would become one of two possibilities: a relationship or a haircut.

Almost every time, the guy ended up being merely a sex partner.

I found it easier to ask a man if I could shave his mustache off than it was to ask if I could cut his hair. I suppose it was less of a sacrifice and the odds of finding a participant were much greater. There were also many more guys walking around town with mustaches than long hair. Six months after moving to Chapel Hill, I met a guy with a beautiful mustache in the men's restroom of Gardner Hall who seemed very interested in getting to know me. His name was Thomas. Meeting him presented me with a huge dilemma: shave him or date him?

Thomas was about seven years older and seemed very nice. He was handsome and had thick, dark hair that was cut short and a dark mustache that was full and accented his face nicely. The afternoon we first met in the restroom he was quick to motion me outside to talk. He seemed lonely and asked in his strong southern accent if I would be interested in going to dinner that evening. I agreed and we exchanged numbers.

A few hours later he picked me up at my home. He was a complete gentleman, opening doors for me and holding my hand in the car. I loved the attention, but I knew I should make a decision quickly as to whether to date Thomas or pursue the mustache. I was certain that if I chose to date him, I could never face the embarrassment of explaining my obsession to him. If I chose to pursue the shave, I knew that as soon as I asked, whether he said yes or no, our time together would be limited by my post-shave embarrassment.

We talked on the telephone a couple of times the following week and it seemed that he liked me. However, he was a little dry and boring for my taste. I realized that even without the mustache, I wouldn't date him for very long before losing interest. I would be happier with a younger, free-spirited boyfriend. I liked guys with a sense of humor. I couldn't remember Thomas ever laughing.

I found myself staring at his lip. It was apparent that I was more driven to pursue the shave rather than the relationship. I found it difficult just to spring such an idea on him, since I gathered that Thomas was a pretty conservative Southern gentleman. It was clear I was going to have to approach my proposition with care. He touched his mustache a lot and it was obviously important to him. I assumed he'd had the mustache for a long time, and convincing him to shave it would not be easy.

The following weekend we had another dinner date, which included an invitation to spend the night at his place. That evening I played with his mustache a lot during sex. I could tell he had no idea what I was thinking. I felt bad about the deception. I had to find out if he would let me shave him soon, because the guilt of leading him on was outweighing the embarrassment of asking him to let me shave him.

I finally sat on top of his chest, held two fingers over his mustache to hide it, and said, "I wonder what you would look like without the mustache?"

Thomas stared back at me. "I don't know." I could tell that he wasn't processing things.

"Can I shave it off and find out?" I asked in an upbeat tone.

"Oh, I don't know about that," he said, sitting up in bed.

"Please?" I said, "It would be so cool. It'll grow back."

He hesitated. I continued to make the request, cheering him on. It was obvious he didn't want to do it. The more he didn't, the more turned on I got. He couldn't help noticing my erection bouncing around. I continued to touch the mustache and cover it up. I was campaigning fiercely, playfully badgering and charming him as much as I could.

Finally he said, "Okay, the next time we get together, you can shave off my mustache."

"When will that be?" I asked. I didn't believe him and he knew it. He was truly scared, and I was very turned on. I wasn't going to take no for an answer. I knew that if it didn't happen immediately, it never would. I wouldn't have the guts ever to see him again, even if he still wanted to see me.

There was a lot of energy and tension in the bed. I had never had to work so hard at seducing a guy. I do not think anyone had ever tried so hard to seduce Thomas before, either. We kept discussing the shave as I massaged and caressed his whole body. Each gesture I made always made its way back up to his mustache. I reassured him that he didn't need the mustache and that he would look good without it. I said anything I could to convince him that he had to let me shave that mustache. It took over an hour of foreplay and psychological manipulation on my part, but Thomas finally agreed.

I immediately ran to his bathroom and found a beard trimmer with adjustable settings. I got back into the bed and straddled his chest and briefly played with the mustache for the last time. I slid the gauge on the trimmer to the lowest setting, which was for shaving rather than trimming. Thomas looked stunned and lay very quiet with his eyes closed. I turned the clippers on and plowed them right down one side of his lip.

> *He doesn't know what I'm all about.*
> *I bet he thinks I am just a regular guy.*
> *But I am not.*
> *Am I a bad person?*
> *I don't know if I'm a bad person or not,*
> *But I am in control right this minute.*

Little hairs flew all over his face. The clippers had to work really hard to chew through the hair. After half of it was gone, I stopped and really looked at him, comparing both sides of his face. This made Thomas very uncomfortable and he pleaded with me to finish the job. I

135

quickly mowed the other half off and wiped the cut hairs from his face. I tossed the clippers off of the bed and gave him a long passionate kiss. I felt relieved and exhausted. He was unresponsive. I jacked off alone while he ignored me from the other side of the bed.

Thomas got out of bed naked and ran to the bathroom to examine his face for the first time. He came back into the room, having put on a pair of underwear, and lay back down beside me.

"What do you think?" I asked.

"Well ... it's different," he answered sheepishly.

I could tell he didn't like the new look. I wasn't lying when I said he looked good without the hair on his lip. He was, in fact, a very attractive man without the mustache. However, I was no longer attracted to him. For me, the mustache made him appear more masculine. I decided against spending the night after all. Both of us were pretty wiped out from the experience, so we dressed and he drove me home, saying very little about what just happened. It seemed clear that we were done with each other. Whatever admiration Thomas had for me had been replaced with confusion. It was like he didn't know what had hit him.

Shaving Thomas' mustache was much more enjoyable than the guy at ISU.
He was resistant and I triumphed.
I had an impact on him.
I don't feel ordinary.
I don't want to be ordinary.

I was shocked a few days later when the phone rang and it was Thomas. My stomach became queasy as he spoke to me. He was like a new man. He explained that everyone had been complimenting him on his new look. He thanked me for the encouragement and wanted to see me again. His tone made me think that he believed we had a special bond since I had shaved his mustache off. I made up some lame excuse about why I couldn't see him. I didn't remotely want to see him again. He called me a few more times trying to get me to go out with him. I declined.

I knew I had probably hurt Thomas and did my best to ignore any guilt I felt.

What was important to me was trying to figure out where I was coming from with my obsession and more importantly where I was going with it. It was obvious to me that I needed to indulge my obsession to control someone, yet I had no control over my obsession. I experienced a lot of anxiety because I didn't want to feel the way I did. I had no idea how to change.

27-Soft Rape

I got tangled up with a twenty-year-old UNC undergraduate student named Owen who was acting in a PlayMaker's production of Shakespeare's *Love's Labour's Lost*. He was a sweet guy and I was immediately smitten with him and wanted to date him for real. There were no qualities about Owen that fit into my haircutting fantasies. He had very little hair, but I still found him quite attractive inside and out. It was nice to feel like I could get to know him without the distraction of wanting to cut his hair. We became friends and he asked me to design costumes for his undergraduate production of Alan Ayckbourn's play, *Woman in Mind*, for the UNC undergraduate lab theater. I was happy to oblige.

I sensed that Owen was gay right off the bat, but after a few weeks of me trying to pretend I was capable of such a straightforward gay relationship, he informed me he was not gay. I was devastated and did not handle the rejection well. I refused to believe he was straight. By the time the show opened, we were at odds. I was angry and hurt and became seriously depressed. It seemed so easy to blame all my anxiety on Owen. To cope, I found myself spending a lot of time looking for sex in the well-known cruising restroom of Gardner Hall on campus.

On the heels of Owen, I met a guy named Martin while cruising the restroom. He was about ten years older that me. He was built rather average, but I was immediately attracted by his full, thick beard. We immediately hooked up and left the restroom together. He walked me to his gold, beat-up Chevy pickup truck a few blocks away and took me to his apartment in nearby Durham for a few hours of sex. I wanted to forget all about Owen and try to manipulate Martin into letting me shave off his beard. I had rarely touched a whole beard and certainly hadn't shaved one off.

While getting to know Owen, I knew I was pretending to be normal and want all the same things gay guys wanted. On the flip side, my pursuit of Martin was the same as with Thomas; it was all about the hair. The dark hair on his head was certainly a distraction, but that beautiful beard was like sweet icing on a cake. Perhaps shaving Martin's beard and mustache could make up for Owen's rejection.

Martin and I dated for a week or two, but I was empty inside. Every time we got together, it was a token dinner date or coffee and then back to his place for redundant sex. I decided I didn't like having sex with him. He was very much a top and seemed bent on taking all the control away from me. I felt powerless to say no to him. Every time I saw his pickup pull into my parking lot I felt a little sick; I was going to have to submit. I was confused. Even his beautiful beard was no longer inspirational.

Martin seems like a reasonable guy.
Why don't I just tell him I don't want to see him anymore?
Is he the problem or am I?
Am I really on the rebound from Owen after all?
He's like all the other guys.
I'm going to be single my whole life.

As each date got shorter and shorter, I caught on: Martin was more interested in sex than getting to know me on a personal level. What else could you expect from someone you'd met in a public restroom? It made me uncomfortable. I wanted it to be the other way around. I decided I had to be done with him once and for all. One evening, after a quick coffee, I asked Martin to take me home rather than return to his place. He did as I asked, but insisted on inviting himself into my apartment. It only took a few minutes after we got inside for me to realize that he wasn't going to leave without sex. I decided to go ahead and submit to his needs and get rid of him as quickly as possible.

We went to my bedroom and began making out. I was hesitant, but we both stripped to our underwear. I couldn't hide my dissatisfaction, and he got more aggressive. I realized that I was now his challenge. He violently pushed me down on the bed and crawled on top of me. The dark hair and thick beard that had so attracted me only a few weeks earlier now made him look like the Devil. He had a fire in his eyes, and I was truly disturbed and getting angry. He started biting me. I tried to grab his beard, perhaps to take control of the situation. He slapped my hand away and quickly pinned me to the bed on my stomach with one of my arms behind my back.

I decided the best thing to do was to relax. I didn't want to have sex with him, but I didn't exactly fear him, either. I didn't feel in danger, but the longer his aggression showed, the more anger and humiliation I felt. I hated him. He seemed so turned on by my disdain.

I understood Martin at that moment. We both preferred to "win" in our sexual adventures, but he was stronger than I. I was being manipulated and I was not happy. Martin slipped a condom on his cock and lubed up my ass. He enthusiastically tried to penetrate me without success. I clenched my ass as tight as I could. The situation began to deflate. After a few more semi-careful attempts, I asked him politely to stop. His tone changed and he complied without incident.

We lay close in my twin bed and exchanged some form of pillow talk for a few minutes. I didn't hear a word he said. He got up, put his clothes on, gave me a sweet hug and kiss, and then dismissed himself from my apartment.

I had no idea what had just happened. I still hated him. Had I just been raped? I wasn't sure. He had stopped once I'd finally said no. Was there such a thing as soft rape? I certainly don't think Martin thought he had raped me. He had hurt me and I was a little sore, but had I consented by not saying no soon enough?

> *I know I was raped when I was seven years old.*
> *There are definite similarities between then and now.*
> *I wondered if being a victim of Glenn Stickney years earlier led me to this very night.*
> *I feel like I'm a victim of Owen, too.*
> *Owen and I have never had sex.*
> *Did I set this up with Martin because of Owen or Glenn?*
> *Am I asking to be raped again?*
> *Is this why I am always single?*
> *Martin looks like he could be a Stickney.*
> *That thick, dark hair.*
> *Kory had the dark hair of a Stickney too?*
> *Is the comparison fair or am I crazy?*
> *I don't know which emotion to pick.*
> *I never feel like my emotions fit the circumstance.*

When my roommate, Pilar, came home, she could tell I was upset. I was overwhelmed but didn't know why. I didn't know what to do with myself. She asked me what was wrong.

"I was raped," I said. Without saying a word Pilar went and grabbed a phone book to find the number for the Chapel Hill police. I begged her not to make me talk to the police. Despite proclaiming I had been raped, I still wasn't sure I had been. Pilar's concern grew and she started talking to me a mile a minute. I got scared and started to cry. I spit out a few details of the alleged rape to her and she became ultra-supportive and nurturing. The more she talked to me the more I cried. I began to realize that this was the attention I was due for being raped by Glenn Stickney in 1972.

I wish Pilar had known me before when I was little.
Perhaps Pilar could substitute for my mom.
This is the comfort I have craved all these years.
I never had the support I needed.
I never got to be the victim.
This feels right.
Maybe Dad was right;
I should have told them about the Stickneys as soon as
it happened.
This is all just in response to the wrong man, at the
wrong time.
I am indeed a rape victim.
I have just substituted tonight's rapist for Glenn
Stickney.
I am so angry and hurt.
I am completely humiliated.
I want revenge, but I still want to be lovable.

Pilar packed me up in her car. She thought it was best if I got away from the apartment. She made some calls and by 11 o'clock that evening she found a place for me to stay the night with a classmate of hers. I slept on a cold, strange floor with a spare blanket and pillow and cried the whole night.

Pilar alerted my boss at the theater what had happened. When I got to work late the next morning, she called me into her office and told me how sorry she was and offered any support she could. It was another warm, heartfelt message that seemed eighteen years late. It felt good. I wanted more sympathy so I quietly told another coworker I was friends with that I had been raped the night before. Several hugs and sad eyes later, I was beginning to feel better as I collected all the overdue sympathy from selected peers.

Whether it had been Martin's intent to rape me or not, whether I had been right or wrong by not telling him sooner, it didn't matter. I allowed myself to fill with rage, anger and humiliation. If I couldn't control Martin, then I wanted to be his victim. I wanted to feel all the feelings I had been unable to feel when I had been molested by Glenn Stickney.

I also made sure that Owen knew that I had been date-raped. His condolences were bittersweet. My shift in thinking was working. I was the victim I always wanted to be. No one in North Carolina knew that I had been molested as a child. No one would be the wiser.

I wore my rape on my sleeve. I began to irrationally fear running into Martin. I gave my apartment managers a description of his truck. I threw away the clothes I wore the night of our last date. I also trashed the sheets from my bed. I filed a "blind" police report without giving my name to be used against Martin if anyone filed rape charges against him in the future. I even rented and watched the movies *Extremities* and *The Accused* in private just to pick my old wounds and cry even harder. I freshly hated Glenn and his whole family for what had been done to me. I hated everyone.

But all the torture I put myself through didn't stop me from going back to Gardner Hall for more anonymous sex. I wanted to shave and cut more than ever.

My needs were somewhat met when, on hiatus from PlayMaker's, I was hired at Seaside Music Theater in Daytona Beach, Florida, for the summer. I was to be the Wardrobe and Hair Manager for five large musicals. I was indifferent to the sun and the sand, but was privately aroused by the prospect of giving upwards of fifteen resistant long-haired surfer guys short, 1920s haircuts for the production of *Cabaret*. However, I was still aching for an understanding of why it felt so right and wrong at the same time.

28-Love or Bald

I had first set eyes on Eric Ingle in the fall of 1989, not long after I had moved to Chapel Hill, while he was performing in a play. He was a UNC drama student playing one of the many New York street characters dabbling in hustling in Lanford Wilson's drama, *Balm in Gilead.* I thought he was the most charismatic guy I had ever seen. I couldn't help noticing he had a beautiful head of dark-brown hair, which I would have loved to cut.

The Evita Corkscrew (Inset-Eric Inale)

I spent the summer of 1990 working at a summer stock theater company in Daytona Beach, Florida. When I returned in the fall, our paths crossed again. For a drama class, Eric was assigned to work backstage on PlayMaker's production of the George Bernard Shaw play, *You Never Can Tell.* Eric was the only gay boy that I met while living in the south who had a flamboyant personality and didn't seem hung up on being gay and having a feminine side. We quickly became close, and his friendship helped me put the Owen and Martin messes behind me.

As with Owen, I wanted a relationship with Eric that wasn't soiled by my fetish. The fantasy of cutting his hair became secondary to being his best friend. Eric was special. I had never connected emotionally with a man the way I did with him. I never felt judged by him.

143

*If I had a choice of buzzing all of Eric's hair off or
being his boyfriend,
I would be delighted to be his boyfriend
But it's not that easy for me.
I get a hard-on looking at his hair, but I also get hard
looking at his face and body, too.
I don't know where to place him in my heart, and that
concerns me.
Sex and love have never fit together in my life like they
should.
That has nothing to do with Eric.
I don't want to scare him away.
I just want to understand.
I want an opportunity to be like everyone else.
I want to be loved.*

One night at Eric's house, I was delighted to discover
he was as big a fan of the musical *Evita* as I (and Stefeny)
were. We played the soundtrack and each pretended to be
Eva Peron, singing and dancing around the kitchen while
making dinner. I realized that Stefeny was back. However, I
felt like it was okay—perhaps even acceptable—for me to be
Stefeny as Eva, for Eric. I wondered if Eric was introducing
me to his own version of a Stefeny. The humor and honesty
of our playtime was inspiring. I found myself falling deeper
and deeper in love with Eric that evening.

As the soundtrack played, I noticed a metal corkscrew
on Eric's kitchen counter. It was the kind of corkscrew that
had a circle that looked like it could be a head, and two arms
that move upward, pulling the cork out of the bottle. I
suddenly got a brilliant idea. I grabbed the opener and ran to
the bathroom.

Minutes later, I returned on cue with the music, having
made a white, strapless dress out of toilet paper for the
corkscrew, just like the one Eva Peron traditionally wore for
the famous number, "Don't Cry for Me, Argentina." The
Evita corkscrew doll was Stefeny and she knew every word of

the song. Eric quickly produced two spoons for Corkscrew Eva to use as microphones. The toaster became her balcony.

She did all the choreography and the corkscrew doll proudly raised her arms at the end of the number, just like a Patti LuPone (NOT Elaine Paige). Eric was speechless. Both of us didn't know whether to laugh or cry. I didn't formally introduce Stefeny to Eric, but it was the first time anyone had ever witnessed her. It felt like a special night.

The room was alive with possibilities the rest of that evening. I loved Eric and I felt the love back. I wanted to make love to Eric, but I didn't know how to go about it. Affection with a man I loved was completely foreign to me. The soundtrack ended: Eva Peron died and so did the moment of possibility.

Eric and I were never intimate. I was still having anonymous restroom sex. Sex had become cheap and almost meaningless for me. I think that is what I liked the most about my time with Eric. By not adding any sexual ties to my friendship with him, I knew that every moment I got to spend with Eric was real and sincere. Unfortunately, I could tell he didn't love me the same way I loved him.

There were moments of tension and jealousy between Eric and me. My already fragile self esteem wasn't strong enough to process the situation. My entire life began to unravel.

> *I don't think about cutting your hair off as much as I think about kissing you ... except when you make me unhappy, then I want to make you bald.*
> *Sucking your dick would be too much like what I do to all of those men in the restrooms.*
> *You have become a symbol of a lot of things to me.*
> *You have become a hopeful model of "men" when I haven't had any hope or faith in "men" for a long time.*
> *I love you very, very much.*
> *I love you so much that if you wanted me to go away, I would.*

By the beginning of 1991, my unrequited love for Eric brought on a serious and dangerous depression. I was suddenly reintroduced to panic attacks. My first exposure to them had been when my mom had tried to take me to get a haircut years earlier. The feeling I was now having was very similar to the panic I had experienced at the possibility of being humiliated by getting my hair cut in a salon on that day long past.

A panic attack was like an overload: all the intense pressure in my mind would transfer itself to my body in order to give my mind a break. The attacks became more frequent and more intense. To make them stop, I found myself wishing I was dead. I bought a bottle of sleeping pills and carried them around like a loaded gun. I was comforted knowing that I could take them if I felt too bad. At first I didn't think of wanting to "kill myself" so much as wanting to stop the exhaustion and pain. I think that's why I chose pills, which people often take to feel better. Eventually, the possibility of suicide became a way to get back at Eric.

An ex-boyfriend of Eric's reappeared, and I was overwrought.

Eric obviously still had a great deal of affection for the man. I couldn't tell if he and his ex-boyfriend were going to be just friends or rekindle their romance, but they started spending a small amount time together. I was convinced I was going to be replaced, despite the fact that my friendship with Eric was still very much intact.

Then one day, with little explanation, Eric canceled dinner plans with me at the last minute, and I had the most serious panic attack I had ever had. I was convinced he was going to spend what I considered "our" time with his ex-boyfriend. I had no proof that was what was going on, but had merely been waiting for an excuse to act out. The trigger had been pulled and I was ready to take drastic measures.

I'm too tired to go on.
I want to die.
I have a twisted-up life where I can't stop thinking
about hair.
I really wanted Eric to be the guy that changed all of
that.
I'm so angry and I cannot imagine what I did to
deserve this.
I want to be a good and well-adjusted person.
I want to be happy.
I want to be loved.
Instead, I'm dealt this hand of cards that I can no
longer play.
I want to cut guys' hair.
I want to cut Eric's hair just to make him notice me,
Listen to me,
Respect me,
Or even fear me.
But I'd prefer he just love me.
There is absolutely no way I can think of to make him
love me.
Every day is another day of dealing with men:
Men to have sex with,
Men to fantasize about cutting and men who don't love
me.
Men who don't want to even look at me.
I want to be dead to stop all of this.

I went home alone after Eric canceled our dinner. I
started taking the sleeping pills that I had been hanging on
to for so many weeks. The timing was perfect because Pilar
was out of town. I took one pill every ten minutes and lay on
the couch and cried harder than I had ever cried. I didn't
really want to die. I just wanted a good reason to live.

After about two hours I had taken close to a dozen
sleeping pills. My body was shutting down, but my mind
continued to race. I was sick to my stomach and having
terrible head tremors. I couldn't open my mouth. I hated the
way my body felt but had no remorse for my dangerous

actions. I was scared, so I stopped taking the pills. At that moment, I wasn't sure if I was living or dying, so I just closed my eyes and decided to let fate take it course. I decided that if I didn't die, I was going to have to make some changes in my life.

When I woke up the next morning, I couldn't move. I had thrown up in the middle of the night. I lay in bed and contemplated my future. The more I thought, the more my body loosened up. I wasn't sure what my next step was to be, but I decided to take things slow, both physically and emotionally. I called in sick to work and found the suicide hotline in the front of the phone book. I explained everything that had happened the night before to a compassionate volunteer. I asked for her help. She recommended a counseling program that utilized UNC graduate students as therapists. The fee was only nine dollars a session, so I put myself back into counseling.

The next day I went to work like nothing had happened. I took a long dinner break and hooked up with a wonderful counselor named Candice whom I credit with helping me through this very rough period. I didn't tell Eric about my suicide attempt. He knew I was in love with him and he knew I was in pain, but I didn't want to create more pressure in our friendship than what already existed.

As spring approached, I sank so low that my therapist brought up the possibilities of hospitalizing me and getting me serious psychiatric care to keep me from killing myself. I was agreeable to the suggestion and kept a small suitcase packed in case Candice couldn't be reached and I felt like I had to check myself into the hospital to feel safe. Luckily, I never had to take such action.

I spent most of my sessions talking about Eric. He had become a curtain blocking out the rest of my life, namely my obsession with haircutting.

Nothing was getting better. I realized my life wasn't going to change unless I took drastic measures to fix it. I had kept in touch with my friend Jim from SIU-C. Back in 1990, Jim had moved to the Seattle, just as I was settling into Chapel Hill. I adored talking on the phone with him about once every two weeks. The day after my suicide attempt in 1991, I called and told him everything. He was horrified at what I was doing to myself and repeatedly suggested I move to Seattle. He didn't come out and say it, but I think he wanted to keep an eye on me.

He told me his roommate would be moving out that summer, so I could move in with him. Jim also agreed that I needed to get away from Eric. I wasn't feeling any better and therapy was only valuable in the short term. I had to evaluate my future. The timing was right and I finally accepted his offer. I knew that I wasn't going to heal immediately, but I was very excited about the change of scene.

I told Eric I was moving the Seattle the following May. He didn't seem to believe me at first, but after the idea sank in, he was supportive. I believed him when he said he was going to miss me.

"I've never met anyone like you. You are an original," he said, giving me a big hug.

I made a special gift for Eric before leaving town. I bought a corkscrew and made a wig, jewels, and white satin dress for it, to remind him of our *Evita* evening. When I gave him the gift, it was the first time in weeks I had been able to look him in the eyes and not feel pain. He was touched. I knew Eric and I would be friends no matter where I chose to live.

Truthfully, I wasn't sure if I was running away from my problems or actually fixing them. I didn't care. Only two weeks after making my decision, I had lined up a job with Jim working in the costume shop of Seattle Opera. I told my parents about the move but didn't elaborate on why. They never really asked any questions, but bought my plane ticket across the country.

Every couple of days, I would ship a box of my stuff to Jim. As my apartment became emptier and emptier, my head began to clear and I felt better. The panic attacks had stopped. I was back to my usual obsessed self.

29-An Exit Haircut

I continued the hunt for anonymous sex as I prepared to move across the country. A week before I left, I met a guy named Hank in the Gardner Hall restroom. He seemed very interested in having sex with me. He had shoulder length, thick dark hair that I was very interested in cutting. Looking at his hair and thinking about the prospect of cutting it all off made my cock hard. His hair was slightly longer than Eric's.

Considering the fact that I was leaving town in a matter of days, I took a chance and passed him a note written on toilet paper under the stall partition: "Can I give you a short military haircut in exchange for sex?"

This was the first time I had ever asked a guy to let me buzz his head in a sexual context. A note was easier than saying it out loud. I figured I had absolutely nothing to lose by asking.

I could tell that he was taking me seriously when I got a note back saying, "Sure!" He then asked where we would go to do the haircut. We obviously couldn't do it in the restroom. For something I fantasized about doing so much, I was totally unprepared to actually do it.

Luckily I hadn't shipped my haircutting equipment to Seattle. But I didn't want to take him to my home for fear of Pilar being there. If this was really going to happen we had a lot of details to discuss, so I arranged for him to meet me outside where we could actually talk freely. Once outside, I introduced myself using a false name. He immediately admitted that he had second thoughts about getting his hair cut. He was nervous and fidgety, which excited me.

Hank wanted to know why I wanted to cut his hair.

"I get sexually excited cutting men's hair. I would get very turned on if I could buzz your head while we have sex," I said. It was such a relief to say it out loud, despite being terrified of what the guy's reaction was going to be. I expected him to be disgusted. He sounded fascinated about the sexual part, but he was still very hesitant about the short haircut. It seemed my proposition wasn't meant to be.

He then asked me again where we would go to have sex and do the haircut. I remembered there was a cheap motel very near my apartment and suggested we get a room there for privacy.

"I'll only let you cut my hair if I can stay in the room for the night," he said very earnestly. He explained to me that he had just gotten into Chapel Hill from out of state that afternoon. He had no place to stay and sounded quite desperate.

I quickly agreed he could keep the room for the night, and we walked to the bus stop that serviced my neighborhood. He didn't have money for bus fare, so I had to pay both our fares. We were unable to sit together on the crowded bus. I wouldn't have been surprised to see him get off the bus and flee, but he was keeping an eye on me as much as I was keeping an eye on him. I figured he needed the room as much as I needed to cut his hair.

I got off the bus and he followed me. We were both nervous as I checked us into the motel room. I paid for the room with a credit card. Once inside I told him to stay put while I ran home to get all of the tools to do the haircut. He agreed. My heart was beating quickly as I walked the two blocks to my apartment and gathered up the clippers and scissors and put them into my book bag.

What am I doing?

Am I insane?
He could rob me.
He could hurt me or kill me.
I shouldn't let him stay in the room unsupervised.
He could vandalize the room.
He could steal something.
The room is in my real name and my credit card has
already been charged.
He could invite anyone into the room who could also
do any number of things

Even if I had wanted to, it seemed too late to back out now.

I finally had an opportunity to experience my obsession without being inhibited. I had gotten a small taste of this when I shaved Thomas's mustache off months earlier. This time I had a whole head of hair at my disposal. Something told me this guy wasn't going to be a problem. Hank seemed sincere. I left a discreet note for Pilar with the name of the motel and the room number alongside my wallet on the bedroom dresser, just in case.

When I got back to the hotel, I found Hank lying on the bed, calmly watching television and wearing only a towel. He had taken a shower while I was gone. We made some nervous small talk while I approached the bed and dug the clippers out of my book bag. I snapped on the half-inch attachment guide. I found a wall socket that was close enough to plug them in and still reach the bed. I sat down on the edge of the bed with my feet still touching the floor. Hank was still lying down. He unbuttoned my pants and started fondling my crotch from behind. I stopped him.

"Sit on the floor in front of me facing my crotch," I demanded. He did as he was told.

Hank quickly pulled out my cock and started sucking on it. I felt a wave of energy shoot through my body. I ran my fingers through his long, damp hair. The clippers were only a few inches from my leg. I let him continue servicing me for several minutes. It seemed like he had let his guard down and perhaps wasn't thinking about the haircut. The timing was perfect for me. I grabbed the clippers, turned them on, and gently slid them right down the center of his scalp, from forehead to crown.

It's finally happening.
This is intense.
What must this guy be thinking about me?
I can't see his face.
I don't want to see his face.
From this angle, he looks just like Eric.

I was enthralled as long folds of hair fell all around his head. He winced, yet continued to suck on my cock. I started cutting another path down his scalp to the right of the first one while fantastic tremors shook my body. It was the most incredible sensation I had ever had. I could tell Hank wasn't enjoying himself anymore. As I was on my third pass with the clippers, he gasped like he was coming up for air and pulled my cock out of his mouth.

I stopped cutting. "Are you okay?" I asked.

"Yes. Finish what you started," he snapped. His mood had turned sour.

How dare you stop?
I don't want you to hurt me, but you better keep going.
I finally feel something.
Running the clippers through your hair makes me feel in charge.
You have to let me do this or you don't get the room to sleep in.
I know neither one of us will ever forget this.
You don't deserve this punishment, but someone does.
If we had met any other way, you would never have noticed me.
This is the only way I can get your attention.
You must remember me, you must respect me.

*Every time you look in the mirror, you will remember
who did this to you.
I wonder what Eric is doing right this minute.
Does he have any idea what I am doing?
I wouldn't have to do this if he loved me.*

I continued buzzing his hair. He had stopped sucking,
but was halfheartedly stroking my cock, which was covered
with his fresh cut hair.

There were huge piles of long hair all around him. The
man had only the slightest bit of stubble left on his head.
Hank was upset. After his head was completely shorn, he felt
his head with his hand and crawled up into the bed and lay
on his back. I had not cum yet, so I spun around and lay next
to him, surveying what I had done to his head.

"Well, go ahead and touch my head. I know that's what
you want to do," Hank snapped, still pretty uptight about
was happening.

*You snap at me?
Are you trying to take some control away from me?
I don't want you to hurt me.
Your hair will grow back, but you look pretty ugly
now.
I was so turned on because you hated what I did.
I'd rather be turned on the way everyone else is turned
on.
I don't want to be weird.
Why do I care what you think?*

I rubbed his head and jacked off until I shot a large
load of cum. I had to focus on what he looked like before and
what I did to change that, rather than what he looked like
now.

We both lay quietly in the bed for about half an hour. It
was over. I didn't know what to do next. I was exhausted and
felt like I was going to choke. Hank looked terrible and I was
sure he resented me. I felt a small amount of satisfaction

from his contempt, but felt ashamed of how I had used him. I cleaned myself up in the bathroom and packed up the clippers. I told him that I would be back in the morning to check him out of the room. I made sure to keep the room key, noticing the door automatically locked after it closed. Once I left the room, I felt relieved.

The next morning, I was nervous to go back to the room. I wasn't sure what to expect when I opened the door, but he was dressed and ready to leave. I took a quick look around the room and everything seemed to be in order. I checked out of the room, and there was an awkward pause as we prepared to go our separate ways. I broke the ice and wished him well. He seemed grateful, shook my hand and thanked me for letting him stay in the room. I couldn't bring myself to thank him for letting me cut his hair. It seemed silly. I felt a little confused and empty, and I think he had grown a little bitter. We both had gone to a lot of trouble to accommodate each other. I said nothing and watched him walk away.

The evening I spent with Hank gave me a dose of guilty pleasure.

It was sexually satisfying, but I felt like I had done something terribly wrong. Reminding myself that everything that happened between Hank and me was consensual didn't seem to help me feel any better. I think I expected that when I finally got the opportunity to experience satisfaction from my haircut fantasy, it would finally go away. It hadn't. If anything, I was ready to try it again and make the next time bigger and better.

A few days before I was scheduled to leave Chapel Hill, I called Jim on the telephone and told him about the experience and confessed the details of my obsession with hair. I was expecting his reaction to be negative. Jim was the first friend I told. Being open-minded, he didn't flinch, but was fascinated. He even suggested that Seattle might hold even more opportunities for such activities.

I certainly saw a light at the end of the tunnel as far as my turmoil over Eric. We remained close friends right up to the day I left North Carolina for good. We perhaps got even closer after I announced I would be moving away.

On May 15, 1991, Eric took me to the Raleigh-Durham Airport. We said our goodbyes, and I didn't look back. I missed him before the plane even left the ground, but I knew I had made the right decision. When Jim picked me up at the airport in Seattle later that day, I felt like an orphan who had just been adopted. I knew I was in good hands.

After I had lived in Seattle a few months, I found a paperback romance novel entitled *Chapel Hill* in a department store. I couldn't help but buy it. It seemed like a typical weepy melodramatic novel that was written in the same formula as all romance novels, only the descriptions were specific to Chapel Hill. There appeared to be nothing original or creative about the book. It was restricted by its formula. I felt the exact same way about my time spent in that city. I wasn't sure if the restrictions I had experienced during the two years I spent in the south were good or bad.

My mom had always enjoyed romance novels, so I mailed the book to her.

30-Two Hundred Dollar Trim

I wanted to be as gay as possible. I was having more sex in Seattle than I had ever had in my life. I had begun to frequent Club Seattle—a bath house on Summit Street—as well as a few restrooms on the campus of the University of Washington. I kept expecting something wonderful to come out of all of the experiences. Nothing ever did. After shaving over a dozen mustaches, cutting one off offered only limited pleasure. It did allow me to get more comfortable with my obsession, though.

I decided to journal my sexual experiences—the haircutting ones as well as the experiences where I didn't indulge my fetish. I hoped I would learn more about myself by documenting my exploits.

My first entries were in September 1991:

CLUB SEATTLE - ROOM 176
*Blond hair (thinning and curly; layered; medium to short)
*Chunky; average height, 20s
*Smoker
*Slight mustache, pleasant face
*Wore big plastic glasses
Met in TV bedroom and went to his room. Heavy kissing, affection; he sucked me some; very fixed on putting his fingers in my ass. I wouldn't let him. He came on top of my chest. I didn't cum. I might do him again.

UNIVERSITY OF WASHINGTON—SMITH HALL
*Early 30-ish name Bob
*Balding, geekish blond man
*Short small frame
*Glasses
*Slight short mustache
*Wearing dress clothes and a tie
Met in restroom on first floor; he agreed to let me give him a haircut, and we went to the fourth floor to a private restroom. We kissed some; lots of touching. He sat on the toilet and sucked on me, but backed out on the haircut; I didn't suck on him; neither of us came; I would only do him again if I could give him a haircut. I gave him my number and he said he wanted to call me for a haircut on Saturday.

UNIVERSITY OF WASHINGTON—SMITH HALL
*Blond, thinning, wavy hair
*Big build, tall, early 30s

*Glasses

*Mustache

Met him in first floor restroom and asked if he would let me trim his mustache short. He agreed and we went to Gowen Hall restroom. He said he was a top. We kissed some and did a lot of affectionate touching. I sat on his lap facing him on the toilet and trimmed his mustache as short as I could with scissors. I enjoyed it but it wasn't overwhelming. He held me tight and kept telling me to relax and calm down. "We were going to be okay." He kept jacking me. Neither of us came and I left him. I might be interested again.

* * * * *

I realized I was carefully picking and choosing the men I asked to participate in my haircutting scenes. I would determine by a guy's personality during foreplay whether I thought he would let me do it before I went through the embarrassment of asking. Eventually it became routine to ask every man that I had sex with and who sported a mustache to let me shave it off. Either they would agree to it or not. I realized that no matter what, life would go on for both me and my partner, with or without his facial hair.

I never forgot the experience of shaving Hank's head before my cross-country move from North Carolina to Seattle. In fact, I continued to utilize that memory during masturbation. Despite Hank's halfhearted willingness, I still assumed cutting head hair was not negotiable with most men. Unlike my experiences with mustaches, I was still intimidated at the thought of asking a man to shave his head, and I couldn't imagine a man agreeing to it easily. It didn't help that I wasn't merely looking to trim a guy's hair. I was mostly interested in drastic haircutting situations. I was starting to get desperate for any sort of situation I could get. Even playing with long hair without the possibility of cutting it seemed better than nothing.

I saw many ads for escorts in the *Seattle Gay News*. One particular ad for a long-haired guy named Chuck interested me. I thought about it for a few days. Hiring an escort would strain my budget. The newspaper indicated that they ranged in price from $80 to $150 an hour. This was an amount of money I ordinarily wouldn't have. However, I had recently received my income tax refund so I decided to give the ad a call and investigate.

It turned out that Chuck worked through an agency. A very friendly woman answered the phone and obviously served as the madam. She was curious as to how I had found out about the agency, and I explained that Chuck's ad in the gay newspaper caught my eye. I was told that he wasn't available at that time, but she offered to tell me about several other men who were. I explained that I was interested in Chuck because his ad said he had long hair. It turned out that Chuck was the only escort at that agency with long hair.

I asked her about rates and boundaries when hiring an escort. She told me that $150 was a guy's rate for his time and implied that anything beyond that would cost more, but gave no price list. The agency wanted no knowledge of what an escort did on a "date." That was left up to each escort's own discretion. I didn't bother to explain to the woman on the phone that I had a sexual interest in cutting hair. I asked about possible times to call back and hook up with Chuck. Her answer was politely vague.

I knew I would never convince an escort to let me cut his hair, so I didn't plan on even asking. My expectations were that I would hire a gorgeous, long-haired escort and completely confess my fetish to him just to see what would happen. I felt confident any conversation about his long hair would be at the very least interesting and perhaps arousing. I was also interested in some uninhibited hair play. I thought perhaps shampooing a man's hair could be a substitute for cutting it. Actual sexual contact with the escort was interesting to me (especially if he was attractive), but secondary to the hair activity and seeing what his reaction to me would be. I had exactly $200 to spend, and I wanted to get my money's worth.

I was also nourishing a psychological curiosity. Naively, the word "escort" implied "model" or "beautiful" to me. Although I now lived in a city where beautiful people were a dime a dozen, I was still a small-town boy who had never rubbed elbows with the likes of a model or escort. I had also never had the undivided attention of an exceptionally long-haired man. I expected this guy to walk off of the cover of a romance novel and make my day by reading my mind, then say and do the right things to turn me on and get me off. I wasn't sure where this date was going, but I was more than willing to pay money to find out.

I called the agency for Chuck a few more times before the madam told me he was available. I gave her my number and she told me he would call me in ten minutes. A few minutes later, the phone rang, and it was Chuck calling from a cellphone while driving on the Interstate 5 toward Seattle. He seemed very nice and I explained to him what I wanted to do—wash and play with his hair. He thought that was great and I gave him directions to my apartment. He told me he would be over within an hour and I was to have the cash on hand. I had just enough time to accomplish my mission before Jim got home.

I waited patiently for the intercom to ring, when all of a sudden there was a knock on the front door. I couldn't imagine who could be stopping by from within the building. I opened the door and it was Chuck, who had been let into the building as someone was exiting. He stood about six feet tall and was wearing jeans and a T-shirt. A baseball cap was hiding most of his hair, which was in a ponytail. He had a muscular body and was handsome, yet nothing about him screamed *escort*. He gave me a firm, pleasant handshake, and I invited him into my apartment.

He asked if he could look around and make sure I was the only one in the apartment, and then asked to see my identification. Everything seemed to meet his needs. He then asked to use my phone to call the agency. I had to repeat my telephone number back to him to give to the madam on the line. He hung up and announced that our hour was to start right then. He asked to see the money and requested it sit on the dresser in the bedroom where we both could see it at all times. I dug the money out of my wallet, counted three fifty dollar bills out for him, and placed it in the designated spot.

With all of the business out of the way, he smiled and asked how I wanted to start the hour. I said I wanted to wash his hair.

"Great. Let's take our clothes off," he said.

The first thing Chuck did was take off the baseball cap and pull the elastic from his hair.

"My hair is dirty today anyway," he said, shaking it out.

This was the first look I got of his hair. It was naturally blond and hung about twelve inches below his shoulders. He had some layers and bangs around his face, which I always think is rather unattractive on men. His hair seemed very healthy. I could sense that he liked having long hair and probably got a lot of attention because of it.

He continued taking his clothes off and I took mine off, too. When we were both naked, we rushed to the bathroom and got into the large, old fashioned tub. I felt rather ridiculous being with him. He had an impressive, tanned gym body that seemed perfect except for some acne scars on his back. I, on the other hand, had a doughy, pale body. We made a silly-looking pair. I felt weird. Even though I had the money, he was in control. I quickly realized I hadn't hired the power I wanted.

I sat on the edge of the tub, and he bent his head over while I got his hair wet with the shower nozzle. He commented on how much he liked my apartment, and we politely discussed rent in the city while I shampooed his hair.

He seemed like an intelligent, outgoing guy. I massaged his scalp and ran my fingers through the long lengths of hair. He began playing with my penis, barely getting it hard. He occasionally glanced at me, his face showing little expression. We got out of the tub and dried ourselves off. I approached him face to face and gently touched his chest, trying to break the ice. He froze and said nothing. I gathered he didn't really want me to touch him, but he didn't tell me not to.

We went back into the bedroom and got into bed, naked, side by side. I began playing with his hair again.

"For another fifty dollars, I'll suck on you with a condom. Do you have a condom?" he asked. I declined his offer, explaining I wanted to just play with his hair. He seemed rather pensive. It became tense in the room. Our date didn't seem to be going anywhere and neither of us was comfortable.

"Do you want to give me a trim?" he asked.

I was shocked.

"Sure. How much do you want me to cut?"

"Just an inch; my ends are a mess. For an extra fifty, I'll let you give me a trim."

I pondered his offer.

"How about you give me a blow job with a condom and I trim your ends for an extra fifty dollars," I asked.

Without hesitation, he agreed. Time was running out, so I jumped out of bed and quickly grabbed a chair, comb and scissors and set up a makeshift haircut station beside the bed. I got back into bed, and Chuck began stroking my penis, getting it hard. I reached into the nightstand drawer beside my bed, grabbed a condom, and put it on. He began sucking on me very unenthusiastically. I was quickly bored and suggested we move on to the haircut.

I asked him a couple of questions as we got out of bed and prepared.

"Is this the longest your hair has ever been?" I asked.

"No, it used to be a little longer, and I didn't always have bangs," he replied, playing with the ends.

"Have you ever gotten a bad haircut?"

"Oh, yeah. This one woman really butchered it one time," he snapped. " I said, as I began to play with my cock again.

He then launched into a story about a terrible haircut he had gotten several years ago. I couldn't tell if it was true, or if he had pinpointed my kink and was patronizing me. For the first time since he walked into my apartment, I was feeling genuinely aroused. We finally had some spark between us. He sat down and quickly flinched because the metal folding chair was very cold against his naked butt. I placed a towel over the chair for him to sit on.

I began combing his hair and I got very nervous. I felt like I was in a dream, watching myself outside my body. It was a feeling I knew well.

"Now don't take off more than an inch," he warned.

I grabbed the scissors and leaned over and froze. All of a sudden, an inch meant nothing to me. I stared at the wet hair stuck to the back of the chair.

This whole situation is fake.
Chuck is fake.
I am fake.
He doesn't care for me.
He's pretending to be my pal, just to get my money.
He couldn't care less about my satisfaction.
I am a dollar sign to him.
He's a prop to me.

I cut a four inch chunk from the ends of his hair. The damp, freshly cut hair made an audible clap on the hardwood floor below. I had just stolen some control back from him.

"That didn't sound good," he said calmly, as he stood up and look at the hair I had just cut, sitting on the floor.

"Oh my God! That's way more than an inch. My hair hasn't been this short in a long time." He kept saying the same thing over and over for about five minutes. He was obviously stunned.

I hadn't actually finished the haircut. I had only taken one slice and it was uneven. I started to tremble. His hair was by no means short. It was still a couple of inches below his shoulder. He continued to babble on about the drastic cut and kept looking at me in amazement.

"Do you want me to finish it, or leave it like it is?" I asked.

"Go ahead and finish it, but don't cut it any shorter," he said and nervously sat back down in the chair.

I did as he asked and just evened the back up. It actually looked fine, just shorter. He got up and looked in the mirror and seemed to calm down. I couldn't tell if he was really mad or not. I even suspected he was overreacting for my sexual benefit. Whatever was going on, I was not enjoying it and was ready for him to leave.

"I really am sorry. I thought that was an inch," I offered dumbly.

He ignored me and started getting dressed. He put his hair back in the ponytail, and popped the hat back on his head. His attitude had changed, almost as if nothing had really happened.

He looked at me and smiled. "Well, I guess it will grow out."

He walked over and took the $150 off the dresser. He asked about the additional $50, and I took the extra money out of my wallet. The phone rang and I answered it. It was the woman at the agency; our hour was up. He shook my hand and even told me to call him again some time. Then he left. I had no interest in ever seeing him again.

> *What the hell just happened?*
> *I can't believe what I just did.*
> *Escort is another word for prostitute;*
> *I guess I hadn't thought about that.*
> *I just spent $200 on humiliating myself.*
> *I only have myself to blame.*
> *All I have to show for my money is my memory of cutting his hair.*
> *I wish I had cut his hair much shorter.*
> *Instead of a few inches, I should have cut a big hunk out of it.*
> *Then, HE would have never forgotten me.*
> *It would be very scary to let go of myself like that, but also very arousing.*

I deeply regretted the situation I had placed myself in that day. For the first time, I had been introduced to the dark part of my psyche that can severely impair judgment. As drug and alcohol addicts build up tolerance, the risks they take to meet their needs become greater. I was no different. My drug of choice was raping men of their power and vanity by robbing them of their hair.

31-Disconnected People

Who was the real victim?

Within the first year of living in Seattle, I became addicted to reading *The Advocate*. Inches from the classified ad for the Men's Hair Club, I discovered a couple of mail order gay porn video companies that dealt exclusively with hair.

Manco Golden Images was a company based out of Los Angeles that was directed more toward men's body shaving enthusiasts and had only a few sporadic head haircutting scenes. Katsam Productions was a New Jersey company that specialized in S&M and unusual kinks, including scat, water sports and sex with food, to name a few. Some of their movies had silly story lines and the tapes were very poorly produced. These haircutting video companies were not terribly interesting to me, and tapes were expensive, but it didn't stop me from ordering them.

My favorite company was Barber Shop Videos. The owner was a southern man named Craig who operated out of Louisiana. I had a few pleasant telephone conversations with him while placing my orders and enjoyed listening to his thick accent, despite my recent distaste for the south. He produced several videos of haircuts, most of which were performed in a real barbershop with real barbers. There was no sexual content in the tapes (although he later branched out with a separate company that did combine haircutting and gay sex). Craig simply solicited men to get their hair cut and then videotaped the event. He obviously liked watching long-haired guys getting sheared, just like I did. Many of the tapes featured drastic haircutting scenes. I always wondered if the men in the tapes knew that their video appearance was geared toward a fetish market. I loved the tapes, but his company was terribly disorganized and it took forever for Craig to complete the orders.

Despite the apparent innocence of the subject matter, and because these videos couldn't be bought in stores, owning them made me feel like I had a dirty little secret. I have to admit that was part of the appeal. My video library grew and I ordered every tape I could get my hands on. I would get terribly impatient waiting for my video to arrive and often called Craig to remind him to ship my order. Jim thought I was berserk to get so wound up over a tape that only featured fully-dressed men getting their hair cut, without sex or even so much of a handshake between the barber and client.

Almost a year to the day after moving to Seattle, I began working at Intiman Theater as the Wardrobe Manager. The job required me to work more seriously with theatrical wigs and hair. I was at the theater six nights a week and generally got off work late. I didn't have a car, so my primary form of transportation was walking. The walk home from work every night was cruising time. I walked right through downtown and Freeway Park—a known haven for anonymous gay sex. I would occasionally meet someone and have sex before continuing home from work.

FREEWAY PARK
*Tall Latino type boy
*20s—30s
*Long dark hair
*Mustache
*Solid build
Came up to me at my bench and asked me to have sex with him. We went to a private corridor outside by the parking garage. We kissed and he sucked on me very briefly. We jacked off and he came. I gave him my number.

FREEWAY PARK
*Older man, pleasant face
*Gray short hair
*Medium build
Came up to my bench and offered me $20 to let him suck me off. I agreed and took the money. He told me he would pay me again if I came to his hotel room tomorrow (more money). I told him I would consider it. His name is Bob and he said he is staying at the Executive Inn on 6th and his room number is 201.

FREEWAY PARK
*Late 30s—early 40s
*Big beefy guy, tallish, (sorta fat)
*Brown Hair, nice mustache
*Not that interesting or good looking
I followed him to a dark corner behind some bushes. He didn't give me head. He kept telling me I was "erotic." I asked him about his mustache. He had never been without it. He flinched a lot when I combed it with my teeth. He left after a while.

* * * * *

One evening I stopped and sat on a park bench to check out the action.

There wasn't a lot of activity that particular night, just a few of the regular pedestrians who used the park's path as a transition from downtown to the nearby neighborhood. Sometimes, if it was a slow night, it was nice to just sit in the park and relax. The park was built over a freeway and the sound of the cars zipping by underneath could be quite soothing.

As I was sitting there, an extremely drunk guy stumbled past me. He appeared to be in his twenties and looked a little worn, but I was attracted to him. He had long brown hair. I watched him veer off toward a row of bushes by a concrete wall in a dark corner of the park. I waited to see if he came out of the bushes. When he didn't, I figured that he would pass out drunk back there. Without much thought, I went into the bushes to investigate. He did indeed seem to be haphazardly down for the night.

I crawled into the bushes and sat cross legged at his head. He was obviously very out of it and mumbled something incoherent right to my face. I stroked his hair soothingly, and whispered to him, "It's going to be all right."

I sat with him for about half an hour just thinking, as I often did in the park late at night.

This man is probably just floating through life, just like I am.
Maybe he used to drink as a hobby.
From the looks of him, I bet it is now his lifestyle.
He is probably no more happy a person than I am.
There is no reason for him to have long hair.
He doesn't need the hair as much as I need to cut it.
It probably doesn't mean a thing to him.
Cutting it would mean a great deal to me, but I don't know why.

I reached down, and took the scissors from my bag, and began to cut big chunks of his hair off. I could tell in the darkness his hair looked bad. He soon began to regain consciousness and tried sitting up.

"What are you doing?" he asked. I got frightened.

"Nothing," I said as I quickly got up and exited the bushes. I felt victorious and very aroused. As I calmly walked away with an obvious erection in my pants, I heard him calling after me in a deep voice, "You're dead! You're dead!" However, when I looked back, the drunk man was having a hard time even standing up.

About a month later, I found another haircut possibility while walking home from work late at night. I began to take notice of a cute, small-framed young man in his early twenties that I would see sleeping in the doorway of an abandoned building that was once the Coliseum Theatre on Fifth Avenue and Pike Street. He was usually just going to sleep in his sleeping bag as I passed him on my way home each night. He was Native American, seemed pretty clean and had beautiful, dark hair, well past his shoulders. He dressed somewhat like a hippie—tie-dyed tee shirt, bell-bottom jeans, and beads. He didn't necessarily strike me as a down-and-out, drunk street person—just someone who lived on the street almost like he was camping. I never saw him panhandle.

I began to acknowledge him kindly each time I saw him on my way home, making sure he noticed me. He seemed like a cheerful person. He smiled and would occasionally say hello, since I walked by almost every night. I really wanted to cut his hair and thought about it constantly. Since we had built up a small rapport, I pondered the idea of just asking him if he would be interested in a haircut. Perhaps, since he was sleeping on the street, I could offer him money to let me give him a haircut.

"Excuse me. I know this is an odd question, but would you mind letting me give you a short haircut?" I asked politely.

He declined with a grin. "You should ask the skateboard punks over at Westlake Park. They might let you do something like that."

I smiled back and walked away.

A couple of nights passed. I got depressed and started to feel like I was falling apart. His refusal reinforced my desire. From the time I woke up in the morning until I walked home and went to bed at night, I thought about the guy's long dark hair and constantly fantasized about cutting it all off. I couldn't control or change my desires. I was soon daring myself to act out. Perhaps satisfying the desires would make them go away.

> *I feel like I'm at a fork in the road.*
> *Both of the paths are extremely frightening to me.*
> *I can keep trying to resist; do nothing.*
> *It's agony.*
> *I can't stop thinking about this guy's hair.*
> *I feel like the whole world is happening around me,*
> *and I'm in a tiny glass box watching it.*
> *People talk to me, but it is muffled.*
> *I can't breathe or rest.*
> *This obsession keeps me contained.*
> *I can only LOOK at the world.*
> *The only thing I can grasp is my desire to cut hair.*
> *If I act out and pursue cutting, perhaps the glass will break.*

One beautiful July night, the downtown Seattle streets were fairly deserted, except for a few passing cars. As I got closer and closer to the homeless man's usual doorway, I knew I would do something that evening. The guy was already bundled up and asleep. His dark head was poking out of his sleeping bag. I had second thoughts and walked right past him, trying to ignore the fact that he was there. I got a block away and stopped in the middle of the sidewalk. I started shaking.

I turned around and started to walk back, pulling the small scissors out of my bag. I stopped next to him, shears in my hand and ready to cut. I stood there looking down at the sleeping creature at my feet. Slowly, I squatted and gently stroked his long, silky hair with my right hand. I pulled a big section of his black hair out and sliced it off within an inch of his scalp. I quickly stood up, put the hair in my pants pocket and walked away. I stopped in the middle of the next block.

I did it.
I have made a mark on someone.
I'm unaccountable.
This guy is going to wake up in the morning and not know what happened to his hair.
I'm the cutter.
I'm responsible and I LIKE that feeling.
He's a victim and I'm not.
That is powerful.
That matters to me.

I pulled the hair out of my pocket. It was about a twelve inch long piece of healthy hair. I had gotten away with it. I felt relieved and hoped that I could finally stop thinking about the guy. Unlike the guy from the park a few weeks earlier, this guy hadn't woken up and had no idea what I had just done to him.

I wasn't satisfied. I wanted another shot, so I turned and started walking back. There was a lot of adrenaline in my system so things seemed to be moving faster. I knelt down, took a bigger hunk of hair in my hand and began sawing at it with the scissors. I felt myself let go of any control I had. I started feeling anger and rage. I was almost tearing the guy's hair out instead of cutting it. Suddenly, I heard a vicious scream, almost like a wounded animal. I couldn't tell if it was me or the guy screaming. He was now awake. He spun around with a twisted, maniacal look on his face. I let go of his hair and ran down the sidewalk as fast as I could.

He was loudly screaming gibberish as he chased me up Pike Street. We passed a bus stop where about five people stared at us in bewilderment. I wasn't sure what to do or where to run. He was quickly catching up to me and I was out of breath. I saw a row of taxicabs parked in front of the Sheraton Hotel so I ran to one and tried to quickly open the back car door, which was locked. The driver darted out of the car's front door. The guy had caught up to me as I desperately tried to get in the taxi. He swung his fist at me and punched me right in the face, splitting my cheek open. I was in shock. Despite all of the years of being bullied in school, no one had ever punched me in the face.

We were face to face and his eyes were huge and fierce looking. His hair was sticking up and I could see exactly where I had just chopped it off. He punched me again. Then he punched me again even harder.

The horrified taxi driver said, "You had better get out of here, or I'll call the cops." The driver was looking right at me, instead of my victim.

I felt like I was the victim. Why wasn't anyone helping me? The long-haired guy turned and walked away slowly and confidently.

I don't know what to do.
I've been punched in the face and I'm bleeding all over the place, but I hurt more on the inside than the outside.
I don't know how I'll explain this.
I just want to erase the whole evening.
I'm a liar, and I'll believe my own lie.
Pretending is the only way I can deal with this.
I was attacked.
I'm innocent.
I'm a victim.
If I really believe this, so will everyone else.

I got home and Jim was in bed. I went to the bathroom and looked in the mirror. My white T-shirt was covered in blood. My right cheek was split open very, very wide and the whole right side of my head was swollen. I knew I was going to have to wake Jim up, but I spent about twenty minutes trying desperately to get the bleeding to stop. When I finally woke Jim up, he was startled at my appearance. I told him I had been attacked by a homeless man.

My face wouldn't stop bleeding. After an hour, it became obvious I was going to have to get some serious medical care. I was terrified to go to the nearest emergency room, for fear the police would be waiting there for me. I insisted Jim take me to an emergency room on the other side of town.

The doctor who attended me asked what happened and I made up an elaborate lie about falling and hitting my head on a coffee table. We didn't even own a coffee table.

"It looked like you were punched in the face," the doctor said. I knew that I wasn't fooling him, but I didn't want to talk about it and I was still afraid I might somehow get in trouble with the law. The doctor seemed nonplussed and didn't pressure me for more explanation as he put sixteen stitches in my face.

That evening I behaved so far out of character (or what most people thought was my character) that it wasn't hard for people to believe my big lie. I got lots of sympathy, and the staff at Intiman gave me a beautiful bouquet of flowers. I was given a week off work to recover. I knew I wasn't done with my hair obsession even after that disastrous experience because I had no idea how to get rid of the desire to cut men's hair.

The lie was successful with my friends and coworkers, as well as myself.

What should have been a wake-up call was lost in my own denial. I felt like there was absolutely nothing for me to do but to wait for something even worse to happen.

32-Can I Cut Your Hair?

On one of my weekly bathhouse trips to Club Seattle, I encountered a young man who was lurking around Summit Street near the club. He was nervous and obviously checking me out as much as I was studying him. I knew he wanted something, and he didn't seem like a typical panhandler. He was in his early twenties and average looking ... except for a beautiful head of shoulder-length curly hair. He approached me as I got closer to the entrance to the baths. I braced myself as he began his pitch.

"Hey, man, are you going in there to have sex?" he asked.

"Maybe," I replied cautiously.

"Well, I'll suck your cock for twenty dollars."

I pointed out the fact that it only cost thirteen dollars to get into the baths, to which he replied that he would give me a better blow job than anyone in the club could. I took a close look at this guy's shoulder-length hair and saw a fantastic opportunity staring me in the face.

I countered his offer, "If all you can offer me is a blow job, I'd rather get that in the club. Maybe you can help me out with something else."

"I'll do anything. What do you need?" he said. I got very excited because I could tell he had no idea what I was about to suggest.

"Can I cut your hair?"

"Oh, man! Not my hair. No way!" he snapped.

"That's cool. Whatever," I said and continued toward the door of the club.

"Wait. How short do you want to cut my hair?" he asked.

"A military cut. Very short. Basically, I want to mow all of your hair off," I replied.

"Why do you want to do that?" he said with a puzzled look on his face.

"It turns me on. It's a fetish."

"Well, that's going to cost you more than twenty dollars."

"Sure. That's reasonable. How much do you want?" I asked.

"A hundred bucks, and that doesn't include any sex." I could tell from his tone that he thought I wouldn't be interested at that price without sex.

"Great! I'm not all that worried about the sex. All you have to do is sit there. I just want to cut your hair. Let's go," I said quickly. He was stunned that I had agreed. It was almost like he wanted to change his mind.

"Wait a second. Are you sure? I want to see the money first."

"Okay. We'll go to the cash machine first and I'll get the money."

He paused and looked at me like I was crazy, but agreed to the terms. I took the money out of the cash machine, counted the five twenty dollar bills out in front of him, and tucked them deep inside my jeans pocket. Once he saw the money, he seemed relaxed about the haircut.

We made small talk while we walked to my home. He talked a lot about basketball, about which I knew nothing. He seemed to be a rather ordinary guy. I wasn't intimidated or afraid of him. If anything he seemed more afraid of me. I kept reassuring him that he didn't have to take his clothes off or even touch me. I just wanted to buzz his hair off.

I didn't find him all that attractive. I would never have been interested in having sex with him outside of our agreement. However, I was really turned on by his hair. It was a dirty-blond color and hung in little ringlets that you could easily wrap around your fingers. If the hair had been straightened out, it would probably have fallen well past his shoulders. He didn't seem to be the kind of guy to fuss with it much. It was a little disappointing that he wasn't more sentimentally attached to it. I knew I wasn't going to gain much in the way of power out of the situation. Nonetheless, I couldn't wait to start hacking away at those curls.

After we got to my home, we walked right into my bedroom without hesitation. I put a haircut cape around him as he slouched down in a chair in the middle of the bedroom.

"Sit up straight," I said, pulling the curls out of the neck of the cape and placing them on his shoulders. I took a spray bottle, wet his hair down, and began to comb and untangle the curls. My cock was bouncing around in my jeans, so I undid the fly and released it. I spent a few minutes jacking myself off with one hand and running the other hand through the thick, damp hair.

This is the closest I have felt to being in heaven.
I am floating before this head of beautiful hair.

Since I was a child, my own hair has never been all that interesting, so not only do I admire a handsome head of hair, I feel jealous. He sat there quietly looking around the room, not speaking or paying any attention to me.

I don't have to turn all of my feelings off.
This isn't like cutting a friend's hair.
I BOUGHT the opportunity to think whatever comes
naturally.
I bought his attention.
I bought his respect.
I can do whatever I want with his hair.
I am not cutting hair for a show
We are the show.
We are the theater.
That permission is the sexiest feeling I can imagine.

I allowed myself to not worry about haircutting skills or what he would look like when I was done cutting his hair. In fact, for a few minutes, I felt free enough to not worry about anyone but myself. No one would dictate what I could and couldn't do.

What did this punk do to deserve a head of hair like this?
He probably doesn't appreciate what he's got.
My dad would have never let me have hair like this.

I began to allow myself to be irrational as I picked up the scissors and chopped out the first chunk of hair. The young man flinched as the freshly cut hair wrapped around my hand. I tossed the wad of damp cut hair in his lap, forcing him to look at it. It made a loud snap against the cape. I grabbed another hunk and cut it off, then quickly sliced off another. I became more and more aroused as I watched his appearance change before my eyes. His hair began to look chopped up and ugly.

I wasn't actually hurting him physically. I had enough control over the aggressive cutting not to accidentally cut his scalp or stab him, but the sensation I had while hacking the hair off was comparable to assaulting him. With the length of hair reduced to stubble, I took a moment to admire what a mess I had made. I liked the fact that a part of him was severed and lying on the floor. However, he seemed barely interested. I would have delighted in his crying or trembling. Instead he just sat there in an apathetic daze. I hadn't affected him as I much as I would have liked. I plugged in the clippers and evened the hair up, hoping the buzzing would intimidate him.

When I finished, he walked to the mirror and rubbed his head.

"Oh, well. I guess it will grow back," he said glumly.

We put our coats on and I walked him outside my apartment building where I gave him the money. Just before we parted company he said, "You realize there are a lot of guys downtown who would probably let you cut their hair just like I did?"

"Really? Where?" I asked. It hadn't even occurred to me.

"First and Madison ... sometimes Second Avenue, too. That is where all of the guys hang out looking for johns."

"Are there long-haired guys?" I pondered out loud.

"Some. I don't know. You'll have to take a look for yourself." He playfully slugged my arm, smiled and said goodbye. He walked away with an attitude, like he had gotten the better end of our deal.

I hadn't even ejaculated. I hurried inside to finish beating off. When I walked into my bedroom, it was like someone had thrown cold water on my face to wake me up. I had not taken the time to clean up before I walked the guy out. The sight of my normally tidy room was shocking—the chair, the cape, all of the haircutting equipment and long pieces of hair strewn everywhere. It was hard enough to take responsibility for what had just happened in my room, harder still to own what had happened in my head.

I negotiated a deal to attack this man.
It was more of a psychological attack, and the hair
was a trophy.
I am puzzled.
I am not sure that the haircut accomplished what I
wanted,
But I have no regrets.
If I could do it again right this minute, I would.

I didn't know what else to do, so I sat on the floor and masturbated while playing with the beautiful pieces of hair and remembering the evening's events. I was careful not to ejaculate in the hair. I had essentially paid for the hair so I felt the need to save the curls. I found an empty saltine cracker box in the kitchen, and ceremoniously placed the hair inside. Closing the box was almost like sealing a tomb. I buried the box in the back of my closet. I wasn't exactly sure why I was compelled to save the hair or when I would look at it again.

I felt like I had just eaten too much of a very bland Thanksgiving dinner. I was full, yet unsatisfied. Within a few days, I wanted to go back for seconds. This guy hadn't gotten me all that excited, but the information he had shared with me did.

It didn't dawn on me for a few days that the guy was officially a prostitute and I was a john. When I hired the escort from the agency, the whole thing seemed so sanitized that I hadn't given it much thought. It felt more like I had answered a personal ad. Society is quick to point a finger and look down on the oldest profession. My views were no different. Not only did I have a fetish to be ashamed of, but I was participating in illegal activities again. Despite the additional guilt, I was overcome with curiosity about male prostitution.

This could be the most dangerous adventure I'd ever embarked upon. The area the guy had spoken of wasn't the safest part of town. The street people were quite possibly drug addicts or criminals. The whole situation seemed as desperate as I felt. I wanted to hire another young guy and cut his hair as short as he'd let me. I had no idea what to expect, but I was determined to find some sexual satisfaction. There would be no boundaries set by an agency, and the fees would be lower. I also assumed a street hustler would be less concerned about his hair than a higher priced call boy. I naively convinced myself I could handle anything that happened.

33-Rough Trade

The longer I was away from my parents, the more distant I felt from them. They never came to visit. I concluded they were afraid of a trip to the big city, and even more afraid of seeing me for who I really was. Time froze when I stopped being who they thought I was and started becoming something they no longer understood.

To compensate, I viewed Jim as my family—my mom, my dad, my brother and my sister rolled into one. Having both come from small towns in Southern Illinois, we had a lot in common. We had a similar sense of style and sense of humor. We both shared an interest in dolls. Now that we were adults and had our own income, we began collecting and playing with Barbie dolls. We recognized the irony of being adult men playing with dolls. I didn't go into a lot of detail about Stefeny Calvert with Jim, but it was still quite therapeutic to openly play with the forbidden toy of my childhood. We enjoyed the frivolity and even started having Barbie cocktail parties with all our gay friends.

I shared a few details with him about my many sexual exploits. He was sexually active and always had a tale or two of his own to share. I think Jim could tell I was hypersensitive about the subject. He never judged me and I trusted him to keep my private life a secret.

It took a few days to get up the courage to tell him about the boy prostitute I had picked up outside the baths. Jim was just as curious as I was about Seattle's male hustlers, and we drove downtown in his car to investigate. It was the early 1990s and the Grunge music scene was all the rage all over the country. Seattle was the birthplace of the alternative sound and lifestyle. People were flocking to Seattle to see what it was all about. I had high hopes of finding lots of long-haired guys inspired by the look of Nirvana, Pearl Jam and Soundgarden.

Downtown Seattle after dark did not disappoint. Jim navigated the car through the hustler area and we would stare and speculate about which boys were for hire and which were not. He would slow the car down so we could get a good look. It became common to check out the scene on our way to and from our everyday errands. It was just silly fun for us, because we never would have picked up a guy together. We were only "window shopping." I always pretended to be coy, like I would never really pick up a guy and pay him for sex. I'm sure Jim saw right through that, but said nothing. This routine was also allowing me to check the area out safely from a car before heading down there on foot.

Even though I hadn't been too impressed with my first hustler pickup, I felt as if I absolutely had to attempt to find a another potential haircut. I had never been more nervous as I prepared for my first walk downtown. My legs were shaking, and I could barely speak. I made a conscious decision to carry no ID or cash, but to take a cash advance from the one credit card I carried if I were to meet a guy who fit my criteria.

Sure enough, the first night I went downtown, I found a guy on the corner of First Avenue and Madison Street, which happened to be on the same block as a porn shop called Taboo Video. He introduced himself as Tony. His hair wasn't as long as the guy I had met outside the baths, but I agreed to pay him sixty dollars to come home with me and allow me to buzz all of his hair off. We started walking to my apartment, and he started to reconsider. He kept touching his hair and panicking about losing it. I was extremely aroused watching him rethink the decision. Finally, he said he would go through with the haircut because he couldn't pass up the money.

After I started Tony's haircut—unlike my last hustler haircut—he became very upset. He was obviously humiliated and almost in tears as I sliced off the first big hunk of his hair. The sight of his hair falling in his lap was overwhelming for both of us. The image lifted me to a sexual peak, while Tony was inconsolable. I had a fantastic orgasm while jacking off within minutes of his fuss. He pouted and said nothing as I handed him the money he had earned for his humiliation.

I had opened Pandora's Box. I was instantly ready for more. After that, I hurried down to the area as fast as I could every night after work. I quickly got the hang of picking up guys. Neither the time of night nor the day of the week seemed to have any impact on whether or not a boy would be available. The guys were generally young. There seemed to be as many attractive guys as there were unattractive ones. I was fascinated by the guys I would meet. I loved to talk to them about their hair. I continued my journal, but it became easier to document the hustlers than it was to document me.

* * * * *

SEATTLE—FIRST AVENUE AND MADISON STREET
"My hair is the one reason men like to date me. That could cost me a lot of money in lost business. I want a thousand dollars to lose my hair."

SEATTLE—FIRST AVENUE AND MADISON STREET
"You can shave my whole body except the hair on my head ... for $150."

183

SEATTLE—FIRST AVENUE AND SPRING STREET

"I can't do anything for a small amount. I need to come up with $100 by tomorrow. Plus, my girl will kill me if I get a buzzcut."

SEATTLE—SECOND AVENUE AND SPRING STREET

"Not sure 'bout losing my hair. How much would you be willing to pay? What is the most you would offer?"

* * * * *

It became obvious that there was a steady flow of johns circling the area in their cars. Because I was on foot, some of the johns thought I was a hustler. They would circle in their cars trying to pick me up as I walked around. I became less and less afraid of the seedy environment. I spent a lot of time walking around and thinking, not only about finding the perfect subject for my fetish, but about my life in general. Some nights there would be no one to pick up, so I would walk home disappointed.

Sometimes, once I got a guy in the chair, I would hand him the scissors and make him take the first slice out of his hair. This always baffled them, since I had made it clear that I was the one who liked to cut hair. It was a test to see how attached the guy actually was to his hair. Guys were usually timid about cutting their own hair and would cut a tiny piece off. If this happened, I demanded that they take a bigger cut. A few actually refused to do it. Yet other guys were delighted with the opportunity and would start hacking away at their hair. I quickly took the scissors away from the enthusiastic participants. I was turned on by making the guy do what he didn't want to do, while reinforcing my need for control of the situation. This distraction could be an exciting build up to my buzzing their heads.

* * * * *

184

SEATTLE—SECOND AVENUE AND SENECA STREET
"Sorry my hair is kinda important to my image and style. But thank you."

SEATTLE—FIRST AVENUE AND MADISON STREET
"Sorry, Bud. I love my hair too much and respect my looks to let anyone touch my hair. My hair is perfect."

* * * * *

I never felt the need to ask a guy to take his clothes off for the haircut.

Some would voluntarily take their shirts off to keep from getting hair inside it.

Occasionally, I found a guy rubbing his crotch or playing with his nipples under the cape while I was cutting. A few would play with my cock or just touch me affectionately. I wasn't opposed to the guy showing me affection while I cut his hair, but I was usually too deep in concentration to reciprocate. I think some guys hoped that by distracting me sexually they would make me forget about the haircut. That never worked. Since I never completely stopped having sex at the baths, parks and restrooms, I never felt the need to indulge in more than masturbation with a prostitute. In fact, I was so engrossed with the hair that sometimes it didn't even occur to me to pleasure myself until later.

Very little talking would take place during a haircut. Most guys simply sat there with their arms crossed and watched in disbelief while I worked in a trancelike state on their heads. When the haircut was done, I rubbed my hands over the stubble. I wasn't as sexually aroused from the sight of a freshly buzzed head as I was from trying to figure out what was going on in a guy's mind. I would ask them if they liked their new haircuts. They almost never said they did, even if I could tell they did. Most of them never actually came out and said they hated it, either. I think that they were in shock and didn't know what to say. I wished I could be privy to their comments on their new looks the next day. They certainly didn't know what to think of me, so they said very little. They were always glad when it was over, and tried to hurry up the process so they could get their money.

When the haircut was done, I would sweep the floor. Most guys kept looking at themselves in the mirror until I was done cleaning up. Others avoided looking at themselves at all. Often, a guy would ask me if I had a hat around. I never did because I didn't want them to cover their bare heads.

* * * * *

SEATTLE—FIRST AVENUE AND MADISON STREET

"I do many things for cash, including bondage or letting a guy shave my ass, toys, dress up. Not sure about my hair though."

* * * * *

Some guys wouldn't agree to anything unless they were paid first. This was a common conflict. I quickly learned the hard way that if I gave them money up front, they would walk away before I got the chance to cut their hair. Eventually, I found that it was best to dismiss the guy if he had to have the money up front. More often than not, once I dismissed him, he would change his mind and agree to my terms. If he didn't agree, then I reasoned those were the guys to avoid anyway.

When I handed over the money, every guy automatically counted it. Once the transaction was over, everything lightened up, and it was like nothing had happened between us. I never, ever cheated a guy out of whatever fee he and I had negotiated. I certainly didn't want to piss anyone off and put myself in further jeopardy. Most hustler dates went off without a hitch. Some of them even shook my hand when they said goodbye.

Only half of the experiences I had picking up hustlers proved sexually gratifying. Often I would just cut the hair and not be motivated to masturbate. I would either feel empty when it was over or completely forget about it the next day, even though I was spending all my money. Despite the expense, risk and frustration, my need to act out in this way was escalating. I spent way too many hours a week chasing after something that I couldn't define or experience release from. I began to realize that people didn't comb the city streets for hours and hours late at night to find anything good for themselves. I lost interest in cruising for plain sex at the baths. I was building a double life. When I was invited to go out with friends or attend a party, I struggled to choose between the event and looking for a head to shave. I was so ashamed, I couldn't even tell Jim. I knew I was in trouble.

34-The Hustle

SEATTLE—FIRST AVENUE AND SENECA STREET
"Can you give me a #1 on the sides faded up to a #3?"

SEATTLE—PIKE STREET AND BROADWAY AVENUE
"It took me a year to grow it this long so I would have to do it for a lot of money."

SEATTLE—SECOND AVENUE AND UNIVERSITY STREET
"Interesting. I just got a haircut yesterday; I got a couple of inches left. I guess it depends on what you can give me. I really like my hair."

SEATTLE—PIKE STREET AND SUMMIT STREET
"My birthday is October 22nd. I am going to need my hair for that day. After that you can cut it all off."

SEATTLE—PINE STREET AND SUMMIT STREET
"No, thanks!"

SEATTLE—FIRST AVENUE AND MADISON STREET
"I can't cut my hair because I just became a model."

SEATTLE—FREEWAY PARK
"$80."

SEATTLE—PIKE STREET AND BELLEVUE STREET
"Look, I really need some money and this will help me out. If you want, why don't we go somewhere? If you change your mind there is no problem."

SEATTLE—PIKE STREET AND CRAWFORD STREET
"Where do we go? Looking to do anything sexual?"

PORTLAND—COUCH STREET
"That wouldn't work for me. Best of luck."

SEATTLE—SECOND AVENUE AND PIKE STREET
"$500."

SEATTLE—FIRST AVENUE AND MADISON STREET
"I'll do it but not now. Next week."

SEATTLE—SUMMIT STREET
"Go fuck your mom."

SEATTLE—FIRST AVENUE AND PIKE STREET
"I have a barber. I don't like anyone else cutting my hair. I like it to be perfect."

SAN FRANCISCO—MARKET STREET
"$200."

SEATTLE—FREEWAY PARK
"Wow, I like you. Good luck with that. I hate to tell you but cutting my hair is the one thing I would not do for any amount of money. I haven't cut it in ten years."

SEATTLE—PIKE STREET AND BROADWAY AVENUE
"All you want to do is give me a haircut and you are going to pay me?"

SAN FRANCISCO—MARKET STREET
"$2,000."

SEATTLE—FIRST AVENUE AND UNION STREET
"Umm I love my hair. A lot. I need $300 or $350 upfront, and I don't know about buzzing it all off. Is there any way we can make a deal? Like a Mohawk or something? Are there any other services I can provide for you?"

PORTLAND—COUCH STREET
"My lady loves my hair so you would have to offer me $1,500 to cut it all off. I have had this hair for 15 years."

ATLANTA—TENTH STREET
"Sorry, my hair is a part of who I am. I have been growing it for 5 years. Thanks for asking."

SEATTLE—FIRST AVENUE AND MADISON STREET
"Are you a hair stylist? I was planning on letting it grow but I need some cash and I don't care. I just wonder if you are a professional hair stylist."

SEATTLE—FIRST AVENUE AND UNION STREET

"The hair is a no-go. Maybe I would let you take off my goatee and some of my sideburns, but not unless you plan on paying me a fucking ton of money."

SEATTLE—FREEWAY PARK

"I'll let you buzz my hair but it's got to be a #2 from the sides and #3 from the top. $250. Believe me; having sex with me is way cheaper."

SEATTLE—PIKE STREET AND BELLEVUE AVENUE

"I've been needing to get a haircut and what a great way to do it. I just love kink."

SEATTLE—SUMMIT STREET

"I hope you ain't gonna make a huge penis or vagina with my hair."

SEATTLE—FIRST AVENUE AND MADISON STREET

"Thanks for the reminder and the memory of having my hair cut off and shaving when I joined the military."

35-Photo Shoots

"No, I am not a cop."

"I do not have the money on me."

"I promise no one else will be there."
"Really ... I don't want to have sex with you, I just want to cut your hair."

"I like to do this because it turns me on."

* * * * *

The first couple of drastic haircuts I gave to hustlers proved minimally satisfying, yet still interesting enough to get me hooked on finding more encounters. I just needed to find the perfect head of hair to cut, attached to the perfect subject to humiliate. I had become a haircut junkie.

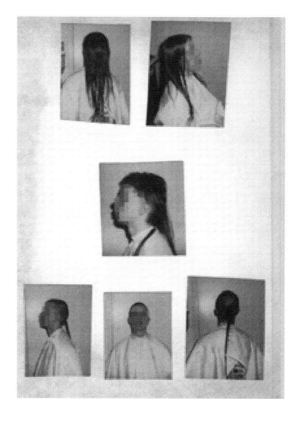

I had to keep looking for my haircut fix no matter what. I found myself on the prowl through rain, sleet and snow. Even Christmas night—a night when only the most desperate of hustlers could be found working the streets— was not a night off from my obsession.

Each night as cruising time approached my breathing became shallow. I could feel my heart beating harder and faster in my chest. I became dizzy and my attention span narrowed. People could speak to me, and I wouldn't listen. I was tired and my body ached all the time. I trembled at the possibility of meeting a guy with long hair to cut, but I also trembled with fear at the risks I was taking; I could get killed trying to fulfill my needs.

Most evenings were a bust. Even when I did hook up with a guy, I felt like I had little to show for my efforts. After several months of combing the streets for gay hustlers who would let me cut their hair, I decided I needed to take pictures of the haircutting process for my masturbation enjoyment.

The pictures eliminated the need to masturbate in front of the hustler, essentially eliminating any sexual contact. It was all about documenting the humiliating haircut for later.

* * * * *

SEATTLE—FIRST AVENUE AND MADISON STREET
"Wow. That is definitely a new one. You want pictures, too? The interesting thing is that I have been letting my hair grow. I am interested. Thanks for being so creative. You wouldn't believe how boring these guys get."

* * * * *

Looking at the pictures in private was like admiring a trophy I had won. When I wasn't aroused, the pictures were evidence of a crime and needed to be hidden from everyone's view, even my own.

I was way too ashamed of my fetish to use a camera that required me to take film to a lab to be processed, so I bought a Polaroid camera. In fact, I was so uncomfortable documenting my experiences at first that I found I couldn't even look into the camera to aim properly. I kept my eyes closed and shot the pictures randomly.

I nervously made sure to mention to every guy I negotiated a deal with that I wanted to take pictures of him. Most guys would ask what they were for, so I simply told them the truth. Surprisingly, few had a problem with the request. Guys were less likely to resist my request for pictures once I reminded them the pictures were from the shoulders up and were only to demonstrate their hair before and after I cut it. They were always alone in the pictures (you could see me in the reflection of the mirror), and there was no nudity unless the guy chose to take off his shirt.

Before I cut his hair, I would take pictures of the guy standing up from the front, side and back. More than once a hustler pointed out that these poses were similar to police mug shots. This made some of them uncomfortable. Then I would sit a guy down and put the cape around him. I would wet his hair and, if were long enough, arrange it on the cape and take some more pictures. I loved the cape pictures because they really showed the beginning of the process. Guys were usually the most nervous when I put the cape on them, and it always showed in the pictures.

I would perform half a haircut then take more pictures. I enjoyed the sight of cut hair on a guy's shoulder. If the hair didn't land there on its own, I would pick it up off the floor and put it on his shoulders for the pictures. After finishing the haircut, I would take more front, side and back pictures. I always took a picture of the hair on the floor. If the guy had a ponytail, I would take a picture of him holding it up like a prize. These shots reminded me of a fisherman holding up his catch. The bigger the ponytail or pile, the more valuable my catch.

For many guys, taking pictures of their haircuts only added to the humiliation, which in turn added to my enjoyment. There was no way to really know what was going on in a guy's head after being picked up for a haircut, but the pictures captured a tone I wasn't always aware of while in the moment. Once a guy was gone and I could study the pictures, my experience was heightened. Viewing the photos could be more exciting than the actual haircut. Gaps in what I knew about the guy could be filled by my imagination. The memory was often far more sexual that the reality.

I'm completely responsible for this event.
This guy is under my control.
He has to do what I ask, or he won't get any money.

I can tell from the photo he is nervous.
I can tell he hates what is happening.
He fears me.
He probably hates me, too.
He likes his hair.
He would never allow such a radical cut if it weren't
for me.
Each picture chronicles him looking worse and worse.
His hair and his face change.
He says very little as I buzz all of his hair off,
But his face says everything.
I love the transition; the contrast between long and
short hair.
The guy looks uncomfortable.
The last picture, when his hair is gone, exhibits
finality.
He is stuck being shorn for a long time to come, and
it's all because of me.

Most of the time the guys looked solemn, and wouldn't even look at the camera while being photographed. A compromise was sometimes reached with guys who didn't want their pictures taken by letting them cover their face, photographing only their hair. Other guys flipped me the finger for their picture.

Much to my initial disappointment, some guys didn't mind being photographed and even wanted a "before" picture of themselves to remember what their long hair looked like.

Polaroid pictures are seldom flattering, and it didn't take long to build up a sizable library of unflattering pictures of some very unhappy people. One of the first times I took pictures of a haircut, the only Polaroid film available at the store that particular night had a colorful, preprinted birthday-party border that would surrounded your picture after it developed. The pictures of that particular haircut have a surreal quality, depicting a miserably unhappy street person getting his long hair cut inside a cheerful frame of bright balloons and streamers.

Polaroid film was expensive, so I never bought it until I needed it. There were a couple of twenty-four-hour stores in the area that sold the film. Film shopping also gave me more time to sound the guy out and make sure he would really go through with the haircut. Cruising on foot could make it a lengthy event. If I felt unsafe, I could abort the situation before we got too far along. The transit time was when I learned about the guy's personal life. Most had no problem confiding in me, despite knowing me for only minutes.

I bought an inexpensive photo album for all my haircutting pictures and was very concerned with getting them in chronological order. I began cropping the pictures down to just the haircut subject with little else in the frame. Since the album was for me alone to look at, I wasn't too careful while cropping, and many of the shots were oddly shaped. Picture placement on the album page was never symmetrical either. The cheap, generic album began to take on a deranged personality of its own as I filled it with dozens of jaggedly cut pictures.

Jim bought a video camera for himself and I wasted no time borrowing it, with and without his knowledge. At first, I could not believe that a guy would actually let me film myself giving him a haircut. Just as with the still pictures, I never asked anyone to perform sex acts or pose nude. I was always more uncomfortable documenting the event than most of the hustlers were being documented. I loved watching the haircut videos I had created. I was racked with shame. I had to stop and remind myself: "It's just a haircut."

36-Santa Monica Blvd

After a few years working as the Wardrobe Manager at Intiman Theater, I got the opportunity to do an apprenticeship in theatrical wigmaking with a very talented wigmaker at the Los Angeles Opera. I had experience with wigs as a dresser, yet I had never been trained in actually constructing a theatrical wig from scratch. I had been fascinated with wigmaking ever since I made the yarn wig for my hippy Halloween costume (pretending to be Cher).

Wigmaking is an art all its own that hinges on a process called ventilation. Ventilation is the craft of actually hand-tying the hair onto a foundation of net, one hair at a time. Most theatrical hairpieces are made from human hair. The

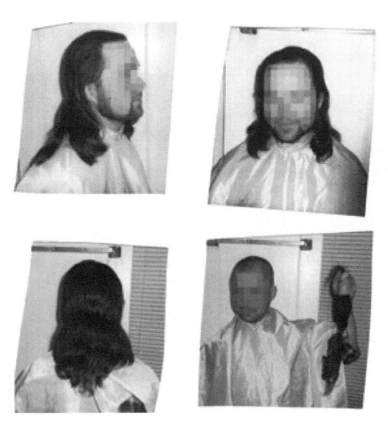

finished product is a hairpiece that looks and acts like hair growing right out of someone's head. For several years I had wanted to learn the process and become a full-fledged wigmaker as an artistic outlet. I arranged for housing, took out a small personal loan and moved to Los Angeles for six weeks early in 1995.

Having never been there before, I was nervous and excited about living in Los Angeles. I knew the apprenticeship would change my life and give me skills that would make me very marketable in theater and possibly film. I also knew that Los Angeles was home to a large prostitution scene. Santa Monica Boulevard in Hollywood is famous for gay hustlers. Within days of arrival, I was avidly searching for guys to pick up for haircuts. I lived in Los Angeles as frugally as possible, making my loan money stretch far enough to pick up as many hustlers as I could.

* * * * *

LOS ANGELES—SANTA MONICA BLVD AND NORTH HIGHLAND AVENUE

"$200 you can cut my hair. Pubes, too."

LOS ANGELES—SANTA MONICA BLVD AND NORTH CHEROKEE AVENUE

"I hope you are a good barber. My hair won't be easy for a novice since it is so thick and wavy"

LOS ANGELES—SANTA MONICA BLVD AND LA BREA AVENUE

"... to be honest, I am a little hesitant on the whole cutting off all of my hair thing, but a haircut would be great. Is all you are looking for to do is shave my hair off and nothing else? Are you interested in any fun at all?

* * * * *

I was house-sitting for a friend of a friend, so I had a private housing situation near Hollywood. This made it easy to bring people home without explanation. Unlike in Seattle, where hustling mostly takes place after dark, on Santa Monica Boulevard it is a twenty–four-hour business. In my spare time, I combed the streets both day and night for long-haired hustlers. Initially, my perception of a LA hustler was that he would be rougher and more dangerous than a Seattle hustler, but I quickly learned that there was no real difference in attitude. A gay hustler is a gay hustler. Other than one guy backing out at the last minute, I had no issues or problems with the men who participated in my fetish.

Hair had been an overriding part of my life since childhood, but I was surprised by how much I didn't know. I learned a great deal about hair as an artist's medium during my apprenticeship in Los Angeles. Most hair for wigmaking comes from countries outside of America (some impoverished) and is bought from vendors by weight. The longer the hair, the more it weighs, and the more it can cost. The most common type of human hair used is Asian, which is always dark to begin with, but is then stripped and dyed different colors. Asian hair is more plentiful and economical than European hair, which is softer and holds a curl better. Non-chemically treated blond, red and silver hair is more valuable than brown and black. Hair can be bought in any texture imaginable. It needs to be at least eight inches in length and pretty healthy to be useful for wigmaking.

After cutting the hair from the head, my sexual interest in handling it seemed to expire. Since most theatrical wigs are human hair, I decided while in Los Angeles that I should start saving the long hair I was buying off the heads of guys. After becoming familiar with guidelines for buying and selling hair commercially, I found that I was often influenced by my knowledge of the market when deciding whether to pick up a street hustler and how much to pay him to participate in my fantasy. When bartering with a guy on the streets, I tried to get the best deal possible, but I had no problem paying him top dollar if he had healthy, valuable hair.

My apprenticeship at Los Angeles Opera was a success. I came back to Seattle with a new career path and a new staff job title at Intiman: Wardrobe and Wig Master. I also had half a dozen hanks of usable hair for wigs. It was important to photograph my work and assemble a portfolio to show prospective employers. I considered the irony of having pictures in my wig portfolio of a beautiful wig that had I made by hand as well as pictures in my fetish album of the guy whose hair it was. Cut hair was creepy to me at first, but after I started making wigs for a living, this hair, no matter what the source, became a tool of my job. After that it wasn't very sexy. I stored and sanitized all the human hair I used for wigs—whether it was from a trick or vendor—in one place in my office. Only rarely do I now know the source of the hair I use in a wig.

Even now, I am delighted to buy hair from non-hustlers who call me, especially if the seller is an attractive man. There is an emotional cycle one usually goes through when making the decision to cut off one's long hair. When a guy comes to me to ask about selling his hair, I am almost always willing, if not aching, to be the one to perform the cut. If he hasn't already made his final decision, I like watching him agonize over the choice. It becomes a privately arousing game for me. I try to appear unbiased and let the guy come to his own conclusion. It's a delicious turn-on if a guy talks about how nervous he is to get it done. A guy's tone and body language can change dramatically when he talks about getting a drastic haircut.

Having never had extremely long hair myself, I cannot totally identify. I always wonder what's going on in his mind. Almost always, if a long-haired guy goes to the trouble to discuss cutting his hair with me, he will eventually go ahead and do it. Yet, I have waited as long as a year for a guy to make that decision. Knowing that he can make some cash if I buy his hair for wigs will often swing the deal.

I am always nervous on the day of the long anticipated haircut of a non-trick. However, I maintain my composure and am sympathetic during the process. I always ask before I make the first cut if the man is sure, because I want to hear him say "Do it!" The reaction after the first cut is as diverse as a person's fingerprint—relief, horror, denial, humor. As the cutter, I never know what reaction the man will offer. Some guys like to watch me do the cut, others don't. I certainly like to observe his face and body language. I always sense that the guy is a little bit better after the experience, whether he is a friend or a trick. But it can be frustrating to experience the haircut and not be allowed to be sexual.

37-Crisis Accounting

Most of the guys I pursued for haircuts had made a career out of street life. However, others had jobs and fairly average lives. They treated prostitution as a second job to earn extra cash. Since I conducted my obsession in an almost business-like fashion, some of them freely shared information about their daytime jobs, telling me exactly where they worked. I even got a few business cards. I've pandered with electricians, car detailers, construction workers, plumbers, and several hopeful musicians.

I heard many stories of broken homes, lost jobs, friendships gone bad, and incarceration. Despite their many woes, some guys I picked up were quite charming and smart. I began to question which of my two worlds were more important to me. Which one did I belong in?

My career in wigs was beginning to take off. I was building a good reputation around the country. When I was hired to do wigs and hair for shows in Tucson and Louisville, my haircutting impulses followed me.

* * * * *

TUCSON—UNIVERSITY STREET
"I am thinking around $50."

TUCSON—TRAFFIC ISLAND
"If you can do a good fade I'll do it for cheap."

LOUISVILLE—GARVIN PLACE
"What is your limit? I want to get a couple of video games."

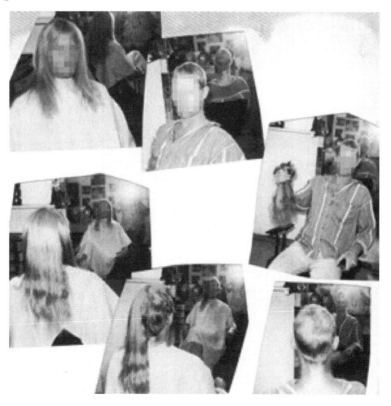

* * * * *

I was also offered a number of projects around Seattle and asked to teach a class in wigmaking at the University of Washington. I was even doing a few shows by mail—making the wigs in Seattle to specifications and mailing them to theaters across the country. For the first time in my life, I had to have my own business cards printed up.

Jim began letting me borrow his car with little supervision. This was a dangerous act of kindness. It did help me save time and energy running errands, but also made it very easy to shoot through downtown looking for a head to shave late at night. It was important not to let a trick smoke in the car, since neither Jim nor I did. Some hustlers had body odor, which would require me to roll down all of the windows and drive around for a while after he got out of the car. I tried to be very careful with Jim's car, even if I was just running around town. If Jim thought I was abusing the car privilege, he might cut me off.

Jim dropped hints that he knew what I was up to, but I still found myself lying about my behavior. Every time I lied, I felt a little part of me being eaten away. The guilt over the obsession was bad enough. Compound that with guilt over lying to someone I cared very much about. It was terrible.

Johns are often identified by their cars, and I was quickly becoming known by a car that was not even mine. Eventually, I earned enough money from my new freelance wig career to get my own car. I was relieved to be rid of the fear of something bad happening to Jim's. My car happened to look very much like his, so I don't think any of the street regulars knew the difference between his red Ford Festiva and my red GEO Metro.

It didn't take long before buying hustler's hair to create wigs got me into trouble financially. I was spending an average of eighty to a hundred dollars a trick and making less than ten dollars an hour at my theater job. Therefore, most of my bad-habit money was coming from credit. It took less than a year for me to start maxing out my credit cards. I would make a credit-card payment and then take a cash advance after the payment was credited. Luckily, due to my freelance wig work, my income was dramatically increasing every year. I was staying afloat—but just barely.

I was approved for a loan to consolidate all my credit cards into one payment. I thought this would help me organize my finances. There was a large amount of money left from the consolidation loan, and the company even supplied handy checks to make it easier to spend the available balance. However, one couldn't write a check for less than one hundred dollars. I would often turn a sixty or eighty dollar trick and be forced to write a check for a hundred dollar advance.

My job at Intiman required me to carry around a couple hundred dollars worth of petty cash at all times for work supplies. I would borrow from petty cash for a hair date, then pay the work money back by buying supplies when needed on my department-store credit cards.

One evening, I went scouting for a guy to hire, and found two guys who were friends. Both had really long hair and agreed to let me cut their hair only if I would do both and pay them $150 a piece. I was absolutely crazed because I knew I had only a hundred dollars left on a credit card to spend. At that moment I had no other credit, no petty cash, nothing to tap except my rent money. I agreed, without question, to go through with the deal. It didn't matter that I had to spend my rent money; I had to cut their hair and get the pictures. I cut their hair and paid them as agreed. The haircutting experience was sexually rewarding, yet I was mortified. I had never been unable to pay my rent or any of my bills.

I called my parents later that night. Although I had told them I am gay, they were never comfortable with it and seldom acknowledged it. Whenever I mentioned something specific about my sexuality, I got silence in return. It was as if they hadn't heard a word I said since I divorced Jessica in 1987. We had been having the exact same conversation once a week for almost ten years. Our topics were limited to the weather, who in the family was sick or in trouble, and the fact that there was nothing they liked on television anymore.

Even though I felt my actions had been stupid and irresponsible, I was curious to hear what my parents had to say about what I had just done. I decided that now was as good a time as any to tell them the whole story about how I had lost my rent money, including the part about my sexual peculiarities.

It was after midnight in their Midwestern time zone, and I knew my parents would be asleep when I called. My mom answered the phone.

"Mom, I'm in trouble. I have something to tell you that's kind of unusual, and I'm scared you'll think badly of me."

"What's wrong, Denny? You know you can tell me anything," she said. I did know I could tell her anything, but I wasn't sure she would actually listen and hear me.

I hesitated and said nothing for a few beats. The less I said, the more worried my mom got.

"Come on, son. What's going on? You can tell me. Whatever it is, it'll be all right."

I just blurted it out. "I have a sexual obsession for cutting men's hair, and I've been picking up male prostitutes downtown and paying them to let me cut all of their hair off."

I paused and took a breath. I didn't sense any hostility coming from my mom, but there was silence on the other end of the phone.

I continued, "I've had this problem for a long time. I used to pick men up other places. But it's hard to find men who will let me do this."

I couldn't believe I was actually telling my mom all of this. Even more shocking was that she wasn't freaking out.

I continued my story, "I found an area downtown where a lot of young guys hang out looking for men to pick them up and pay them to have sex. Once I found out that I could pay men to let me cut their hair, I couldn't stop myself from going down there to look."

"Where were you looking for the guys before that?" she asked, quietly and intelligently.

"Well, there are a few public parks, sometimes the sex clubs. I never had to pay men that I met at either of those places," I answered.

"Well, Honey, why don't you go back to trying to find men in the park for haircuts?" she offered.

I couldn't believe what she had just said. I couldn't tell if she really understood, but I was touched that she was trying. I explained that I had just spent my rent money on a guy that evening, and I began to cry. It really hit me hard.

My mom calmed me down and said she would send me the money. I said that I needed more than just financial help, and my mom encouraged me to do whatever I could to feel better. For however much my mom chose to keep herself naive about my sexuality, I knew that she loved me. My dad loved me too, in his own distant way.

We never discussed the subject again.

I had hit a low point that evening. I felt better that my parents were at least trying to understand and would probably love me no matter what. I made myself two promises that night: that I would immediately try to get counseling, and that I would never ask my parents for money again.

Right after I got off the phone with my mom, I called a crisis hotline and exploded into tears and hysteria. My parents had solved my immediate financial problems, but I needed to change myself, and I knew this wouldn't be a quick or easy process. I got set up with a mental health screening appointment for the next morning.

At the appointment, I told my story. I also explained that I had no health insurance. I made a small wage, and the very habit that was causing my problem had drained most of my money. It was frightening to learn that even counseling based on my $8 an hour wage wasn't affordable. The woman at the mental health agency didn't know what to do with me. She was used to evaluating people who couldn't get out of bed in the morning or hold a job. She leveled with me that I was at the wrong agency. She suggested I find an individual counselor who had a sliding scale.

I looked in the *Seattle Gay News* for such counseling. I made some calls and found that unless I was ready to blow my brains out that day, there was a long wait to see most therapists. I started asking around about reasonably priced counselors. A few days later I told a friend that I was having some emotional problems, without going into any details. I knew she spoke highly of her counselor and asked her for a recommendation. She called her therapist personally in order to get me in as soon as possible.

I went to the first appointment, which was free, and told my story again.

The middle-aged woman, who was very kind, said she could see me within a few weeks. She was frank with me, explaining that she would have to charge forty dollars a visit. I felt that was totally fair, and it was less than what the sliding scale would have cost me at the first agency. The problem was that I didn't know how I would pay for it, considering I had just used my rent money to support my habit. I had nothing left. I didn't trust myself to stop the cruising and devote the cash to therapy. I was scared of getting in another financial bind.

Unbelievably, I still hadn't fallen behind on any other bills. I just had no money left over. I considered using bill money for counseling but decided against it. Sadly, there was also a part of me not ready to deal with the situation quite yet. I had told my story to my mom and two counselors. I was beginning to feel like my wounds were still fresh, and I didn't think I was strong enough to work on them in therapy. Using money as an excuse, I told the counselor that I would have to do some financial figuring to pay for her services. I didn't follow through. I felt that, with a little soul searching, I could manage without professional help.

A couple of days later, I was back looking for heads to shave.

38-Blackmail Is Illegal

I met a guy named Stewart who not only agreed to let me cut his hair and shave his mustache, but also wanted to pimp future haircut tricks for me. He was a skinny guy in his late twenties, and dressed in colorful clothes that had been fashionable fifteen years earlier. He operated like a very convincing used car salesman, always talking faster than I could think and gesturing a lot. He told me he could find a lot of guys who would let me cut their hair. Stewart seemed pretty trustworthy, so I naively gave him my home phone number. I thought he could save me the trouble of looking for guys, and I was more than happy to pay him a finder's fee if he produced suitable and cooperative subjects. He indeed produced three new guys for my pleasure. However, Stewart vanished after a few weeks.

I didn't think anything of his disappearance until he called me at home one evening from jail. He was crying and wanted me to come visit him. I got the feeling he really was lonely and considered me a trustworthy friend. Of course, Stewart also wanted more money. I felt bad for him, but I refused to give him money or to come see him. I felt our relationship should stop right there or I might never get him to leave me alone.

He continued to call me regularly from jail for over a month. I finally had to tell Jim what was going on. Stewart had stopped asking me for money, but had started acting like we would be close friends upon his release. I was suspicious and didn't believe him, but always remained polite during our brief phone calls to avoid escalating the situation. I never asked why he was in jail. I didn't want to know. After Stewart got out of jail, he had obviously lost my phone number, but he continued to bring guys to my secured apartment building at all hours of the day and night. He would throw tiny rocks at my bedroom window to get my attention. I would go to the window and wave him away. I never did business nor spoke with Stewart again, but saw him around the streets for years.

Another hustler didn't let my secured building slow

him down. One morning he somehow got into the building and knocked on my apartment door. He was a chunky blond guy, and I didn't recognize him at first because I had cut off all of his hair. The guy had had long hair and a mustache when I first met him. It had been over a week since we had met, and he had to spend a few minutes reminding me who he was. I wouldn't let him into my apartment, so we talked in the hallway. He was clearly under the influence of something. The guy's clothes were dirty and he smelled terrible. He was fidgety and not making sense.

He wanted more money and made it clear to me that he wasn't leaving without it. He looked like he had been through hell since I had met him the week before. There were fresh cuts and bruises on his face and hands. I am sure he could have used some money, but I insisted that I wouldn't give him any. He thought he could blackmail me and threatened to tell all of my neighbors what I had been doing. He also threatened to tell "everyone" that I was gay. I surprised him by telling him everyone already knew I was gay and that I doubted that anyone cared that I was giving haircuts in my apartment. He got frustrated and said he was going to tell my building manager a bunch of lies. I didn't budge; I still refused to give him any more money. After half an hour he got angry and left in a huff. I wasn't really afraid of him, but it alarmed me that he had gotten into my building. I reevaluated bringing men into my home for haircuts.

Not bringing a hustler home presented a new problem—finding another location to stage my activities. I really didn't feel safe going to a location of the hustler's choice. Since all my encounters were after working hours, I decided to take them to my office at Intiman. I was all set up for doing haircuts there, anyway.

I did everything I could to be safe and keep the building secure. I was also careful not to get caught by my co-workers. Seldom was anyone around late at night, and my office was a locked room within another locked room, so there would be plenty of warning if someone was coming. Upon entering the building, I always announced to a trick that there were security cameras all over the building (which there weren't). I would take them in one door and out the other side of the building to confuse them. I felt that most hustlers would be too intimidated to stalk me at my workplace—a public theater in a busy part of town.

Out of dozens and dozens of pickups, only one man ever showed up at my work site uninvited. I had picked him up one evening and cut his hair without incident in the privacy of my office. The guy was young and looked somewhat like "the boy next door." He was well-spoken and even seemed pretty pleasant. He had beautiful dark curly hair that looked well maintained—until I buzzed it all off.

The next day Jim had met me at work. We were leaving the theater on our way to get dinner when the guy appeared. I didn't acknowledge him, and he followed us. As we approached the restaurant a few blocks from the theater, he stopped me and said he wanted to talk to me. He came across like he was a panhandler, so Jim ignored him. However, I knew exactly who he was and what he wanted and hoped he would be gone when we left the restaurant. At dinner I made sure we sat away from the window, so the man would not see us. I worried about what was going to happen. I felt like I should leave before Jim and deal with the guy alone, since I didn't want to explain to Jim what I had done with him the night before.

After giving Jim a flimsy excuse, I left the restaurant. Sure enough, the guy was still waiting for me outside. His face was all twisted with anger and he looked very different than the pleasant person I had met previously. He told me, in so many words, that I was a terrible person who was taking advantage of street people by cutting their hair off. He said he wanted sixty dollars from me immediately or he would go to my employers the next morning and tell them what we had done in my office. He told me he was going to get me fired.

I was scared. Not of getting fired; I was scared he was going to try to hurt me. He was very angry and larger and stronger than I. We were in the middle of a business district, so I was certain that he wouldn't try to hurt me right there, but since he knew where I worked, I was scared he would try something later on. I didn't think it was going to be easy to get rid of him, so I started walking toward the theater. He proceeded to mock me about my obsession with men's hair, claiming I was sick, twisted and should be institutionalized. He found my emotional buttons as he followed me down the sidewalk. I was just ashamed and insecure enough about my behavior to almost agree with him. When he noticed he was pushing my buttons and getting me upset, his jeering became exaggerated and ridiculous. He asked if I was a murderer and started calling me a child molester. I didn't know what to do but stand there and take his abuse.

We stopped right outside the theater, where he kept insisting over and over that I would get fired if I didn't do what he wanted. He told me he would tell my boss we had sex, even though all I had done was take pictures of the haircut. I knew that it would be my word against the word of an obviously crazy man. The worst-case scenario would be that I would get a stern warning about bringing strangers in the building.

The longer our exchange lasted, the more aggressive he became. He angrily spit on me and demanded I give him money. I was hesitant because I felt certain he would return for more money in the future if I surrendered to his demand this time. I stood my ground and told him I would not be blackmailed and that I didn't care if he told my employer. His face turned bright red. My statement made him even angrier. I was beginning to get angry myself. After all, he consented, without argument, to letting me cut his hair. We didn't have sex, he didn't get hurt, and he got paid the exact amount that had been agreed upon.

After about thirty minutes of bickering, it was obvious I would not get rid of him unless I paid him. I went to the cash machine and gave him the sixty dollars he wanted. I still didn't trust that he wouldn't come back, so I went into my office and called my boss, Donald, at home and told him the story, with a few alterations. I explained to him that I had met the guy in a bar and that he asked what I did for a living. When I told him that I worked with hair, he'd asked me if I would give him a free haircut. I sheepishly admitted to Donald that I was under the assumption that when we went to my office for the haircut, we would have sex, too.

Donald seemed annoyed, but not angry. He pointed out that having sex was not illegal or grounds for getting fired. He said he stood by my work and told me never to do anything like that again. I agreed. He also told me that if the crazy guy did show up again, I should give him his name so he could deal with him personally.

"After all, blackmail is illegal," he said. I am sure Donald would not have been so understanding had he known I was bringing prostitutes into the building.

I was relieved that I didn't get fired. But the situation was a hard blow for my ego. I knew I had been lucky, but I was becoming paranoid. I hadn't really learned my lesson. After a brief stint of bringing guys back into my apartment, I returned to utilizing my office at Intiman for hustler haircuts.

39-The Haircut Guy

Most of the hustlers I picked up seemed to know each other, and after a while they all knew about me. Every time I met a new one and explained what I was looking for, I got a knowing look. They would say, "Oh, yeah. I've heard all about you. You're *The Haircut Guy.*"

I would always ask exactly what they had heard about me. I reportedly had a good reputation with the hustlers and was considered an honest businessman. Meeting me was almost an initiation for the new hustlers in town. Within a few days of their hitting the streets, I would surely find them and ask to cut off all their hair. Some short-haired guys claimed to let their hair grow out just so I would be interested in cutting it off and paying them. I was pleased that I had a good reputation but would have preferred to have no reputation at all. I had gone beyond maintaining anonymity and was very nervous about being known on the streets, especially since Jim was the only one who had any idea what I was doing.

Most men could be found working the streets for a few months; then they would vanish. Guys would give me unsolicited reports on hustlers I had previously met—who was in jail, who had left town and who was dead. I preferred not to know what had happened to these guys because their fate was almost always unfortunate. Most of them already had rough lives before they ever started hustling. I was saddened to watch a few young men grow up on the streets, starting out as teenagers and turning into men.

I remember a young man I met on Pike Street outside Benson's Grocery who, when I cut his hair, was an adorable guy with sparkling eyes, a nice smile, and a fresh demeanor. He was a handsome, sturdy guy in his early twenties who looked like he could have been a fashion model. When I picked him up he confessed to me he was a heroin user. He was very vain and concerned how he would look with a buzzed head. Even shorn, he was an attractive guy who could easily turn heads. A couple of months later, he was still working the streets, and it looked like he was rotting away. He had sores on every visible part of his body and his teeth were gone. He could barely walk and struggled down the street with a bad limp. He probably weighed less than a hundred pounds.

I met another guy on First and Pike who had beautiful, dark, curly hair almost down to his waist. Without a doubt, he had the longest and most attractive hair I had seen on any guy I encountered on the streets. When I saw him on the corner, I started shaking at the mere possibility of cutting off his gorgeous hair. He was in his late twenties and dressed rather nicely in a bulky sweater, jeans and dress shoes. He was clean shaven and, with his long hair and small frame, he looked androgynous. I walked by him a few times and stopped about a block away. I figured it was better to play coy and let him approach me. I leaned against a building and casually watched traffic go by, pretending to mind my own business. Within minutes he came over and struck up a

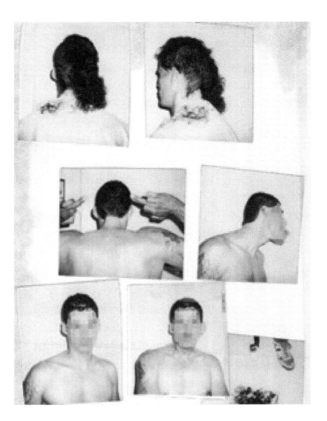

conversation. He had a routine that I'm sure he used with all the potential johns who passed by him that evening. The conversation led to him announcing that he was low on cash.

I played along, and went through my own routine of telling him I would pay him to let me give him a haircut. He was stunned by my request, even making a sour face like he would rather let me cut off his arm. He freaked out and started shaking his head, wanting absolutely no part of it. I politely excused myself and continued on my way. He followed and stopped me a few yards away to ask how much I would pay him and how short I wanted to cut it. We bartered back and forth for a few minutes and landed on a figure of $200 for a crew cut. I could tell he was really wrestling with the idea of short hair. This made my heart almost stop because I was very consumed with the idea of chopping off his hair. The more he debated, the more excited I got. Finally, he reluctantly said yes. However, he insisted on buying some drugs with part of his fee and claimed he had to get high before he would let me touch his hair. I agreed to give him a small portion of his fee up front. By the time he finally made his decision, I was so worked up by the beauty and length of his hair that I would have agreed to any of his conditions.

It shocked me to find out that he had a car, albeit a very beat-up one. He was the only hustler I ever encountered while cruising who had a car. I got in his car and we went to a seedy part of downtown for him to make his purchase. He left me alone in the car while he dashed into a rundown apartment building. He quickly returned with something in his hand that he did his best to hide from me.

I gave him directions to my home, but he ignored me and drove around downtown aimlessly for a while. I was afraid to push the issue. We didn't speak. I'm sure he was trying to figure out how to avoid getting his hair cut. I had told him before we left that I didn't have the rest of the money on me. I would only go to the cash machine after I cut his hair. He parked the car in a remote parking lot in the Belltown area of downtown Seattle and smoked his drugs out of a homemade Pepsi-can pipe. While nervously sitting in the car, I watched him get more and more paranoid. I gently encouraged him to finish his business so we could get out of the area. He still wasn't speaking to me. We left about fifteen minutes later.

I could tell the drugs were affecting his judgment. His driving became careless. Luckily we didn't have far to go. By the time we got to my place, he was a mess, and I had run out of patience. I had already paid him some money and was extremely aroused, so I didn't want to forget the deal. I had helped him with his addiction, now it was time for him to help me with mine.

Jim wasn't home, and the guy made a beeline for the bathroom once inside the apartment. I left him unsupervised for only a minute then opened the door and walked in the room to check on him. He was peeing and yelled at me for interrupting. I told him to leave the door open, then stepped outside to watch him from the hall. He came out of the room even more paranoid and firmly announced he wasn't going to let me cut his hair after all.

I was disappointed but not surprised. I was relieved because I was afraid this guy would go off the deep end and hurt me if we did get around to the haircut. There was nothing I could do. He was sweating, shaking and seemingly terrified of me. He didn't even ask for the rest of his fee. I calmly told him to leave my house immediately. It wasn't until after he had left my apartment that I realized that during the brief moment I had left him unattended in the bathroom he had stolen Jim's watch.

When negotiating with a desperate hustler who needed a fix, it always came down to who was more desperate—him or me? I have never done an illegal drug in my life, but I went on many drug buys in Seattle and Los Angeles for the sake of a haircut. I did finally wise up and stop allowing any drug usage in my presence, keeping my eyes on the hustler at all times.

I met one guy lurking around First Avenue downtown who wasted no time approaching me, explaining he was in need of money to get a bus ticket to California. He felt the need to prove his identity and showed me his driver's license and a stub from a used one-way ticket to Seattle that had his name on it. He didn't explain his business in the city and sounded desperate to leave quickly. It wasn't hard to convince him to let me cut off all of his curly, shoulder length hair. We settled on sixty dollars, which was exactly what he needed for his return ticket.

He was a tall, good looking guy and had a very elaborate tattoo covering his left shoulder. He couldn't have been more than twenty five years old. He seemed perfectly calm with the idea of losing his hair until I put the white cape around his shoulders. His eyes became big and he started making an alarming and rapid clicking sound with his mouth. I asked him if he was okay, and he reluctantly explained to me that he had a nervous tic. He seemed fine on the outside, but as I prepared for his haircut and took the "before" pictures, he continued making the clicking noise in unison with the clicks of the camera.

The instant I turned the clippers on, the clicking became louder and more assertive. His mouth was making more noise than the clippers. The noise was really exciting me. After I'd made two or three swipes with the clippers, the clicking began to resemble a scream, yet his mouth remained closed. I took more pictures of him with a half buzzed head and encouraged him to relax. I found the succession and volume of the tic to be very erotic. It told me exactly how vulnerable he was at any given moment, clearly measuring his anxiety level. I couldn't have asked for a better monitor of the effect I was having on him as I butchered his hair. I had an orgasm without even touching myself. When the buzzing was complete, he looked at me spitefully out of the corner of his eye.

His mood changed dramatically as I took more pictures of his newly shorn head. He clowned for the camera, sticking his tongue out and flexing his muscles. The tic was gone and he didn't seem to miss his hair in the least. I wanted to ask him questions about his tic but was afraid to piss him off. I dropped him off at the bus station and never saw him again.

I ran into a blond guy on Second Avenue who was in his early thirties in the hustler zone of downtown Seattle. He had uninteresting, medium-length hair; it was his mustache I really wanted to shave off. We chatted for a few minutes, and I found him to be quite charming. I did my song and dance for him, but he made it clear that he wanted no part of a shave and a haircut. He loved his mustache and said he would never shave it off for anyone. He laughed at me and told me I was crazy. I accepted his answer and went on about my business. I didn't argue with him or really take anything he said seriously. He was too pompous and a waste of my time.

I saw him again a week later, and he flagged my car down. We had a friendly chat. He was very flirtatious. He confessed that he was a drug user and had just been fired from his job, which I got the impression was a somewhat high-paying blue collar job. He was straight and didn't look like a street person. He looked like he should be sitting in a sports bar, drinking a beer. He would only let johns suck him off. No reciprocation. He started asking me questions about why I like to cut and shave men's hair. I explained that I didn't really know why, other than I found it arousing. I could sense he had been thinking about my offer, but I didn't push him to do it. He kept smiling and joking with me and saying I must be insane. I enjoyed our chat but kept thinking to myself that I couldn't be any crazier than he was. We went our separate ways again.

I continued seeing him every time I happened to be driving around, and noticed he was always wearing the same clothes. I could always count on him giving me a funny look and sincere wave as I drove by. Eventually, he flagged me down and said he would let me shave off his mustache and buzz his head, but he had to have the money up front. I explained my rule about not giving any money in advance. We went back and forth about the money. Eventually, he said that if I gave him the money up front, he would let me keep his shoes until after the shave and haircut was complete. It was winter and I had been seeing him in the same clothes for a long time. He claimed that he washed them out every night in a sink before he went to bed and often wore them the next day still wet.

I didn't offer to pay him a large amount of money. I figured if he backed out, I would have his shoes in my locked car. That would surely be incentive to go through with the deal. I gave in and paid him, locking the shoes out of his reach. He walked the two blocks barefoot from the parked car to my office on the cold winter ground. I performed the shave and haircut and we walked back to the car. I gave him back his shoes, just as we had agreed. I saw him for a couple of months after that, and he always gave me the same silly look and wave. I think the guy really did think I was crazy, but liked me nonetheless. He never grew back the mustache that he had so desperately wanted to keep months earlier.

One fall evening, I found myself having a frank discussion with a guy who seemed almost too willing to tell me he had just been released from Walla Walla State Prison for armed robbery two days prior. Stealing cars and embezzlement had landed him in prison four of the last six years in both Texas and North Carolina. I thought he was cute. He was 27 years old and had shoulder-length brown hair and a mustache. His southern accent tipped me off that he was not from Seattle.

We sat on a bench at a bus stop on First Avenue and talked for about an hour, and I found myself really connecting with him. I wanted to be in love ... with him. Even for just one night. I actually found myself undecided about my usual practice of cutting and shaving. Eventually I invited him home with me and fed him a sandwich. There had been no mention of money.

We talked some more, and I finally got around to asking him if I could take a shower with him and shave his face and give him a haircut. He enthusiastically agreed. He held me and kissed me in the shower. I shaved his face clean and gave him a good, normal haircut, no humiliating buzz. We went to bed and listened to music while we messed around. I fell asleep in his arms not knowing if he would rob and kill me while I slept. I didn't care anymore. I was in love.

The next morning, I made us breakfast. His clothes were disgusting so I gave him some of my own clothes to wear. He didn't have a home or a phone, but I gave him my phone number and kissed him goodbye behind my apartment building as I threw his old clothes in the dumpster. I never saw him again.

Maybe I was going crazy. The truth was I didn't feel that different than those folks on the street. I was conducting my life like an addict, helplessly waiting for the worst to happen to me but hoping for a lifeline. My judgment was going down the drain. I certainly wasn't happy, and I was as desperate for a fix as any of the people I was meeting on the street.

40-Their Own Version of Normal

I was in my fifth year of obsession, although it was hard to pinpoint exactly how and when I had become obsessed. It was even harder to tell if it would ever end.

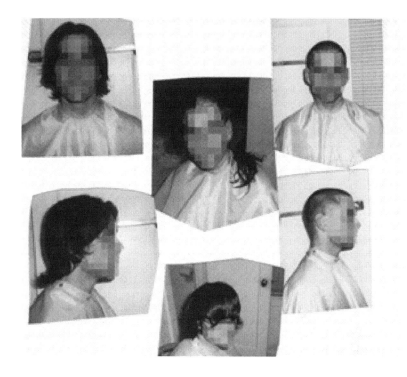

It was surreal to drive through downtown Seattle and see over a dozen sad young guys walking the streets with no hair. The cruising area looked like a concentration camp. Even seeing a guy with buzzed head out of context in the daylight in other parts of town caused me to pause and wonder if I had been responsible for the guy's severe haircut. I felt drunk with power, yet guilty and sickened.

I was paying an average of a hundred dollars a trick. The most I ever paid a hustler for his hair was $300. That was the largest amount of money a cash machine would give in one evening. I got pretty comfortable with the negotiation process, even when they started off in the thousands of dollars. Price dickering was always part of the fun and could make a difference in how sexually excited I got. The more money a guy wanted, the more attached he was to his hair. Like any good negotiator, I learned that the two feet I stood on were the same ones I could walk away with. If a shorter haired, less desirable boy wanted too much for his hair one evening, chances were good he would flag me down the next time I saw him, ready to get his hair cut.

I never begged a guy to let me cut his hair. It didn't suit my agenda. I still needed to be in control. Instead, I applied some heavy persuasion and let the candidate come to his own decision. It was a delicate balance for me to find a guy who needed the money enough to go through with it, yet was still emotionally attached to his hair.

There were some men I could offer a million dollars to, and yet they would never let me cut their hair, even if their hair was already short or unimpressive. There were others with long hair down to their waist who didn't bat an eye at my offer of money to shave their heads bald. My approach was simply to look them in the eye and confidently and calmly tell them exactly what I wanted to do. I always respected their answers; I tried never to waste their time or harass them.

Often, after I hired a guy for a haircut, he would want to date me again a few days later despite the fresh haircut. In my mind, I had no reason to hire him again until his hair had grown out. Some hustlers did not understand this and would get angry with me. If a guy confronted me, I would tell him to wait a year and let his hair grow; then we would do business again. Even though I owed them nothing, it could be hard to say no, unless they were rude or tried to blackmail me. It was especially hard if I sincerely enjoyed their company and they needed the money. I had been known to give a guy a few dollars to grab a bite to eat if he said he was hungry and I believed him.

A few long-time hustlers became repeat customers.

Getting together for a yearly haircut was an interesting reunion. I met John around 1993, the first year I was combing the streets. He was working with a partner, Jason. Both boys were in their late teens and very cute. They both had long, dark hair. Neither one of them appeared to be living on the streets, but simply worked the streets for money. Despite selling drugs, I don't think either of them used drugs heavily beyond pot and booze. I think both were bisexual and may have even been lovers off and on.

The first time I approached them was on foot at Second and Madison. They were very suspicious of me. I was attracted to both of them and really wanted to cut their hair. When I told them what I wanted, they both looked horrified. They firmly stated they liked their hair long and planned to keep it that way. That declaration turned me on even more. I didn't push the offer and left them alone. I saw them both again a couple of more times. Each time they offered me sexual favors for money, but I was firm about just wanting to give them haircuts.

Weeks later, I ran into John by himself for the first time. That evening, I could sense that John might go through with a haircut without Jason around. John was the older of the two and treated Jason like a little brother. He asked me if I still wanted to cut his hair. I said yes. We discussed the length of the haircut I was proposing. He didn't want it too short. I agreed that I would leave it a bit longer on the top, but the rest would be very short. He said he had to walk around the block and think about it. I knew he was going to do it.

A few minutes later, he came around the corner and said he would let me cut his hair for $175. I didn't care about the money. I had to cut all of his hair off. I had a strong sense John really hated getting his hair cut, so I was extremely aroused. When I got him home and set up for the haircut, John was pretty uncomfortable, and I thought he was going to back out. As I buzzed his hair off he tried his best to be cool about it, but I could see he hated every moment of the experience.

A few weeks later, I ran into Jason by himself. He flagged me down. He seemed excited to see me, and told me he had seen John's haircut. I asked Jason how John liked his haircut. He reported that John really hated his hair short, but he thought I had done a good job. I asked Jason if he was ready to get his hair cut. Jason said he would let me do exactly what I did to John for the same amount of money. He also wanted to see the pictures of John's haircut. I agreed to everything except showing him the pictures. I wanted to keep that private.

Jason was much more relaxed about his haircut, especially since John had already submitted to a cut. He wasn't as attached to his long hair and sat there quietly as I chopped it all off.

Years later, I ran into John. He was drunk and walking the streets alone. I had a car of my own by this time, so I picked him up. He was very upset because he had gotten into a fight with his sister. He started crying really hard, so I pulled the car over and sat and held him while he cried. I liked feeling needed. I hadn't felt that way in a long time.

He told me a rather involved story about the fight and asked me if I would give him a ride to his house in Federal Way, which was almost twenty miles away. I was more than happy to help him out. He thanked me for listening and gave me a kiss as he got out of my car. John and I were not really friends, but there was a part of me that hated seeing him so upset. It somehow didn't matter that I didn't cut his hair that night.

The last time I saw Jason was in early 1998. He had gotten into a fight with his dad and was leaving town for good. He was in good spirits and claimed he was desperate for the change of scenery. He showed up at my office with his bags all packed and wanted me to shave his head for money to help him get out of the city. He was too enthusiastic about the buzzcut for me to really get all that aroused, but I was glad to help him out. He didn't tell me where he was planning to go but was adamant that he was never coming back. He gave me a hug when we said goodbye.

I'm glad to have met Jason and John. Not only because they let me cut their hair, but because they represent a shred of ordinary humanity in the harsh world of prostitution, drugs and street life. At first glance, they appeared to be like a lot of the guys I met on the street. Perhaps I'm assuming too much since I didn't really know them, but they seemed like lower-class guys with troubled family lives. What sets John and Jason apart was that they seemed to maintain and survive street life for a number of years and still be their own version of normal. Their longevity must have been an indication of some degree of strength. Their lives had obviously been hard, but they never appeared hardened by their circumstances. They were fighters, and presumably winning on some important level. Many of their peers were not.

I found a lot to admire in John and Jason. The guys were not role models by any means, but they were survivors who seemed to know who they were. So did everyone around them. I was a mystery, even to myself. My mental state was becoming weaker and I was losing my will to live.

Whether as an act of solidarity or a gesture to punish and humiliate myself further, I took my clippers and buzzed almost all of my own hair off.

41-The Triangle

I drove around Seattle nightly until I was exhausted. I was hesitant to stop cruising and go home for fear I would miss an opportunity. If a guy wouldn't let me cut his hair, it became impossible to accept the failure. When suffering with insomnia, I would get out of bed in the middle of the night to go back to the streets.

My guess is that I hired and cut the hair of well over three hundred men and unsuccessfully approached several hundred more. Between 1993 and 1998 I probably spent over $27,000 on my addiction. Those were not huge figures when compared to the cost of other addictions like drugs and alcohol. The only thing that kept that figure from being much larger was the difficulty I had in actually finding what I was looking for.

Shorn and dangerously depressed, I was running out of money. An empty bank account really didn't matter though, because I was also running out of hustlers to cut. There were very few men looking for action in my usual spots that I had not already cut. I had some luck finding a few panhandlers outside the movie theater on Sixth and Pike, but if I was going to continue to cut, I was going to have to rethink my territory.

As I began to lose my grip on reality, I started getting bolder and bolder. I was ready to try anything with anyone to get what I wanted. I made a late-night triangle between three different twenty-four-hour grocery stores in Seattle. I went from the QFC in one neighborhood to the Safeway in another, then over to the ShopRite a few blocks from my apartment. I would sit in the parking lot with my scissors close by and watch people go in and out. After midnight was when things got interesting. It was as if the air changed and possibilities began to present themselves ... or so I hoped. I would walk right up to suitable men in their cars and do my routine:

"Hey, Man. Can I ask you something? Can I cut your hair short?"

"I am looking for guys who will let me give them a haircut. Do you want to help me out?"

"Wow. Look at your hair. You should let me cut it."

Even the most seasoned night owls would be caught by surprise as I rationally gave them my pitch. Most guys were too confused by me to be rude. I could tell they were expecting me to ask about drugs. What they didn't realize was that haircutting was a drug to me by this point. I thought I was being reasonable. I could make my pitch with a straight face. Everyone politely declined my offer and went on their way. After about a week of playing haircut roulette in the grocery store triangle I had set up, I was ready to up the ante.

One fall evening I drove down University Avenue near the campus of the University of Washington. I hadn't looked for opportunities there since the old days of bathroom cruising. I figured there had to be some young street kids or skateboarders on the street who would consider my offer.

I saw a young guy with long red hair loitering in front of the post office. I circled the block a few times until he noticed me. I slowed down, stopped right next to him and rolled down my window.

"HEY ... DO YOU WANT A HAIRCUT?" I shouted from my car.

"WHAT?" he said, cupping his ear like he couldn't hear me.

"DO YOU WANT A HAIRCUT?" I repeated. He paused a beat and flipped me the finger. I flipped him the finger back. He puffed his chest out and started walking toward my car as I sped off.

A few blocks away I saw a young white guy with dreadlocks almost down to his nipples. I waved at him and smiled as he walked up to my car. I rolled down the window and engaged him in polite chitchat for a few minutes. He seemed like he might be as interested in me as I was in him, but for entirely different reasons.

"This is a weird question, but can I touch one of your dreads?" I asked.

"Sure, go ahead," he said with a smile.

"You know, I have never really touched a dreadlock in my life," I said, playing coy. He selected one of the longer

ones and playfully waved it in my face. I gently touched it …
then I started tugging on it.

"Can I keep it?" I asked.

"Keep it? What do you mean?" he said.

I increased the tension on the long dread and wrapped
it around my fist. "Keep it. Let me cut if off and keep it," I
said quite seriously.

"No you may not!" His face changed and he pried his
dread out of my fist.

"Come with me. I want to take you with me and cut all
of your dreads off," I said almost bursting into tears as he
walked away from my car.

I drove back to the Safeway on Capitol Hill to continue
my triangle. It was very late. I couldn't remember what day
it was. My face hurt from gritting my teeth during the hours
I had been out combing the streets. As I parked my car I saw
a young man in his thirties pull into the parking lot in a nice
sports car. When he got out I saw that he had thick, healthy
hair—similar to that of my old high school crush Brent. He
flipped it out of his face as he locked his car and went inside.
I got out and followed him in with my scissors hidden in my
hand and jacket cuff.

The store was almost empty, except for a few people
waiting to check out. He quickly grabbed a soda and got in
line. I grabbed a candy bar and got in line right behind him.
I stared at the back of his head. I was so close I could touch
him. I wanted to touch him. I wanted him to turn around
and tell me I was not a bad person. I would have killed for a
hug and a kiss. I reached for a magazine and almost brushed
his arm in a pretend clumsy gesture, but didn't quite make
contact. He turned around and shot me a dirty look; he knew
I was stalking him. I backed off, but I was tense. I was mad
at him for being a normal guy. He had a nice car, a lot of
confidence, and beautiful hair. I felt I had nothing.

I watched him ask for a pack of cigarettes. I got tenser
because the cashier was a handsome man with a mustache.

The two men exchanged small talk and flirted with each other. I noticed my hand was wet; I had cut myself while hiding my scissors and I was bleeding. I had stabbed my wrist without knowing it. I backed out of line and quickly left the store. No one even noticed that I had not paid for the candy bar.

I walked to the man's car and waited for him. I put the candy bar in my jacket pocket and managed to get blood all over myself. He came out of the store tapping the pack of cigarettes against his palm.

"Excuse me, sir. I cut myself. Can you help me?" I asked. My wound was not the motivation to approach him.

"Get away from my car," he demanded.

"I'm bleeding." I held my hands out so he could see them.

"Get the fuck away from my car!"

The man wasn't playing my game. I changed my tone, "Listen to me ..."

"No, you listen to me. GET THE FUCK AWAY FROM MY CAR!" he snapped. I quickly went to my car and got in. I noticed him pulling out a cellphone as I drove away.

I had never felt so pathological in my life. Something was different about that night. I wasn't scared anymore because I couldn't think straight. I hatched a plan.

More determined to cut hair than ever, I drove down to the ShopRite on Madison Street. Somehow I knew this would be my last stop of the evening. I pulled into the empty parking lot. I grabbed a few tissues and cleaned the blood off my hands and the steering wheel. I took the bloody wrapper off the candy bar and ate it. There were already three candy bar wrappers on the floorboards from earlier in the evening. In the mirror I noticed that I had blood on my face. I could not see well enough in the rearview mirror to get it all off.

I got out of the car and propped the hood open, pretending my car battery had died. I was putting on an act for an empty parking lot. I improvised to myself how mad I was by the inconvenience of being stranded. I waited. A woman pulled into the parking lot. On her way into the store, she asked if I needed help.

"No, I'm fine. Help is on the way," I said. I got in and out of the car as other groups of people came and went from the store. It took almost an hour before the right guy came along for me to unleash my plot. The guy was driving a pickup truck. He was around twenty years old and had shoulder-length blond hair and a goatee. With my bloody scissors cupped in my hand, I asked the guy if he could help me out with a jump start.

"Sure. Can I help you on the way out? I'll only be a minute," he said with a friendly wave. I watched him walk into the store. I decided I was going to grab his hair and cut if off while he was bent over my car. I didn't care if we got in a fight or even if he killed me. I was ready to go out with a bang.

He came out of the store with a small paper bag and sat it on the seat of his truck.

"Do you have jumper cables?" he asked.

"Yes, I do. They're in the back," I said as I followed him to the back of my car. I lifted the hatchback and we were both stunned to see six wigs on wig blocks. They were all styled in eighteenth-century hairstyles. I had completely forgotten about the freelance show I had been working on for the last few weeks. The wigs were done and ready for delivery across town.

"What are those?" he said with a twinge of surprise.

"Oh, they're wigs for a play," I answered quietly.

"What play are they for?"

"*The Good Natured Man*, at the U-Dub. I do wigs for the School of Drama there," I said in a cheesy way.

There was an awkward pause. I was ready to abort the whole plan.

"You know, I just realized I don't have jumper cables. I'll call a tow company," I said, slamming the hatch closed.

"Oh, okay. Well, have a good morning." He was right; it was almost four in the morning. I went home, went to bed and cried. As I watched the sun rise through my bedroom blinds, I realized that something had to change. If I could have had one wish, it would have been to have the whole fetish cut out of my head.

42-Paraphiliac

I had bottomed out. The odds of me being in the wrong place at the wrong time were high. I was waiting for something tragic to happen to me, perhaps even to be murdered in embarrassing circumstances. I felt so strung out, my body constantly ached from the stress. On a couple of occasions I tried to get help, without much success. I was suffering alone and in silence. I was losing track of time and space. I was told by many that I was very talented with hair and I received praise for my wig work. However, looking at and touching hair all day in my job only reinforced my after-hours impulses. I was weakly pretending to be the *Together Homosexual of the 90s*. Nothing could have been further from the truth.

At age 33, I decided it was time to get a better grip on my life and at least try to make changes. I hadn't been in continuous therapy since I'd lived in the south eight years earlier. My therapy in North Carolina had been focused on the crisis over my unrequited love for Eric. I had been suicidal at that time, and she had just tried to keep me alive. I had never talked about the fetish in my previous therapy, because I hadn't been ready to admit it. I had barely acted upon my impulses, so it wasn't a problem that needed fixing at the time.

When Intiman Theater changed insurance providers, I found that the new plan would allow me up to sixteen counseling sessions at a cost of fifteen dollars per session. The catch was that I had to go through a telephone screening. My evaluation would determine how many of the sessions my insurance would cover. I decided even before I made the call that I wasn't going to go into the fetish during my evaluation. I was very direct during the telephone call, indicating that I would probably be dead very soon if I didn't get help quickly. I insisted on talking to a female counselor. I was terrified of getting an attractive male therapist with long hair.

By the end of that day, I had the phone numbers of three counselors and twelve sessions approved. I chose a female therapist named Dr. Cook. My first appointment with her was less than a week away.

I decided to not tell anyone I was going into therapy, simply because I didn't want to discuss why. I was nervous but enthusiastic. I didn't have unlimited sessions at my disposal, so during the first one, I rattled my fetish story off to Dr. Cook in record speed. She took notes and asked questions very quickly. I was honest about everything I told her. I had no time to lose.

She dug out a thick psychology journal and looked some things up, splitting her attention between the book and my nonstop talking. Then she sat down beside me and showed me a page from the book. She explained that I was suffering from what was properly known as paraphilia—a condition where someone is aroused by an act or behavior that is atypical or extreme. It sounded so serious. I had only heard of my situation referred to as a fetish, which is being aroused by a specific object or part of the body.

It was obvious to both of us that my need to act out hinged on other things. We discussed professional stress levels. We discussed relationships.

232

I opened up about being bullied and molested when I was a child. She immediately offered two discouraging prospects: I probably would never entirely be rid of the urge to cut men's hair, and I might never know why I have these unusual fixations.

Dr. Cook explained that, although unusual, my paraphilia wasn't the end of the world. I wasn't actually hurting myself or anyone. With a few exceptions, the haircuts were performed with the permission of the recipient. We both decided that the most helpful thing I could get out of therapy would be to learn how to manage my obsession. She pointed out that I was doing a fairly good job of that, considering the obstacles. I was surprised by her remark. I thought I was failing.

"Picking and choosing men off the streets is dangerous, but so is picking someone up in a bar or anywhere. A stranger is a stranger," she said.

We agreed that using my best judgment in the selection process was very important to my safety. Having a bad gut feeling was something I should never ignore. Being fair and non-threatening with the men I picked up was key to my personal safety, and she commended me for always practicing that behavior. Generally, if a guy agreed to participate in my paraphilia and get his hair cut for money, it was in his best interest to cooperate and get paid. Most guys probably felt it was a bargain.

She agreed that bringing someone to my home was the riskiest choice.

She was also concerned about me bringing people into my work place. There was no real alternative, except going to a hotel, which was more expensive and ultimately unsafe. Cheap hotels were breeding grounds for crime. My office was my turf and put me at the home court advantage. Although not the best idea, we decided that if I was careful, the risk of me getting caught or hurt was minimal if I continued to use my office.

One day, I brought my hustler haircut photo album into the clinic to show Dr. Cook. There were over sixty men in the book. I told the story of how I had met and cut the hair of each guy. I had never shown anyone the pictures. It was embarrassing. Her overall reaction to the photographs was that I had done all those scraggly haired boys a favor by giving them haircuts. She felt they all looked better afterwards. I almost laughed out loud when she saw one guy's picture and said, "Cute haircut." She thanked me for bringing in the book of pictures, understanding how difficult it must have been. I realized she was giving me permission to stop feeling so bad about my condition.

I was really enjoying the work I was doing on my life with Dr. Cook. She was a much better counselor than I had ever encountered before. Also, I was in a better place in my life to do the homework I needed to do to feel better about myself. I was resigned to the fact that my motives for my sexual situations would probably stay mostly a mystery. Yet I wanted to change.

The elephant in the room was that I had been a victim most of my life. We zeroed in on my being molested when I was seven and the bullying after. There wasn't much time to analyze the whole awful rape, but something clicked in my head, and for the first time, I could totally see how that summer in the station wagon had affected my whole life and certainly shaped my paraphilia. Being called a "Stickney" or any other gay slur was like being raped. Being bullied was a serious trauma, too. It was time to let go of the pain and fear and stop being at the mercy of something that happened almost thirty years ago. It felt a little bit like Dr. Cook had pulled my treatment out of a magician's hat; easier said than done. However, it made sense. I knew she was right.

Our plan was for me to concentrate on finding a relationship. I didn't work nine to five like most of the world. I had one day off a week. I was taking on more and more freelance work and turning into a workaholic. My schedule made it difficult to date normally. She encouraged me to find a great guy, then worry about matching schedules. Dr. Cook pointed out that meeting a mate almost always came from an introduction to a friend of a friend, or from work situations. My problem was that I needed to get out more and stop hiding from my personal life. If I wanted to change that aspect of my life, I had to make it a goal and work on it just like anything else.

In the meantime, my grandma (my childhood yarn and paper-doll enabler) died in September of 1998. Due to her advanced age, it wasn't a shock, but I was hurt by the loss. I felt as if she was the only family member who had loved me despite my effeminacy. With my parents I discussed going to the Midwest for the funeral. I didn't go there very often—once every three or four years. I had long since stopped thinking of Robinson as my home. I always hated going there and became seriously depressed every time I did.

I casually slid the topic of my grandma's death into a conversation with my therapist, only in reference to maybe rescheduling an appointment. I made a big deal about how unhappy I was every time I went back to Robinson. She immediately noticed that it was the first time I had ever mentioned my parents or my hometown in therapy. It hadn't dawned on me. She asked me if my parents knew much about my life and I began making excuses for them: they're older, they're small-town folks, they're blue-collar workers, and my dad's health is bad. She asked me flat out if I liked my dad. I was stunned and almost burst into tears. I knew that I didn't like him at all, but I had never said it out loud. The question hit a nerve. Dr. Cook knew it and I knew it. She told me that what I needed to do was to write a letter to my dad, knowing that I didn't ever have to let him see it. I was to honestly say everything I wanted to say to him. This was a huge assignment.

I left Dr. Cook's office that day feeling scared. I had never allowed myself to disrespect my dad externally. He always made me feel like I was a child. It finally dawned on me that I was an adult and he could no longer punish me.

43-The Truth

My dad

Fulfilling my assignment for Dr. Cook, I sat down and wrote a very long letter to my dad. Since I was writing the letter knowing I would never actually have to show it to anyone, true honesty was the goal. She directed me to write the letter as fast as possible without concern for grammar, punctuation or spelling. The idea was to put things on paper before the conscious mind had the opportunity to censor it. Everything started pouring out of me:

* * * * *

I've spent years fantasizing about cutting men's hair against their will. Exactly what you did to me when I was a child. You thought it was essential to turn me into a boy, but you never really participated in my life. You just humiliated me for being more like Mom. You punished me for being myself. You were ashamed of your sissy son, and cutting my hair was getting even with me. I was a defenseless child, and all I could do was secretly hate you.

I was seeking revenge toward all the boys who criticized me for being a sissy, just like you did. This role as barber is the closest I can come to ever being like you. Maybe that is why I don't understand it. Maybe that's why, deep down, I don't really enjoy doing this to men. I don't really want those men to hate me for cutting off their hair like I hated you.

Our power struggle over my hair set the tone for our relationship for the rest of our lives.

* * * * *

Writing the letter to him, I realized how angry I had been at him for years over the unfortunate experience of haircuts. My anger was much bigger than I had thought. I had tried to be the boy my dad would be proud of, and I had failed miserably. I had no interest in sports, fishing, poker or any of the things he liked. I simply didn't have it in me to be masculine and resented him when I tried. Likewise, he had no interest in the things I liked. I know it bothered him to see me enjoying feminine things.

* * * * *

Your son likes to play with dolls and pretend to be a girl. SO WHAT? Would it have been so terrible to have provided me with a doll? Would it have been so terrible for me to have played with a doll in the living room in front of you while you watched TV? If dolls hadn't been such a big deal, it might not have been so important and such a source of shame. Who was I hurting? I wish I'd had a dad who tried to understand me. A dad who wasn't afraid to ask me questions. A dad who participated.

I needed a dad who said, "My son and I do not like the same things, but the things that make my son happy are okay with me and I can appreciate that" or "My son isn't like a lot of other boys, but he is a charming and talented person who I enjoy talking to and spending time with."

If you had been active in my life, then perhaps I wouldn't have started shoplifting. I wouldn't have been afraid of you. I wouldn't have spent my life seeking validation from men. Perhaps I wouldn't have an obsession with hair. An obsession that often makes me feel like my head is going to pop off.

I would love to hear you say to me now, "I know you're gay and I still love you. I want you to be responsible and take care of yourself. Being gay isn't bad or wrong. Be proud of who you are."

* * * * *

As a child I had assumed that if he was disappointed in me there must be a good reason. My dad was a large man with a gruff voice who barely showed me any love. Small children are dependent on their parents until they become old enough to take care of themselves. Kids want to believe everything their parents say. I had never let myself challenge or openly dislike my own dad. It was now perfectly clear that I didn't have to like my dad or believe everything he had told me. I couldn't change my dad any more than he could change me. It was okay to disagree and still love someone.

* * * * *

When I am buzzing a guy's head or having sex with a guy I don't even know, I am really seeking acceptance and love, which has NOTHING to do with sex. I want men to accept me. I want you to accept me. I want men to be attracted to me. I want men to love me. I don't think that any man on the face of the earth has ever really loved me. I have spent years terrified and convinced no man ever will. I believed there must be something wrong with me because you TREATED me like there was. I have convinced myself that there is something awful and wrong with me all because of you.

* * * * *

I couldn't type fast enough to keep up with the thoughts that were popping into my head. I promised myself to be as pure with my thoughts as possible and not read the things I was writing until I was done with the letter. There were things I wrote about that I hadn't thought about in years.

I finished the first letter and thought I was done. It was five single-spaced typewritten pages long. I sat back and read what I had just written. I was shocked at my frankness. The more I read the letter, the more details came to the surface that I hadn't thought to write about.

My parents had never come to visit me since I had moved out on my own, either to Chapel Hill or to Seattle. My dad refused to look at my wig portfolio. Neither of my parents had ever seen my professional work. They had never met my friends or asked questions about my personal life. It really felt like they had given up on me and chosen to let me go off on my own. I started writing a second letter.

* * * * *

All of this would have been so much easier to take if you had been a blatantly abusive dad. If you had beaten me, or starved me, or said you hated me, or if you had just vanished, I could have found a way to label my unhappiness. The hard part is you were there the whole time, but only by default.

I have made some discoveries and can perhaps piece together my past and figure out how it affects me now. You are still my dad, and I am your gay, sissy son. I have only a few fond memories of you, but have a lot of wounds that I can now let heal.

* * * * *

I cried throughout the process of writing these letters. Everything I had to say was inside of me all the time, but I had never brought it to the surface. I spent an entire evening composing the letters. It was like the words were bullets that I had used to load a gun. Strangely, I was terribly uncomfortable with having the letters around me that night when I went to bed. The next morning, I got up and sealed them in an envelope, took them to Dr. Cook's office, and gave them to the receptionist, explaining that the doctor needed to keep them on my behalf until my next appointment. I tried to put them out of my mind for the time being.

Dr. Cook had read the letters when I saw her next. She was delighted with what they uncovered and congratulated me on such a huge breakthrough. I was relieved but felt a little bitter. She and I reviewed the letters, but there was very little left to say. I had weathered my therapy with success and I was two sessions from running out of insurance coverage. I really felt like I was ready to strike out on my own, using my newfound perspective.

My dad called me a couple of days after I finished the letters, and I didn't know what to say. He, of course, had no knowledge of my therapy. There was no reason to change my conduct. I still loved my dad. The letters didn't change that. I didn't feel it was fair to confront him about the issues I had acknowledged in my writing exercise. It would serve no purpose but to upset him. I wanted to forgive him.

My mom had an essential role in my life. I loved her very much, and she had been a devoted wife to my dad for close to fifty years. To disrespect and attack my dad now would greatly disrespect my mom. I could not bear the thought of hurting my mom in any way, but I knew she wasn't completely ignorant of my pain and animosity toward my dad. She had witnessed it. However, she was a woman raised in an era when wives were expected to obey their husbands for better or for worse. That was her calling.

It was better for me to become strong and honor myself. The best thing I could do was to be the happiest person I could be, despite my parents. I included them in my life only so far as I could maintain that happiness and respect myself. That was to become my calling.

44-Progress

While in therapy, I mentioned my extended bout with shoplifting to Dr. Cook. It was like an alarm went off in her head. She started asking me many questions about my kleptomania and seemed most interested in the fact that I had gotten to the point where I didn't always remember the things I had stolen. She believed that I might be suffering from Obsessive-Compulsive Disorder, a problem that could be controlled with medication.

We discussed the possibilities of putting me on anti-depression drugs. I was all for it, but Dr. Cook was a psychologist and could not prescribe medication. She highly recommended an associate of hers, Dr. Hiatt, who was a psychiatrist. However, he was one of the city's most distinguished psychiatrists, and it would be very difficult to get an appointment to see him. Dr. Cook and I only had one session left, so she started the referral process immediately.

My last session with Dr. Cook ended on an upbeat note. The timing was perfect, because I was really ready to soul-search on my own. I was delighted to have had her guidance. I got a very lucky break: it only took only a month to get an appointment to see Dr. Hiatt.

He had been briefed by Dr. Cook, but when I met him I told my story and did a few memory and word association tests. He thought I was an excellent candidate for medication, not only for Obsessive-Compulsive Disorder, but also for my bouts with depression.

He prescribed Luvox—a relatively new antidepressant. He gave me some free sample packets right out of his office. After explaining the dosage and possible side effects, he told me to come back in a few weeks. I would be building up the dosage gradually and shouldn't expect any change in behavior for at least a month.

I didn't really know what to expect from the medication. It was hard to imagine that I would just suddenly stop wanting to look for a head to shave.

Dr. Hiatt explained that the medication would make the problem behavior seem less important. However, since I spent so much of my time pursuing the behavior, I should begin to seek alternative activities to fill the time I usually wasted. This is where one therapy had to work in tandem with another. I really had to decide what I wanted out of my life. I wanted to date. I wanted to have a boyfriend. Dr. Hiatt helped me map out a plan to come out of my shell and start pursing positive relationships.

I faithfully took the medication as prescribed. The biggest side effect I had was some slight head tremors, nothing I couldn't handle. I was excited for this to work. Just as I was told, I saw no change in my behavior at first. I went to a follow-up appointment with Dr. Hiatt, having just run out of the samples of Luvox. Since I had had no serious problems thus far, Dr. Hiatt gave me a full prescription. However, I learned my insurance would not cover Luvox.

The pharmacy called the doctor and got a substitute. Zoloft was prescribed instead. Dr. Hiatt explained that I had to knock down the dosage of Luvox that I had built up and gradually exchange it with Zoloft.

At first after switching the two medications, I was still cruising men for haircuts. I even did a double-header the third week I was on Zoloft. I ran into two hustlers in the same night. They needed cash and had lots of hair to offer. I was happy to oblige them and buzzed their heads like I had done to so many other hustlers.

Neither the therapy with Dr. Cook nor the medication hindered me from enjoying the experience. However, I fantasized that in the near future I could easily turn such an opportunity down; maybe I wouldn't have the impulse to even look for the situation.

After about five weeks of taking Zoloft, I started feeling different. I didn't have the need to masturbate every day like I had been doing since I was fifteen years old. All of a sudden, it didn't really occur to me to go downtown after work and look for hustlers. The new sensation I had was that I had a choice of whether or not to go downtown. For years, I had felt like I was on auto pilot and simply had to go. The obsession hadn't disappeared, but I had more control. I didn't feel as desperate while I drove around looking. If I saw a long-haired guy walking down the street, I would still feel the desire to cut his hair, only not as strongly as I would have before I started taking Zoloft. It wasn't a perfect fix, but it helped a great deal. I was able to concentrate on other things, like friends and building a new social life from scratch.

I had a totally new lease on life. I was extremely motivated to make radical changes and felt like I had been handed an effective tool to do so.

Taking the sessions with Dr. Cook into account and continuing to take Zoloft gave me emotional strength like I had never felt. The first thing I did was start concentrating on my weight. I had always relied on food as a comfort device and was an avid overeater. I began eating better. After six months, I dropped sixty-five pounds. Having a trimmer body and a new attitude, it didn't take long for people to start treating me differently. I had been absent from the gay scene for a couple of years. I decided to place a personal ad and made a point of going out more often just to be around other gay men. Neither the ad nor the bars produced a significant relationship, but at least I was trying.

Then one day, I got a telephone call from Dr. Cook, who explained that she was relocating her practice out of state. She wanted to casually check up on me and give me the name of an associate of hers if I needed to get back into therapy in the future. We had a delightful conversation, and we both wished each other well. I felt like she had really helped me set up a good foundation for healing, and I'll never forget her.

I was on Zoloft for a year and a half. After a while, I was experiencing side effects I didn't like. I had trouble maintaining an erection. I frequently experienced insomnia. I was also starting to feel almost too calm. I never seemed to feel too happy or too sad. My personality always stayed in the middle. I noticed some weight gain even though I had been so careful to maintain the weight I lost and had continued to eat healthy foods. The pounds started creeping on despite my effort.

I checked in with Dr. Hiatt every couple of months and explained my observations. He instructed me to decrease the dosage of Zoloft and begin taking Paxil in a small amount. Once the Zoloft was out of my system I could increase the dosage of Paxil. I did as I was instructed for two months. Paxil gave me terrible head tremors, very bad dry mouth and made me constantly anxious. After six months, Dr. Hiatt thought Serzone would be better. The whole medication transition began again. A few months later, several friends mentioned to me that I had been quieter than usual and wondered if perhaps I was too medicated.

It was a crap shoot that took a long time to win. Finally I found success taking Cymbalta. It keeps me level and allows my personality to still shine. The co-pay is well worth being able to focus and feel like I have control of my paraphilia. I am open to taking a pill every day for the rest of my life if necessary. I am an advocate for psychiatric medication. I won't say it changed my life but I will say it helped me change it myself.

Newly "sober," I lost sixty pounds and headed off to Oregon Shakespeare Festival to do wigs for a variety of shows. This would be a true test of my paraphilia: there would be no gay hustler population to tap in the remote mountains of Ashland, Oregon.

Once I returned from OSF, my life seemed to coast along fine. I was dating more than I had ever dated in my entire life and had stopped having anonymous sex. I even had a steady boyfriend for a while. I knew I was a strong person when I fell in love with my boyfriend and was later able to accept our breakup with dignity. I wouldn't have been able to do that fifteen years earlier.

45-The Tail of Woe

During the summer of 2000, a new stage technician joined the staff of Intiman Theater. The first time I saw Dean Taylor he was working on stage before our production of Eugene Ionesco's play, *The Chairs*. At first I thought he was a woman. But upon second glance I realized he was an attractive man. He was in his mid twenties and had a thick ponytail of healthy, blond hair down the middle of his back. His body frame was small and his features very delicate.

After a little bit of investigating, I found out that Dean was heterosexual. I was terrified of him. I had trouble speaking to him and looking him in the face after we were finally introduced. Despite the medication and my new outlook on life, I was a distracted by his beautiful hair and the familiar urge to cut it.

There was great irony in Dean's presence at the theater for me personally. The young man he replaced was another long-haired technician named Michael. The two men were about the same size and had similar personalities. I liked Michael, but we never hung out after work. It seemed too risky to get close to him. Michael wasn't the first guy with long hair who wasn't a haircut candidate that I had to filter through in my real life. Why complicate things by inviting a guy with long hair into my life?

Michael was a self-proclaimed hippie, wearing tie-dyed clothing and small, round, wire-rimmed glasses. He had very thin, wispy hair that wasn't at all flattering. It wasn't my sexual urges that made me want to cut Michael's hair; I just felt he would look ten times better with shorter hair. His hair grew very slowly, and he came to me for a trim a couple of times a year. Trimming Michael's hair was a matter of barely cutting half an inch off the ends. He came to me on several occasions to discuss the possibilities of cutting his hair short but was never brave enough to take the leap.

On the other hand, Dean had amazing hair that he nervously played with all the time. His habit made me nervous, too. We would sit in meetings together, and I wouldn't hear a word anyone said as he twirled the ends of his hair. I hadn't been affected by a guy's hair like this in a couple of years. I was experiencing a full-blown infatuation centering on Dean's hair. It didn't help that the rest of him was attractive as well. I was very disappointed in myself for rehashing the old feelings.

One afternoon, while sitting in my office, I noticed Dean passing by my door repeatedly. It seemed like he was looking inside my office every time he passed. We smiled and acknowledged each other. I sensed that he wanted to be noticed. I continued working but couldn't stop thinking about him. Later that day, I looked up and found him standing in my office.

He seemed nervous, but we began chatting. I invited him to sit on the couch while I continued tying hair into the wig I was working on. I found him to be well-spoken and quite charming. He had been raised a small-town guy like myself and had left home to pursue a career in theater. I had some overwhelming feelings as I sat talking to him in my office.

I was intimidated, not only because of his beautiful hair but because he was a beautiful man who was paying attention to me. There was something so open and approachable about him. I was really enjoying talking to him. Still, I felt like I was going to crawl out of my skin. I didn't want to fall for another straight guy, and I didn't want to end up obsessing about giving him a haircut.

Dean excused himself and went back to work. I was derailed by the half hour I had just spent with him. He was very charming guy, but I wasn't sure if the remarkable experience was good or bad.

We exchanged pleasantries throughout the workplace for a couple of days. The next week, he stopped in for another visit. We sat and talked the afternoon away while I made a wig. He asked me many questions about wigmaking. I did a quick tutorial of the craft for him, which he found interesting and informative. I was fighting a meltdown as I worked with a lap full of hair while admiring his ponytail. I made a point of not mentioning his hair in any way. However, I knew the subject would eventually come up.

Being a wig person, I had gotten used to everyone talking to me about their own hair. I have cut many of my peers' hair over the years for extra cash. After my sexual impulses for cutting men's hair diminished, talking about hair lost most of its stimulation value; however, I got chills when Dean eventually asked me where he could go to get his hair cut. The question hurled my progress back five years.

I suspected Dean knew that I cut hair as a side business, and I was certain that he was expecting me to offer to cut his hair for him. However, when I made the suggestion, he looked at me with a blank expression. He actually wanted a salon recommendation. It was an awkward moment that I quickly saved by flipping through my Rolodex and writing the name of a salon on a piece of paper for him. I was made paranoid by his lack of interest in having me cut his hair. Could he smell the obsession on me? If so, why had he brought it up? We continued to hang out that afternoon, and I found myself enjoying his company in spite of everything.

I have had very few close straight male friends. I had seldom, if ever, tried to be friends with a long-haired man. The idea of allowing myself to become friends with a long-haired straight man to whom I was intensely attracted was an intimidating thought. After spending time with Dean, I was ready for the challenge. I felt like a recovered alcoholic who had just gotten a job in a liquor store. I was only just beginning to figure him out.

As Dean and I spent more time together, it became obvious that we were in the same predicament. He was divorced after three years of marriage and really wanted to be in a relationship with a woman. I was actively seeking out a relationship as well. We immediately bonded in our *singlehood*. However, I wondered if I was spending too much time with him. The last thing I needed to do was fall in love with another straight man, especially one with long hair. There was even a part of me that was afraid he wanted me to fall in love with him for whatever reason.

One night at dinner, Dean revealed to me that his only brother was gay.

He and his brother were very close, and that explained why he was so comfortable with homosexuality. Looking across the table at him, I felt something much stronger between us than anything sexual. In fact, I realized that I actually liked having a close straight friend. I respected him for who he was. I was beginning to see a real person under the head of hair. We were, in fact, becoming like brothers.

Eventually the subject of his hair came up again. I learned his hair was very important to him. It was clear after talking about his hair that he was emotionally attached to it and that it made him happy. There was no evidence that he would ever feel compelled to cut it. I was actually relieved to find that out.

It took me a couple of months before I realized that I was flexible enough to maintain our friendship. I wanted Dean in my life. I had room for a straight man in my life as a friend. There was no reason to exclude him because of his gender, his sexual orientation, or even his hair length.

Dean was a good friend as well as a symbol of my recovery. If he came to me and suddenly announced that he wanted me to cut his hair short, I would do it without incident, providing it was something that would make him happy. I have always been curious about what he would look like with short hair. I feel confident he and I both would get through the haircut without incident. Five years earlier, there would have been no place for Dean in my life.

One afternoon, I trimmed four inches off of his hair, as he requested, and we went to dinner just like any other evening. He had no idea about the things that I had gone through with my obsession. I knew I would eventually have to tell him about my past. When I finally did, he asked a lot of intelligent questions. I was able to look him in the eye and answer honestly. When the cards were finally on the table, I felt like we were closer than ever.

46-He's All Man

The last picture I have of my mom, summer, 2006.
She is wearing the wig I made for her
after she lost her hair to chemotherapy.

The year two thousand six started off with both my
mom and my dad being plagued with health issues. They
had been married for 55 years. Dad was 75 years old and still
weighed almost 400 pounds. His whole body was falling
apart. My mom worked tirelessly to take care of him, and
she started having some severe back pain. She, herself, was
no spring chicken at age 73. Finally, it got to be too much for

her. After Dad fell getting out of his chair, the doctors told her it was no longer safe for her to take care of him.

My dad died on March 12, 2006, in the hospital in Robinson, surrounded by his brother and sisters, while I was tending to my mom three hours away in Champaign-Urbana. Two days earlier Mom had been diagnosed with a very serious cancer. After her diagnosis, she was immediately rushed into treatment at Carle Clinic. My mom screamed like a wild animal when I told her the news that Dad had died. She and I were both were devastated that neither of us were there when he passed. I comforted her for an hour and then she insisted I leave her to go back to Robinson to take care of his affairs.

Once I left Mom in Champaign and started to drive, I had lots of time to think. The last time I had seen Dad was in 2004. The big, gruff, scary and unlikable man had turned into a softie whose feet shuffled heavy on the floor when he walked in his house slippers. He had become downright jolly and talked to me like I was a friend. Better yet—a man. I don't know which one of us let go of all the bullshit first, but we both didn't worry about the past anymore. During my last visit home, I overheard him call my aunt on the phone and tell her with pride, "Denny's home. He's got a short haircut. He's all man."

After I got to Robinson I was unprepared for all the stuff I had to do. My aunts and uncles were willing to help me, but I hadn't spent time with any of them in years. I wanted to be left alone. I got settled into my parents' house—the house I'd grown up in—and quickly realized I had NEVER slept in that house without them in it. It was in a very lived-in state. It looked like neither of them had left. Yet I knew neither my dad nor my mom would ever live there ever again.

At the funeral home, I conveyed all that I needed to—cremation, life insurance, obituary. My dad had already insisted there was to be no funeral or visitation. I asked to see Dad, knowing it was to be the last time I would ever be with him.

"Dennis, he had a pretty rough time at the end. I just want to prepare you." I didn't care. I needed to see him.

The director asked for five minutes to prepare his body and then led me into a florescent, clinical work room where Dad lay on a stainless steel table. His midsection was covered with a sheet. His arms were at his sides. The director was right. Since there was to be no funeral, nothing had been done to formally prepare him to be viewed, and he had been dead over twenty-four hours. I didn't recognize my own dad. He was an odd color and very puffy.

I shivered, not because of seeing my dad, but because the room was so cold. I gently touched his hand and noticed that his fingernails were long and almost blue. He hadn't shaved in a while either, as there were sparse white whiskers on his chin. I touched his hair and marveled at how he still had the same low hairline he always had. His wavy salt and pepper hair was soft and uniform like it had always been, even before he started to turn grey. I kissed his forehead and whispered goodbye to him.

The director came in suddenly and startled me. He apologized and spoke softly. He was talking about my dad, but I didn't even comprehend what he was saying. I took one last look at my dad's face and a stream of blood ran out of his nose down his cheek. Without skipping a beat, the director grabbed a towel and gently wiped it away. He asked if I was ready to leave. I was. I had seen enough.

I was thankful that I had forgiven my dad before he died. Despite our differences and the many miles between us, he was the number-one man in my life for forty years. The last five of those were the best and worth the pain of the other thirty-five. All the bad feelings didn't matter anymore. He was gone.

My dad was a good man. Whether he realized it or not he had taught me to be a good man. I think where he and I struggled is how we defined what a good man was. I came to realize as I dug myself out of my paraphilia that the key to being a good man was to be authentic.

My dad was authentic whether he knew it or not. His simple opinions of right and wrong, good and bad, and even boy and girl were all he knew. I know he always wanted the best for me. He wanted me to be happy. Twenty years ago, I bet he would have said to himself, "Why does Denny have to be gay? It is going to be so hard for him."

What helped my dad and me finally bury the hatchet was when he and I both realized that we could both be right yet still be so different. He couldn't change me any more than I could change him. I admired his service to his country, his long marriage to a wonderful woman, his good work ethic, and the sturdy home he provided that was always there for me. I knew that I was his greatest achievement. After all, he chose to adopt me. I was proud of him. And I thank him for being authentic. Perhaps he loved me more than any man ever will.

Despite all the emotional battles I waged over the course of my life, my dad got to see me win. I had my own unique voice, I had found my identity, and I had found a way to make a living expressing myself in my art. I boldly left Robinson and surrounded myself with people who would build me up rather than knock me down. He grew to respect my alternatives. He learned that I had to find happiness in my own way. Despite his worries, I had become a good man. He and I had both learned that being a man had nothing to do with masculinity.

I moved my mom to Seattle after Dad died so that I could be with her during her final days. She had never been on a plane before she left Illinois to be with me. It was a great adventure for both of us and wonderful to get to know her all over again. Through all the futile cancer treatments, she was brave and never complained.

Our relationship peaked when she started to lose her hair from chemotherapy. She asked me to shave her head to keep her from shedding all over herself. I had never shaved a woman's head before. It was very hard, considering all that a severe haircut connotes for me, but I did it to make her more comfortable. I made her a beautiful wig that looked exactly like her hair had looked for the last several years. She wore it with pride. She would tell anyone and everyone who would listen, "My son made my wig!"

She slipped away with dignity on November 10, 2006, only eight months after my dad passed. I was alone by her side when she passed.

I am not biologically related to my mom, but I am very much like her. She lives inside me. All the things I like about myself come directly from her. I feel her smiling at me all the time.

I was surprised to find that I felt like the house I grew up in was like a family member to me as well. With my dad's passing, my mom needed to liquidate her assets to qualify for Medicaid. I was forced to auction off my childhood home, contents and all, on behalf of my mother. My friends in Seattle rallied around my bedridden mother while I flew to Illinois. Over 400 people from miles around came to the auction that day, which was great news.

However, nothing can prepare you for your mom's living-room furniture sitting in the driveway while strangers sit on it like they were in a waiting room. It was heartbreaking to see my parents' whole lives on tables in the yard, with people picking through it like they were at a Farmers' Market. By the end of the day, my parents had been reduced to a dollar figure. I don't know if I will ever get over the experience. I grieved the loss of the house right along with the loss of my parents.

The best tribute I can give my parents is to forgive their faults and be the happiest person I can be. Once they were gone from this earth, I realized that the only one I can depend on is myself. I seriously grieved for over a year. While I mourned their deaths, I worried that I would put myself back on a destructive path. I didn't succumb to the temptations of being a victim or relapsing into paraphilia. I spread all the leftover rage with my parents' ashes and opened myself to the next phase of being Dennis.

I look back at pictures of me when I was growing up and my early adulthood and I am surprised. At the time of some of those photos, I felt ugly, disgusting and unlovable. Now, I see just a confused guy—a normal looking guy with a heart, a soul, blue eyes and a sincere smile when he relaxed enough to smile. I am now embarrassed that I lost all those years. Yet, I am not sure what I would change since I don't know any other me. I believe in my heart that my journey was worth the pain.

47-Vanity and Sanity

There is no way to know for sure what had a greater impact on my unusual sexual impulses—being molested, being bullied, or growing up with a distant dad.

Once control was within reach, I began to feel like maybe I could come up with my own theory on the source of my paraphilia. I did a lot of soul searching and came to the conclusion that it was most likely a combination of factors rather than any one experience that made me who I am.

Years after writing the letter (never sent) to my dad, I felt like the last step of recovery would be to confront the man who molested me in writing. This proved much harder than I thought it would be.

I had cried a lot over the awful events of the summer of 1972. I had cried until I was cried out. Having found a career that I loved in a city with an open mind, I finally learned to accept myself for who I am. But I will never forget that scared seven-year-old boy from the station wagon. He will always be very much a part of who I am, and he deserved to be heard.

My mom and me, summer of 1972. Notice the sticker over my mouth on the end-table portrait.

A Poem for Glenn Stickney

> Here's to you, Glenn
> My dark-haired rapist.
> You have been in and out of my life,
> My heart stifled
> For over thirty years.
>
> You took away my innocence.
> Confused and shamed,
> I cut from others

What was stolen from me
Because of you.

I got back at you in the face of others.
Dark hair and light,
Styles of revenge paid in full,
I do not owe you,
And you no longer own me.

Your lies,
Your penis,
The fear,
No longer penetrate me
Like they did underneath that tree so long ago.

Are we related?
Were you often me?
Brother on brother?
Is that your dark reason?
I will not pardon you.

Trimming the bad,
Clipping my past,
I will now control and understand
Vanity and sanity.
I am Stickneyed no more.

Betsy, Peter and I were all victims that summer. Peter had allegedly been molested by all four of the Stickney brothers. Betsy had no idea the Stickney's were using her babysitting job to provide them with victims. There were many more who suffered at the hands of the Stickney brothers after us in at least two states. I have since found out that the whole family has been punished for molesting children, whether by law or by karma.

That's best the news of all.

48-Epilogue, 2010

I was browsing in the Seattle Goodwill store and found a naked Lester doll. I had not set eyes on a Lester doll since that fateful Christmas when I was a child. He was in pretty good shape, had all of his hair, and cost only three dollars, so I bought him. I couldn't help but see the symbolism. I was determined to take better care of this Lester. I neatened up his hair (without any cutting) and made him an outfit as close to what I could remember his original outfit to be.

In 2001, I was called into a private meeting at work at Intiman. I was scared that I was in trouble. The two leaders of Intiman told me of their plans to start a staff appreciation award. Since I had worked there the longest, they asked me to design the award. They also asked for permission to name it after me. I was the first of many recipients of *The Dennis Award*: a gold statue with an enormous blond wig.

I am still on staff at Intiman Theater. I have been with them for the last eighteen years. Eventually I had to come clean about my unsavory use of my office during my paraphilia years. All is forgiven and I know that I will never return to that extreme behavior.

My work with theatrical wigs still interests me. It provides an artistic outlet, and I'm delighted that I continue to get offers of freelance work around the country. I sometimes wonder if my paraphilia has made me a more intuitive wig designer. Nonetheless, the supplemental income comes in handy as I whittle away at all of the credit card debt I built up from my years of careless living.

Once my parents were gone, I yearned to start over with my birth mom, Janet. She had lost one son to suicide and the other one had suffered a life of turmoil. I wanted to reach out. She was delighted that I did. We bonded, not like a mom and son, but as both friends and family. We are also advocates of each other: no more secrets.

She was both surprised and honored that I had gone to court years before our reunion and legally changed my name to reflect both my birth and adoptive last names. I became Dennis Milam Bensie in March of 2000. Bensie is a rare name, just like I am a rare person. I am very proud to be a Milam, but I tip my hat to Eddie Bensie, wherever he may be.

I can't change anything I've done, but I have been enlightened by the mistakes I've made. I am still a paraphiliac and there have been relapses over the years. If something bad is happening in my life then I can slip back into cruising and haircutting mode very quickly. The medication continues to minimize the appeal of my paraphilia and I try to evaluate the situation clearly and not take dangerous risks.

Some fantasies are better off remaining fantasies. Perhaps the dispatcher from Dial-A-Daddy years earlier was right; I had a fantasy that was impossible to fulfill. I had been chasing my fantasy, when I should have been embracing my reality.

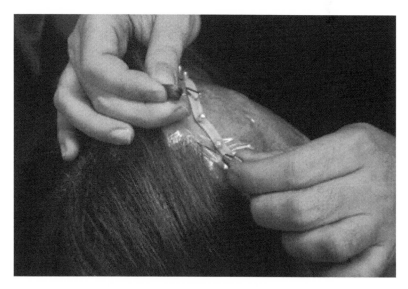

Photograph by Oscar Val Verde, Ovalve.net

Made in the USA
Lexington, KY
14 June 2011